The TRIUMPH of LOVE over EXPERIENCE

ALSO BY WENDY SWALLOW

Breaking Apart

The TRIUMPH of LOVE over EXPERIENCE

A Memoir of Remarriage

WENDY SWALLOW

NEW YORK

Library of Congress Cataloging-in-Publication Data

Swallow, Wendy.
   The triumph of love over experience : a memoir of remarriage / Wendy Swallow.—1st ed.
     p. cm.
   ISBN 0-7868-6860-0
   1. Remarriage. 2. Remarried people. 3. Swallow, Wendy. I. Title.

HQ1018.S93 2004
306.84—dc22

2004042534

FIRST EDITION

Hyperion books are available for special promotions and premiums. For details contact Michael Rentas, Manager, Inventory and Premium Sales, Hyperion, 77 West 66th Street, 11th floor, New York, New York 10023, or call 212-456-0133.

10 9 8 7 6 5 4 3 2 1

For Charlie and the boys.
And for my parents, Chan and Edie Swallow,
who taught me how to love.

~~~ *Appreciations*

THIS BOOK WOULD NEVER HAVE emerged from the lively chaos of my life if not for the vision of my wonderful editor, Leigh Haber, and the support of my wonderful agent, Flip Brophy. I am also grateful to American University for the freedom of a sabbatical year and to my School of Communication colleagues for their friendship and intellectual flint. My patient family (all those wonderful Swallows and Shepards) also extended ideas, suggestions, help, and the occasional shot of bourbon, all at the appropriate moments.

Countless other people contributed to this book, including many therapists and scholars who shared their insights on remarriage and pushed out my horizons. The best stories, however, came from the nearly seventy individuals I interviewed about their own remarriage adventures and hard-learned lessons. To protect people's privacy, I changed names and, in a few cases, a few identifying features, but the stories in this book all come from those interviews. Being a stepparent is perhaps the toughest job in society, and I quickly developed a deep regard for any adult who lovingly opened their heart, purse, and home to support children who were not originally their own. Successful families, indeed, come in many surprising shapes and formations.

But my deepest gratitude goes to my nearly perfect husband, whose willingness to open his life gave the book its heart—and to our four amazing boys. The success of our remarriage has sprung mostly from their abiding goodwill and high humor. They are a continuing joy, and Charlie and I know how lucky we've been.

~~ The Beginning

WHEN I DECIDED TO REMARRY two years ago, I had no idea what I was doing. Sure, I thought I knew about marriage. I knew it would be a partnership, with all the give-and-take that entails. I knew I loved Charlie and that he loved me. I knew I would have more children, though not biological this time but stepchildren. This didn't scare me, because I'm usually good with children. I like children, especially teens, which was what I was getting. I had teens of my own, so it didn't seem like a big deal. What's four teenage boys if you already have two?

What I thought I was doing by remarrying was going home, back into the warm hearth that is the family, and all that American culture enshrines along with its reverence for the family. I thought I was moving back into that sacred circle, that inner sanctum of respectability—that accepted place. Having a partner in the world goes a long way. It means you have someone to stand next to at back-to-school night. It means you have someone else to help with chores and kids. It means you are not an embarrassing fifth wheel at dinner parties. It means you are sewn back into society, no longer vaguely threatening or pitiful in the way single parents often appear to be. People don't have to worry about you anymore. You are safe, you are home.

But in actuality, though, remarrying isn't about going home. It's about going someplace else entirely new, almost as if you've stepped through a looking glass. Things appear normal, but there are all sorts of strange contortions to life, things that aren't readily apparent on the surface. In the end, remarriage turned out to be quite different than I imagined—indeed, from what most of us would imagine—and that is what this book is about.

I should have known remarriage would surprise me. My first marriage surprised me, and when I divorced ten years ago, I found that experience surprising as well. Divorce, when viewed up close, was nothing like what I had imagined back in the unhappy days of my marriage when I sat around fantasizing about being a single mom. The divorce I was living through also seemed quite different from what conventional wisdom had prepared me for, and I soon realized that was because divorce itself was changing, as more fathers fought for joint custody and more mothers worked outside the home. To capture this new landscape of divorce, I wrote a magazine piece for a local publication. Charlie, who had just separated from his first wife, read that piece and knew he had to talk to me.

Within a few months of publishing that piece and meeting Charlie, I got a contract to expand the article into a book, a divorce memoir. This was a challenging opportunity, as there were few memoirs in the divorce literature at that time. My ex-husband and I had worked through a difficult decision to share custody of our boys, and many people were interested in how we learned to bury the hatchet and co-parent successfully. The book, called *Breaking Apart: A Memoir of Divorce,* seemed to fill a deep hunger people had to hear stories about good divorces, those that broke the cycle of conflict and emerged out of the bitterness common to divorce.

Ironically, I wouldn't have had the courage to write *Breaking Apart* if it hadn't been for the love and support Charlie provided during those months. When I told my editor I was going to marry this wonderful man, she suggested I write a similar memoir-style book about finding the love of my life at age forty-five and the consequences of the decision to merge our lives. It seemed like a good idea, a sort of travelogue through this unfamiliar land of remarriage, although at the time I didn't appreciate just how strange remarriage would feel. And then I started living and writing it, and I wondered how I could possibly have signed up for such an assignment.

On sabbatical from my job as a journalism professor at American University, I had no escape from the topic of remarriage. I sat in my study at home reading harrowing reports on the statistics of stepfamilies, then went downstairs and tried to negotiate dinner and laundry and chores and schedules with my patient husband and our four boys. Even though everyone was trying hard, the first year of our remarriage was a bewildering maze of false starts and rewritten approaches. Everyday life was a minefield of potential blunders. The boys had their own adjustments to make, and not always in ways that we anticipated. We all brought our own baggage, our own resentments, our own fears. Together, we worked on the gentlest of bonding rituals—catching a movie together or sharing a pan of brownies.

As I started to write, I also discovered I was in a kind of maze. I had to be judicious about what I said, particularly about the kids. They were all teens now, and curious about what part of their story I was going to tell. Plenty of other people attached to us in a loose, post-divorce way were part of the story and were concerned about what I might say. I worried that Charlie would not be able to live with what I would say. Some days I sat at my desk and thought I should give it all up, it just seemed so complicated.

But I still wanted to know the answer to the big question for remarried people, which was this: Why are the odds against succeeding so high? Why, in particular, do so many remarriages with children fail? What is going wrong and how, oh how, could we avoid the same fate?

So I started looking into that question. My research took me all over the library and into the offices of marriage and family therapists. I interviewed scores of experts, both scholars and psychologists and ministers and counselors. I also interviewed scores of remarried couples and participated in several online communities of stepmoms, remarried spouses, stepdads, and others. I also interviewed plenty of my students, those kids who would sit in my office and tell me about their lives as members of stepfamilies.

And everything I learned I turned over in my own heart. What really works? What feels ridiculous? The advice books are useful, but I wanted to write a book that charted the everyday feelings and dilemmas of remarrying and merging families— from the initial falling in love through the difficult adjustments to the acceptance and relative peace that eventually comes. In the course of writing this book, I ran up against all kinds of questions about what kind of family my husband and I were actually trying to create. I understood for the first time the pressure we were under to do everything right, and the stress that bred. A friend laughed when she heard I was writing about my own remarriage. "Boy, that must up the ante," she said. "Now you really can't fail, or it would be just too humiliating. Having written a book and become an expert, you better be able to succeed!"

I understood what she was saying, but my remarriage doesn't feel that way. It felt like alien territory in the beginning, but now it feels more like my home and my family. Our family is not perfectly blended—and you'll soon understand why—but mostly it works for us.

Perhaps the most important thing I've learned from this journey is that all of us make our own heaven, and each one will look different. What might work for us might not work for another household or another set of children. Our boys brought their histories with them, and we couldn't erase or ignore those. Indeed, we did so only at our peril. The kids are all different one from the other, with different needs and dreams and ways to be loved. We've had to learn a lot, and we still have many more things to get right. But slowly, incrementally, we are creating a shared experience, weaving a web of bonds that will hold us together in the future, I think.

I hope.

I'm coming to believe.

CHAPTER ONE

Love in the Aftermath

WHEN I FIRST MET CHARLIE I felt as if I'd met my double.

I couldn't get over how much we had in common. We were both divorced and had kids. No big surprise there, given that we were middle-aged and looking for love, but we were born the same year, had first marriages that crumbled under many of the same pressures, and each had two teenage sons. Our houses were littered with the debris of boys—gym shoes, basketballs, baseball gloves, sweaty laundry, old Gatorade bottles. On top of that, we were both journalists who had been molded by life at *The Washington Post* and later turned away from it. As writers we shared a strong interest in business and finance. When I met him, he was headed for business school in the hopes that an MBA would help him shift from the newsroom into newspaper management. I had been a business reporter, but left years

earlier to teach journalism at a local university, and I understood his excitement and anxiety about moving beyond the
career he knew. Closer to the bone, we sprang from similar
New England and Midwestern roots. We both spent countless
Sundays as kids sailing around in small boats with our parents,
bored and damp. We gravitated to people, books, learning,
and Schubert. We both played classical instruments and kept
Mozart's operas in the CD player. We loved to walk and would
sneak away to meet in the park for a hike whenever we could.
We would peer at each other sometimes and say, "You do that,
too? Weird." "You went there as a kid, too? That's eerie."

We were so similar, in fact, that we had nearly met several
times before. I left the *Post* just a year before he was hired. We
lived so close by when we had small children that Charlie would
sometimes wait at the bus stop in front of my house while I was
swinging my kids in the backyard. We had vacationed every
summer for many years in Cape Cod towns just a few miles
apart. He worked on a project with my colleagues at my university, and if I hadn't been on sabbatical that year I would
have worked with him, too. Because our careers had criss-
crossed several times, we shared numerous friends. Beyond
that, we had similar personalities and instincts. We were both
wound up in our children, both outgoing and ambitious, both
fascinated by our media-saturated world in Washington and
the problems of journalism at the turn of the millennium. When
I told our mutual friend Nell that I was going out with him, she
said, "That's interesting, because you two are exactly alike."
Our union seemed etched in the cosmos.

· · ·

The irony of this was that I wasn't looking for a double. I wasn't even looking for a man. I hadn't given up men, exactly, but had pushed them decidedly on the back burner. When I first divorced, years earlier, I figured I would soon find someone to love. I tidied myself up, emotionally and physically, then went out into the world, meeting men, being friendly, going out for dinner with a range of guys—some older with grown kids, some who had never married, some like me, divorced with small kids. But I wasn't really interested in getting remarried at that point, certainly not quickly. I knew I had to heal my soul and find my own balance in the world, and that might take years. I had divorced not to follow some romantic dream back into a better marriage, but because getting divorced was the only path I could find to a sane way of life, one without all the tension and anger. I had no idea if I would ever marry again.

Dating, compared to living with someone, turned out to be easy when it wasn't ridiculous, so I dated some men longer than others. Each attachment gave me the chance to examine a different world, to see if I could do it—remarry someone and merge children and furniture and dreams. I wasn't wild about the idea of being a wife again and I knew that remarrying would present new pressures, things I hadn't had to deal with in my first marriage, like stepchildren and ex-wives. I knew enough remarried people to know it would take a measure of patience and goodwill and sheer determination beyond the demands of my single-mom life. So it had to be worth it. The love at the core, the marital relationship, would have to be worth the disruption to my children and me. And when I looked at the men I knew, I knew in my heart that none of them was it. None of them was as wonderful, in fact, as the men I knew who were married, the husbands of my friends. It was true, I decided. The ones who could manage intimacy and help care for their children and live a stable life were, well, living a stable, married life.

So finally, after years on the dating circuit, I stopped waiting for the right guy. I would get on with my life, my dreams. Of all the things I had lost when I divorced, I still grieved the loss of my own hearth. I had bounced from rental to rental—three different homes in six years—and wanted a place I could call my own. A place where I could rip up the carpets if they were too worn, where I could paint the walls and burrow in with my children. A place where I could get to know the neighbors, host a holiday party. So I counted up my savings, picked a real estate agent, and set out to buy a house. I didn't need a man to make my life work.

In short order, I found a split level in my sons' school district, in a cul-de-sac, not fancy but light and airy. I wanted to make an offer, but my real estate agent was worried. She thought the house was overpriced for the neighborhood, and warned that if I sold it again in a few years, I could end up losing money.

What she saw, she said, was a still-young single mom, attractive, with a warm personality and two sweet boys. "You might meet someone," she said.

"But, Mary Lee," I said. "I'm not moving again until the boys finish high school, and by then the house will have appreciated in value. I know what I'm doing. I'm not going to remarry. I've looked. There's no one out there."

"Okay, but just don't come to me next year saying you've met someone and need to sell," she replied.

I laughed. "Don't worry. That's never going to happen."

Three days after I bought the house and moved in, Charlie called. I was sitting on my bed making a list of things I needed from the hardware store. He had read the article I had written about my divorce, which had just been published in a local magazine. "I am both personally and professionally impressed by your piece," he said, sounding nervous but friendly and warm. "I'm a former *Washington Post* reporter, just like you. I had to call and introduce myself."

I was cool at first, as I usually didn't take calls from strange men, but within minutes we discovered we had friends in common, along with our work history. He liked the people I liked at the newspaper. I could have met him at a party, and in fact I was a bit surprised that I hadn't. We talked for an hour and discovered we had interests in common as well, beyond the shared legacy of divorce. Just talking about our boys kept us laughing for twenty minutes. When we ran out of stories about the kids, he asked me to lunch to talk more about divorce and custody issues.

"But I have to go to the hardware store tomorrow," I said, suddenly shy and retreating to my self-sufficient, lone-wolf way. I needed lightbulbs and blinds and extension cords and paint . . . Then something went off in my head, a sign flashing DON'T BE AN IDIOT.

"You know what?" I said. "Who needs lightbulbs? Forget the hardware store. Where shall we meet?"

About a month later, I called my real estate agent. "You're going to kill me, Mary Lee. You were right. I met someone, and I think I'm going to marry him."

How could I possibly have known, after about three weeks with Charlie, that we would marry and build a family together? We didn't talk about marriage directly in the beginning, but it was clear to me after the first few days that we could very well share a destiny.

We met for lunch on a hot summer Friday. My first impression of him was that he was quite tall, with a head of white hair and an open, smiling face. There was something reassuring about his manner as he came toward me, eager yet deferential, happy and curious. Instead of that sinking feeling I usually got on meeting blind dates, I sensed a lift in my spirit. Charlie was good-looking—though not in the way that would make you think him arrogant—just pleasant, and warm.

"That must be you," he said, reaching for my hand.

"That must be me," I said, smiling up at him. He was nearly a foot taller than me, but this didn't feel awkward. I was suddenly glad I had bothered to iron my linen blouse, a last-minute decision to give this date a real chance. We walked to a Thai restaurant and were seated in the window. I noticed that his eyes seemed tight in the corners, some tiredness seeping through despite his smiles. After some indecision over the menu, which I chalked up to nervousness, he relaxed a bit and told me he had been separated from his wife for only a few months. I wondered if it was all too fresh, so we talked about the easy things—our kids, our work, divorce in general. By the time the food was cold, mine barely eaten, we were enjoying each other so much we decided to go for a walk in Rock Creek Park. I got blisters from my sandals but barely felt them. On the walk he brightened even more, and even touched my shoulder at one point. Maybe he wasn't too recently divorced, I decided. Maybe there was a chance. Maybe this would be good.

Finally I had to go, to gather my kids up from baseball camp.

"I have to see you again," he said, gazing down at me. "Can I call you?"

"Sure, anytime," I replied, as if I got this question every day.

When I got home an hour later, there was already a message: "I'll call back around eleven. I can't go to sleep tonight without knowing when I can see you again."

When he called, we talked some more and settled on Sunday. I went to bed with a lightness in my heart I hadn't felt in a long time.

When he showed up Sunday afternoon he said he had a great idea but didn't think I would go for it because it was complicated: a drive out into the Virginia countryside, a hike up some pretty highland meadows, and dinner in Middleburg. Enchanting but complicated. I didn't know it yet, but this phrase would become something of a theme. When I said sure, he seemed pleased.

We drove west, toward the late-afternoon sun. It was exciting just to sit next to him, wondering what the evening would bring. "This is a date, right?" I asked, something inside me pushing to get it out in the open. I could sense that Charlie was drawn to me but simultaneously nervous about being drawn to me. Technically speaking, our original lunch was a meeting to talk about my story in the magazine. This was different, I knew, but I wanted to hear him say it. He smiled at me. "Yes, that's what I had in mind." Getting that said seemed to open the doors of possibility, and I wanted them open.

I didn't really know this man very well, but I already trusted him. He had been considerate from the beginning, saying he knew I might not feel safe with a stranger, so we met that first day at the public library, then walked to the restaurant for lunch so I didn't have to get in his car. Being streetwise and dating weary, I had called several friends who knew him from the newspaper, to make sure he was what he seemed—kind, interesting, aboveboard. Everyone was mildly surprised to hear he was divorcing, and all were enthusiastic about his character. "Grab him quick," warned one. "Once word gets out that he's available, he's going to get snapped up." I didn't know if that was the right reason to go out with him, but took it as a good sign. Maybe one of the wonderful men had busted out of his marriage.

We parked at a nature center, poked around the historic house on the property, then headed up a trail into the meadows to get a better view of the valley. It was early August, hot but breezy, the hillside thick with insects and wildflowers. We hiked farther, up into the low hills and the shade of the trees. As we talked, it became clear that he knew quite a bit about me, much more than I did about him. When I asked him about this, he admitted he had done a web search on me before he called me earlier in the week. This would have made me nervous if I hadn't already known his history as an investigative reporter. Just good backgrounding, I thought, and evidence of a bit of a crush. I was flattered that someone liked me enough to check out my academic résumé, which was posted on my university website. No one else I had dated had ever bothered to look at it. He asked about my teaching, my students, my writing. We talked about our newspaper lives, our stories and frustrations. By the time we hiked down, he had taken my hand. On the short drive over to Middleburg, we stopped and got out to watch a large herd of deer in a clearing. He leaned over and kissed me, then said, "Okay, now that is out of the way. Now I can relax." After which he did, and so did I.

By the end of the next week, and after endless late-night conversations and besotted e-mail, Charlie started showing up at my house for breakfast. The first morning I woke up to find his car in the drive, Charlie snoozing over his newspaper, I knew he was smitten. Fortunately, his boys were away with their mom and mine were vacationing in Vermont with their dad, giving us a rare opportunity to be together without distractions or responsibilities. We walked and made dinner and picked peaches and laughed. We talked now about the harder things, the unbearable dynamics of our first marriages and our share of the blame, our lurch toward a more normal life and the collateral damage to kids and careers. But we also talked about music and our relatively happy childhoods and our desires and fragile hopes. Every conversation revealed new connections, new ways to understand each other.

Although he was clearly eager to be with me, he also struck

me as wary on some deep level, like a forest creature unsure that venturing out into an open area was really safe. He said one evening that he felt disloyal to his boys by being with me. Not disloyal to his ex-wife, as their marriage had ended emotionally years earlier, but to his kids. I remembered that feeling from my own early dates, how strange it was to be with men who felt and smelled different from my husband, almost as if there was some animal instinct to keep the family together. So I just sat still and hoped he would feel safe enough to come to me, which he finally did. By the time my kids returned, I knew our life was going to change.

I was one of those little girls who always had a boy on a string, sometimes just in my head but usually for real. I remember sitting in the dentist's chair rattling on about my third grade boyfriends while the hygienist listened, eyebrows high. I once rode my bike into a parked car while watching my fifth grade heartthrob playing football with his brothers in their yard. In high school my older sister stuck loyally to one guy for years, while I ran through a long list. My father teased me about losing track of my beaux, asking which George it was on the phone when they called. By the time I got to college and switched football players for mathematicians, my friend Jamie suggested drily that perhaps I was dating up the evolutionary chain. I was open-minded, willing to consider all types, looking for the combination of qualities that would keep me engaged, challenged, and protected. I liked guys who could help me feel safe in the world and sought out relationships with men because I needed that support. There was something about me that made men—both nice men and not-so-nice men—feel they could approach me, some lack of boundaries I didn't understand until many years later. So I had boyfriends, one after the other. Some nice, some domineering, but all protective. And by the time I married, I was caught in a box that was as suffocating as it was safe.

Beyond looking for protection, I had a clear fantasy of what I hoped marriage would bring me. I imagined a comfortable middle-class life in specific detail, down to the old Volvo in the driveway and the cats curled on the hearth. I got much of what I foresaw in my first marriage to Ron, but not some of the more critical pieces, the pieces that would hold a couple together, and we didn't hold together. We cracked before the Volvo even had time to age. Our marriage failed for countless reasons: I was too young and he was too old; he was intense and spontaneous, where I was calm and controlled; his family life was so badly managed he left home at sixteen, I came from a family whose wisdom and love extended their influence over me well into my thirties. He was private and solitary, I wanted a life dense with family and friends. He was brilliant, I was not; he was depressed, I was not; he had fought for all the advantages in his life, I had not; he was angry, I was not; I was lucky, he was not. After years of fighting and stress I realized that I was no longer willing to trade happiness for protection, that the best thing I could do to protect myself was to regain my freedom. And then it was time to go.

So I set up my life anew, this time on my own terms. I learned in short order that I could protect myself and not worry so much about what the world would bring me. I learned to do all the hard things I had let men do for me before: mow the lawn; face down auto mechanics, school principals, and mortgage lenders; even single-handedly get the damn Christmas tree in its stand. When I ran into something I couldn't do by myself—such as carrying heavy window air conditioners up from the basement—I asked friends for help. In return, I'd do them a favor. I also learned, ironically, to depend on my ex-husband, who was fully mobilized for child care because he kept the boys half of each week. When one of us was sick or had an emergency meeting, the other took over. My new solitude felt empty and lonely at first, particularly when the boys were with their dad, but in time I grew to love the quiet in my life. On Sunday mornings, one of my days as a noncustodial mom, I would read in bed until I got hungry, sometimes as late as noon, an incredible luxury for a working mother. I had time to work late at the office several days a week, time for lunch out with friends or long runs in the park. I loved the simplicity of my single-mom life, suppers of soup and popcorn, grocery runs that took just fifteen minutes, only a couple of loads of laundry a week. It was life on a scale I could manage. I could focus on my kids and my work without the distraction of a husband's needs or issues. I built a cozy, happy nest for my boys, and they thrived inside it.

But below the surface, I began to miss having a husband. There was no one to talk to late at night after the children finally subsided into sleep. It bothered me that no one would find me for days if I fell off a ladder and knocked myself unconscious while the kids were at their dad's. I pestered friends and family, even my ex-husband occasionally, with meandering conversations, just any kind of contact with someone older than eight. For years I watched my older sister and her second husband, a man of a thousand kindnesses, and I missed marriage. I watched them parent their two teenagers, merged when the kids were little, and knew that they had given those children something strong and precious—the model of parents who loved each other. I watched my parents, married for fifty-odd years and still puttering with their sailboats, and I missed marriage. I watched my brother and his wife, kindred spirits raising three children, and I missed marriage. I watched my youngest sister and her sweet husband just starting their family, and I knew I wanted to do it again. As my older sister said, "We are the marrying kind."

Despite the fact that my marriage fantasy didn't come true the first time, I could sense that meeting Charlie had awakened those old longings, and that if I did remarry it would be more about doing it over than looking for something different. Texas psychologist James Bray, an expert on stepfamilies, hits it dead-on when he calls remarriage "a kind of dream—a wonderful, astonishing dream . . . a dream about making a fresh start, of doing it right this time, of correcting old wrongs, of healing a child's hurt, of reestablishing one's identity and sense of self . . . a dream about love and security and pride and respectability."

I may have put my life together as a single mother, but in some ways I still moved outside the boundaries of acceptable society. As a single mother, I had discovered that teachers and school principals were more likely to blame my kids' problems on my divorce than anything else, even if it didn't even seem related. I discovered that my family sometimes slipped into thinking of me as the maiden aunt—the one who didn't need a private bedroom and could bunk with the granddaughters, the one available to help when my parents were sick, as I was the one who could most easily get away, thanks to my joint custody arrangement. I discovered that I made married couples uneasy, not because I was a potential husband stealer, as I had originally feared, but because husbands saw me as some sort of Pied Piper who might lead their wives off to a never-never land of divorce happiness, where dads sign up for shared custody and the women are finally free to join a yoga class. I discovered that I often felt like the fifth wheel at social events, the one who didn't have a spouse to stand next to and dish about the crowd. I had discovered that I sometimes worried about a lonely old age, about being isolated by illness or becoming a burden to my children.

Truth be told, it is at times terrifying to walk through life as a single adult. Those of us who do it often build intense relationships with our children, inevitably turning to them for the companionship and emotional connection missing from our adult sphere. I also threw myself into my job, taking on too many administrative assignments, staying late at the office to talk with students. I needed to matter to someone, someone beyond the two dependent little boys who filled my days.

I also knew that I didn't want to date forever. I wanted to be more than someone's escort. I wanted to regain my place in society as someone's wife, to prove special enough to be worth being married to. There had been no way to heal this particular wound, despite all the love my children gave me. It was almost as if this was the last remaining challenge in my life: figure out how to have a happy marriage. So many people seemed to handle marriage—why couldn't I? Was I too selfish or petty to be a team player? Was I too whiny and weak, quick to give a guy the upper hand but also quick to resent his dominance? What was it about me? I knew there were things I couldn't learn on my own, that I could learn only from inside a relationship, and those were the things I hadn't conquered. I wanted another chance to try to love, with patience and forever, someone who was not a blood relation.

When I divorced my ex-husband, I was exhilarated by the idea that I could make my life the way I wanted it to be, that the days of unhappy compromise were over. That was true, but only within the narrow confines of what I could conjure up for myself. I could conjure up many good things, but I couldn't conjure up companionship, and in time that world became too small, and not just for me. I could see now that it was too small for my kids, that it would be good for them to see me living in partnership with another, even if it meant compromises. That instead of protecting them from the complications and disruption of my remarrying, a good shaking up was what we needed.

So I fantasized about remarriage, about a bigger house, a fuller life. A life that was intellectually stimulating, filled with music and friends and interesting work my husband and I talked about in bed late at night. I fantasized about a family life where our kids struggled through all the appropriate stages of adolescence yet came through with their hearts intact. I fantasized that our children would see us love each other and learn from that. As we aged, we would travel and enjoy our extended families and fill the house with pets and plants. We would be each other's safe haven, walk together happily into the uncertain future. I wanted to go into my retirement years with someone to hold my hand, even if we were consigned to rocking chairs.

But was Charlie the one? Was I fooling myself to think he was more right for me than anyone else I had met in years—possibly in my entire life? I had long since given up the idea that there was someone out there meant for me, but meeting Charlie made me reconsider. Could it actually be kismet? Did I believe in such a thing? I hadn't before, but the fact that the universe had been trying its damnedest to get us together made me wonder.

In my years of dating I met many nice guys, but every one had untenable quirks or qualities. There was the political speech-writer who was good-looking, smart, interesting, funny . . . and completely hung up on the girlfriend who moved to Montana in disgust after ten years of waiting for a marriage proposal. There was the runner who worked on interesting legislation as a congressional staff attorney, but who said he couldn't date someone who still ate french fries. There was the guy who quit smoking only to take up cigars, the man with the snazzy sports car who couldn't understand why I wouldn't get a sitter for my pesky kids, and the academic who was so enmeshed in his intellectual pursuits he couldn't see past his own glasses.

After this parade of candidates, Charlie seemed as if he dropped out of a movie. It felt like one of those fairy tales where the king is interviewing a string of hapless courtiers in hopes of finding a husband for his daughter and the princess is kicking the table in frustration, yelling "Are you sure there aren't more guys in this kingdom?" when in walks Charming himself. He's not just incrementally better than the others. He's the only one who's her equal.

But if there was anything different about my marriage fantasy this time, it was that I didn't want any old prince, sheltered and arrogant in his inexperience. I wanted a veteran of the divorce wars. I wanted the guy who had just staggered out of the forest of gloom, wiser, more understanding, beaten but returning to life. I dated men who never married or had children, and their self-absorbed lifestyles—mountain climbing in the summers, drinking until late, running out to bike on the canal all afternoon just on a whim—seemed empty and purposeless to me. I wanted a man with a past, even if it was complicated, because I wanted someone who had loved and lost big, who had discovered how hard it was to keep a marriage alive over the course of a challenging life, who had suffered the humiliations of parenthood. Someone like me.

The truth is, remarriage happens today mostly in the aftermath of divorce. There was a time, just a few generations ago, when remarriage was usually born out of death, but that is significantly less true today. The Census Bureau estimates that 43 percent of all marriages in the United States now involve at least one partner who has been previously married; only a small percentage of remarriers are widows or widowers. In fact some people remarry after several divorces. Because of that history, remarriage never quite steps out of the shadow of divorce.

Older newlyweds usually bring more wisdom and self-knowledge to the table, but they also bring more complications—teenagers, ex-spouses, houses thick with the memories and flotsam of other lives. And they bring one of the unsettling lessons of divorce: the understanding that you could divorce again, even as you swear you never would.

Remarriage may appear on the surface like a return to normalcy, but it is actually a gamble, a leap of faith. The failure rate for remarriage is enough to make your blood run cold. According to the Census Bureau, two out of three second marriages will fail, compared to about half of first marriages. And for those remarrying with children living at home, as we would be doing, three out of four marriages fail. Dr. Samuel Johnson famously called remarriage the triumph of hope over experience, and when I read those numbers, I understood for the first time how much hope you have to have. I tend to be suspicious of hope the way I am suspicious of religion—it seems too easy. For a woman who prides herself on her pragmatism, contemplating remarriage felt like stepping off a cliff and hoping that, despite my human biology, I would be able to fly.

So I watched this sweet man and wondered if we would have the courage to make such a leap. As we got more serious and began to wade into the swamps of this new relationship, this promising but challenging terrain, I suddenly saw that whether it was kismet or not was beside the point. The point, instead, was that success wouldn't happen automatically. As soon as it hit me that we could be linked for life—about three weeks in—I was overwhelmed by the feeling that I must be careful of what I said and thought because I was already building something that might have to last forever. That this relationship was no place for bad attitudes or pointed jokes. That habits develop slowly and I must remember to be kind and open and loving every day.

I did not have this feeling in my first marriage, probably because I was too young to understand the weight of behaviors accumulating over time. Back then, I thought there was lots of room for immature comments, mistakes, and resentments. This time I knew that every marriage was a bridge built between two personalities, and it could not withstand unbearable pressure. There was no law that said the marriage must work. Instead, there would only be our promise, the same promise I broke once before. If that promise was to hold this time, I would have to protect it better, value it differently, give it daily attention. I would have to remember it was a promise.

CHAPTER TWO

~*~

The Case Against Remarriage

As SOON AS OUR KIDS folded back into our lives, we snapped to attention, shook ourselves, and faced some hard facts. Despite his professed love for me, Charlie was moving out of town. He had won a fellowship for a two-year MBA program at the University of Virginia in Charlottesville, about a two-hour drive south of Washington. His plan was to keep a simple apartment near the university, then come home every weekend to see his boys and take over for his ex-wife. He was still in the early stages of his divorce, and from my greater distance and experience I could see what he needed to get through before he was really free. Everything seemed complicated for him, caught in a mid-career change with his house in the middle of a renovation. I hadn't met his boys yet, but from what he told me they were shell-shocked and hurt, unsure what would happen next.

I knew they all needed time to sort things out and start to heal.

So I stepped back a bit, feeling self-protective and cautious, because I was suddenly reminded now that it was not just about us—there were lots of other people involved. Besides the kids, I had a job and friends and family, a full life, one with plenty of commitments of my own. Charlie had a thousand questions before him: Who would get the house in the division of assets? Where would the boys live? Would joint custody work for them? Where would Charlie get a job after finishing his MBA? Who would he be after two years of business school? In the days leading up to his departure, Charlie and I bumped along, desperate to be together one moment, pulling back into our children and our anxieties the next. When the day came, I helped him load a rental truck with his desk and some old furniture, a few rugs and pictures, then waved good-bye, went home to my simple life, and wept. How had I managed to do this? Fall in love with someone who was moving away? I didn't know if this was my inner saboteur at work or what. I wasn't getting any younger—could I really afford to wait around? And speaking of younger, Charlottesville was crawling with attractive coeds: twenty-somethings in their running shorts, brainy law students with their sexy glasses and stacks of books. Could any recently divorced normal man be expected to ignore this smorgasbord of opportunity and remember me, older, a bit testy, and far away?

The heady intensity of that August began to seem a bit like a dream. I turned back to my own university, to another year of teaching students and writing articles and attending faculty meetings. As my life cranked back up to full speed and Charlie disappeared into the vortex of business school, I began to wonder what we had done. Charlie's family, saddened by his divorce and protective of their boy, started asking if it was wise for him to start up with anyone so quickly after ending his marriage, no matter how terrific she was. His father, who divorced and remarried at about the same time in his life, cautioned him against the romantic haze of the first affair. I sometimes wondered myself if our relationship was a good thing for Charlie. Maybe he would need what I had needed—months, maybe years, of time alone to regain his footing. Perhaps I should release him to fate and hope he remembered me. Were we really meant for each other, or was that just what it felt like in those first love-soaked days?

What was love, anyway, I thought to myself on one of those nights I stayed up late watching *Seinfeld* reruns and hoping he would call. Did I really need romance in my life? I assumed I did, but sometimes I wondered. My single friends and I all considered love an essential ingredient to a happy life, yet many of us got together for lunch, met at yoga class, or headed off to shop, completely contented with one another's company. Maybe a circle that included children and an extended family of parents and siblings and nieces and nephews, buffered by a tight coterie of loyal friends, was enough happiness to get through this world. Who said we needed romance, particularly at middle age, when the romantic fog was harder to conjure up and faster to disappear? When our bodies didn't support the fantasy? When the idea of merging two lives was overwhelming just to contemplate?

I also worried, late at night after I turned off the TV, that maybe, despite years of therapy, I hadn't corralled all the demons, possibly hadn't even spotted all my negative patterns. While a woman could seem to have recovered from an unhappy marriage by avoiding entanglements, she could still wake up one day to discover she didn't really understand love any better than before. I could see the ways in which I was vulnerable: that old helper mentality that sprang to life in the face of Charlie's problems; my tendency to hog the pedestal, especially when it came to being the "better" half; my need for order and my irritation when chaos reigned. The potential for getting myself into another unhealthy marriage was there unless Charlie and I were vigilant about those old habits. I could feel the tempting tug to fix his life: bring sanity to his upended household, help stabilize his children in their post-divorce life, shower Charlie with the affection he deserved. It could feed all my heroine fantasies, if I wasn't careful.

So I turned to my friends, the circle of wise owls I consulted whenever there was a big question in my life: Was I nuts to be getting involved with Charlie, possibly seriously?

"You say he's cute, bright, successful, really kind and considerate, and not balding?" asks my friend Suzanne, who is divorced with one small daughter. "And you have doubts about this?"

"Well, not doubts, but concerns," I say.

"Enough concerns to let me have his phone number?"

"No. Now, listen, is it crazy to hope this might be it?"

"Probably not crazy," says Suzanne, "but it will be tricky. He has boys?"

"Two—just around the ages of mine."

"Well, that will be exciting. A house? A good job? A crazy ex-wife? Some divorced guys have really bad ex-spouses, you know."

"I don't know yet. We're still—how shall I put it?—in the discovery phase. He has a house, but might not have one when the divorce is finalized. He doesn't have a job right now, but there's no reason to think he's unemployable. So far, his ex seems to be a reasonable person."

"Keep me posted," she says, eyeing me closely.

Most of my conversations went like this. At first my divorced friends greeted the news of a new man in my life, and a promising one at that, as a fairy-tale ending. But I quickly discovered that remarriage, like divorce, was one of those subjects that opened up a cache of fears and desires. Some were openly envious I was in a romance and counseled me to damn the complications and forge ahead. Others heard about the two sets of teenage boys and shook their heads. Instead of a fantasy, this sounded like the Brady Bunch gone bad. A stepfamily disaster in the making.

"What if you don't get along with his kids?" asks Jeanne, a single mom herself and one of the many friends who are curious, watchful, eager to see how my drama will play out. "That was always my biggest problem when I thought about remarriage," she says. "I'm not sure I could live with other people's children."

"I think I would really like the closeness of a marriage, but I'm so used to my solitude, I'm not sure I could do it," says Kate, another divorced friend.

"Marriage can clip your wings," warns Frank, a colleague and divorced bachelor. "When you get out of a marriage, you find out interesting things about yourself. I'd love to remarry, but I'm not going to compromise on those things again. I'm not throwing out the record collection this time. The person I marry will have to accept me as I come, with my baggage."

Underneath these fears I sensed the unspoken but central question: If you are economically stable and secure in your divorced life, why risk it all by remarrying? In this day and age, with more women financially independent and more divorced dads taking on custodial care of children, many of the old-fashioned reasons to remarry have become less important. I didn't need a dad for my kids—they had one, the guy they lived with half of every week. I didn't need financial security because I had that as well, in the house I bought in a safe neighborhood and in my tenured job as a college professor. I didn't really need more children to mother, between my own two sons and the many college students who passed through my life, although I liked kids. And when I thought about it, I liked men, but did I really need a husband?

A husband. Someone to talk with and lean against, yes, but also someone there watching me as I parent, possibly questioning my judgment, suggesting things I didn't have the energy to do, raising the bar on my life. A witness. Possibly a supervisor, God forbid.

One of the dirty little secrets of divorce is that life can actually be easier with only one adult in the house. If I was too tired to make a salad and instead tossed the bag of baby carrots on the table for the third night in a row or we watched cartoons during dinner instead of discussing world events, no one felt particularly cheated or appalled, because no one else was a grown-up. For years I had operated this way, patching together a good enough existence that made room for my priorities and my weaknesses, without answering to anyone.

Most single parents don't like to admit this, because single parenting is also hard in a haul-all-your-own-groceries sort of way. But the secret joy is that the autonomy and independence of single parenting can go a long way toward compensating for the loneliness. Unless a person needs more financial security or just can't bear to live alone, one can make a strong case against remarriage. Several of my friends do just that, even as they congratulate me on finding the man meant for me. Especially for those who already had children, remarriage often seemed like a high-flying stock—too risky to be worth the potential upside.

"It's so much easier to be a single mom because there is no conflict over the kids," says Alice, an old friend of my mother's who divorced years ago and never remarried. "One day I discovered that I could repair wires by myself, and that was a big breakthrough, because then I realized I didn't need a man in the house."

Instead of a husband, Alice had a series of relationships with men who were too young or who lived too far away and thus were often unavailable for marriage in some way. "It was awfully nice to have these very romantic times when we would get together, but those times are romantic in part because you don't have enough time together to get into trouble. For the first few years I wished I had a husband, but the more time passed, the more I realized I had this incredible freedom to stay in bed all day if I felt like it, or to get up in the middle of the night to work without someone worrying about me. Once I had that, I didn't ever want to give it up."

Another divorced dad, a friend I watched go through a grueling custody battle, tells me emphatically that he will not remarry until his two boys leave for college, because he just can't risk the legal complications again. He fought hard for joint custody of his sons and doesn't want to jeopardize that arrangement.

"It was a nightmare just getting my fair share of time with them, and I am not going to complicate my life by trying to accommodate another person, perhaps even another set of kids," Greg says. "It's just too hard. I need to focus on my boys and my work. This feels very precious to me, and I realize I don't have that many years with them. If I do ever remarry, it will be years from now. Maybe when I'm eighty."

But the fears of my once-divorced friends are nothing like the horror stories from people who are twice divorced, those who remarried badly. An old childhood friend told me about her second marriage to a guy who seemed perfect—loving, gentle, attentive—but who turned into a controlling psychopath just days after the ceremony. She had known him only a few months when they got engaged and realized later that she moved quickly because she was desperately trying to re-create the dream of "the perfect white-picket-fence family, with grown children coming home for holidays, bringing the grandchildren—the dream I had just lost by divorcing," as she tells me. It took her more than a year of financial wrangling just to get out of her second marriage, and years to recover from the shame and humiliation of a second divorce.

"I know now that there is no dream family out there if it isn't inside me first," she says. "I'm sorry my children had to be exposed to this guy and go through that awful marriage, but if it hadn't happened I would still be driven by this dream to restore what I lost when I lost my first marriage. If I ever remarry again, I have much more awareness now and the tools to make a conscious choice."

A friend in my yoga class tells me between poses one night that she has finally decided to move out of the house she shares with her second husband. Her twelve-year-old stepson smashed the glass coffee table in anger the night before, and her husband did little more than shrug.

"I can't take it," she says, wiping away tears. "I actually feel unsafe around them. My husband told me yesterday it would be better if I didn't eat supper with them because the kids dislike me so much. This is my home? I can't believe I gave up my wonderful apartment to live like the maid—eating in the kitchen. It's unbelievably humiliating."

I went home that afternoon and pondered my neat, quiet house. The pansies were blooming in the front yard, the boys were out back blissfully whacking at each other with plastic bats. The cat was crouched in the outfield, hoping someone would hit a line drive. In a few minutes, they would all troop in for dinner and we would have our usual—macaroni and cheese, soup, chicken tenders. No one would tell *me* to eat in the kitchen.

. . .

The next time Charlie comes back for a weekend, I take him aside and tearfully tell him I don't know if this relationship is a good thing. I list all the complications, all the unknowns and unknowables—from how the kids might handle things if we got, um, really serious, to where we would live if we ever wanted to, well, live together. I carefully avoid the M word, but he knows what I mean. He looks at me, his eyes serious and sad.

"Who have you been talking to?"

"People. It doesn't always work, you know," I say.

"What doesn't?"

"Relationships like ours. They're pretty complicated. You're in the middle of your divorce, you need time. Maybe things will look different to you a year from now. How do you really know I'm the one for you?"

"Do you think we should split up?" he asks, his voice rising.

"No, no. Not really. I just, well, I want you to feel you have options. I want you to feel free to say you made a mistake if you find you made a mistake."

He pulls me into a hug. "Is that it? Is that what's bothering you?"

"Yes. I don't want you to feel trapped."

"I haven't made a mistake and I don't feel trapped, nothing like that. You are the one thing that is keeping me from going crazy," he says, beginning to smile.

"Well, maybe the relationship is fine, but the timing is bad. Don't you ever worry about that?"

It was hard to deny. The demands of the first semester of business school had left him hollow-eyed and worried; he had little time left for all the other demands in his life—his children, his divorce lawyer, the house caught in mid-renovation when the marriage split up, his dog, his aging car. Me. When he came home on weekends, he raced around restocking the refrigerator, taking his kids to their games and the library and helping with homework and meeting with the workmen. In between, he tried to study and catch up on his sleep. On Saturday mornings, he would slip out and meet me in the park for a run. It was about the only time we had together.

"Maybe I should give you a year to get things in order, let you date around a bit," I say, not really wanting to look at him.

"Date around? I don't want to date around. I only want to see you."

"Well, maybe this isn't healthy, getting involved with me right away. Maybe you need to date some other people to make sure I'm perfect for you."

"I don't need to date other people to know you are perfect for me," he says. "It's not like I've haven't looked around. You're not the only one who has a good idea of what's out there. Look," he said more gently, taking my hands, "I know things are rough right now, but I'm getting my life in order. Give me time."

"Well, it will take time."

He's quiet for a long moment, then looks at me again. "I wasn't going to ask you to do this, but I've wondered if you could get a teaching appointment in Charlottesville for next year and move down there with me," he says.

"Move to Charlottesville? With my boys?"

"Well, I'm really just brainstorming here. Maybe a sort of a sabbatical for you. We could rent a farmhouse or something, have the dog with us there, bring my boys down on the week-ends."

"But I had a sabbatical just a few years ago. Sweetie, that sounds really nice but it wouldn't work."

"I kinda knew that," he says, looking down. "I just miss you."

I fall quiet for a moment, because what I'm really thinking is hard to say. But I have to be honest with him; it's the only way. "I have to tell you something. I hope you won't take this the wrong way, but I'm not going to live with someone I'm not married to. Maybe if it was just me, but I can't ask my children to do that. If you want to live with me, you're going to have to sign up for the whole nine yards."

"Nine yards?"

"Yep, diamond ring, minister, big cake—the works."

"It's going to be a while before I can do that."

"I know. I figure about four years."

"Four years?" His voice tightens again. "I can't wait four years!"

"But you have so much work to do," I counter. "You have to finish your degree—that's two years. Then you have to come back to Washington and settle into being a dad again. That's going to take time. Then if we decide to do this, it's going to take some real planning. I figure four years. By then maybe we'll know for sure."

"I love you too much already to wait four years," he says. "Please tell me it's not four years."

"Well, maybe three." I look at him, softening a bit. "Maybe we can do it in three."

"You don't think we could do this right after I graduate?"

"No, I think it would be hard on your kids. I think they need some transition time, with you back home and a chance to work out the custody schedule. You guys need to be a family together before we show up."

"You mean I'm going to have to learn to cook." He smiles.

"Yep. But cooking's not that hard. Hey, look at the bright side," I say. "If I turn out to be the one for you, you will have divorced and remarried without going through dating purgatory. Now that I think of it, I'm not sure that's fair."

"You're right, it's not fair," he says, starting to smile again. Then he hugs me close. "Lucky me."

And that was when Charlie came up with his plan. He suggested I drive back with him to Charlottesville on Sunday afternoon every other week, then stay over Monday and take the train back to Washington early Tuesday morning. We would get some time alone together, then be able to connect again on the weekends. This was a brilliant idea, because my children were with their dad from Sunday through to Tuesday, and I didn't have any classes to teach on Mondays.

"You really want me underfoot down there?" I asked.

"More than anything. Come this weekend."

We soon were sharing quiet evenings while he studied and I graded papers. "I can't believe I'm dating a professor," he would say. "Do I get an A?" We would take late-night walks through the quiet town, admiring Jefferson's buildings. The apartment was small and worn, but it was our chance for a honeymoon,

our chance to pretend we did not have four children and complicated lives back in Washington. I would grocery shop and
cook him a few meals to leave in the freezer, then kiss him
good-bye in the early-morning mist on the train platform. It felt
like something out of Hemingway.

CHAPTER THREE

Of Princes and Frogs

THE ROMANTIC INTENSITY OF THE first few months of any relationship often breeds the heady sense of intimate connection and deep familiarity that Charlie and I felt, as many therapists will tell you. I knew this, so I was inwardly watchful even as I enjoyed the blissful feelings. Charlie was undeniably a close match, but quick to protect myself from too much hope, still concerned it wouldn't work in the long run, I secretly questioned whether I wanted a man who was a close match.

I had dated someone years earlier who told me, in that early romantic stage, that I was his soul mate. As soon as he said it, I realized he wasn't my soul mate, though I was loath to admit it. I was having too much fun just getting out of the house and having someone think I was sexy. I wasn't about to break up with him right away just because of the soul mate problem. But that relationship left me wondering if you could still be a happy couple even if you weren't soul mates. When I considered the marriages in my own family, being a soul mate team didn't always spell success or even seem to be a requirement for it. My own wonderful parents clearly have a marriage of opposites, though they share a deep core of values and interests. I doubt they ever worried that they weren't soul mates. Frankly, what worked for them was the businesslike way they went about managing their life, without all the doubts that suck at the legs of my generation.

What the hell is a soul mate, anyway? I wasn't sure, so I didn't say anything to Charlie about being soul mates. I didn't want to inspire doubt. But as I got to know him better, it began to dawn on me that maybe we weren't exactly cut from the same cloth, as I had thought. My parenting style is more hands-on, while my self-confidence is lower. He has a head for numbers, the kind of guy who can figure out the tax savings of a particular mortgage in his head. Despite my background as a business writer, I reach for the calculator or, more likely, ask the real estate agent to figure it out. He is a reporter's reporter, endlessly curious and fearless about asking people probing questions, though he always does so politely. I am more hesitant in my work, like to have my facts in a row, am more reserved and shyer. I am a planner, a person who prefers to know the schedule well in advance, while he runs his life by the seat of the pants—filling in time gaps with whatever needs attention next. It drove me nuts, when I let it.

As I began to peer into the darker recesses of Charlie's life, I noticed more differences. His closets, for example, were a nightmare—the type that appears on the EPA's roster of toxic waste sites. Mine were so well organized, I could send my mother in there to retrieve something with just verbal instructions. Charlie's organizational system, or lack thereof, was unsettling, but I couldn't quite understand why. While it was different from the way I lived, it felt familiar. Several months later, the awful truth dawned: I had managed to fall in love with someone not too dissimilar from—horrors—my ex-husband! How could this have happened? Charlie seemed so much like me until, well, until I examined the contents of his garage. If I was hoping to marry someone better than my first husband—which is the point of divorce, after all—how could I have ended up standing there, hands on hip, suggesting curtly once again that someone needed a filing system?

The remarried couples among my friends often joked that their divorce and remarriage amounted to an upgrade, as if spouses could be traded in like cars for a newer model. If divorce is about jettisoning the defective first spouse, then remarriage is about a second chance, about finding the right partner this time, someone you can stay with because, well, this one is easier to love. And most remarried people told me that the new spouse "was nothing like" the old one—except for those disquieting moments when the second spouse was behaving just like the first.

As I discovered during my years as a divorced white forty-something female, the trick to remarrying was not just meeting the right guy, but recognizing that he was a prince even if he had some distinctly froglike qualities. It meant having the confidence that I could pick a partner who would be good for me, despite earlier failures. We might try our damnedest to remarry people different from our first spouses, but how could we know different would make us happy, or which kind of different?

On the other hand, did we need to find someone easier to love or did we need to learn to be more loving, to learn how to kiss a frog? In the fairy tale, it is the kiss that reveals the prince, not the interrogation that precedes it. But I still wasn't sure what I was looking for. Was loving a soul mate going to feel comforting or claustrophobic? If I tried to avoid someone with depression issues this time by jumping into the arms of a cock-eyed optimist, was that going to make me happy? Maybe I liked a little melancholy.

That was the problem—I wasn't sure what I liked in a man, or what I wanted to live with.

My older sister is a pastoral counselor who lives and works in California, land of the divorced and remarrying. She is also divorced and remarried herself, having gone through both crises at earlier stages of her life, so I called to ask her about the soul mate problem, and what it meant that Charlie's closets looked alarmingly like my ex-husband's.

"You two must be getting serious," Annie says. "Have you guys talked about getting married?"

"Well, not directly. We don't use the M word," I say. "But we do use the F word a lot."

"The F word?"

"The future. We talk about the future all the time. But sometimes I wonder if I'm fooling myself. Do you think you have to be soul mates for it to work? To be sure it just won't go bad, like the first marriage?"

"Ah," she says, then puts on her therapist hat. "What I can tell you is that we all operate under the illusion that if we just change partners, everything will work out." As a minister, she does a lot of premarital counseling, and she's seen many couples ride this hope into remarriage, only to wake up a few months later facing problems that feel disconcertingly familiar. "Unfortunately, what I see is that those who haven't really examined how they contributed to the demise of their first marriage are likely to run into similar patterns in their new marriage."

"So it isn't necessarily about Charlie?"

"That's right. It's about you. It is more about whether you can live with messy closets. It's about how you value what else he brings to the table."

"You're saying he could be my soul mate even if he has messy closets?"

"Forget the soul mate business. It's about whether you are ready to make all the compromises that come with remarrying—from how you keep your closets to how you raise your kids and how you spend your money. It all gets messy, honey, the whole thing. Not just the closets. The question is, do you want that? Are you ready for that?"

After my conversation with Annie, I start waking up at night to stare at the ceiling and think about frogs. I feel a little as if by falling in love with Charlie, someone eminently marriageable who very much wanted to be married again, I have stepped on an amusement park ride called Remarriage Fantasyland. It's just inching out of the station, but already I am both excited and scared, calculating the odds of crashing as I smile nervously. I want to be pragmatic and sensible, my usual self, but my hopes and expectations are all jumbled up with my doubts.

So I started poking around in remarriage books and step-family websites, trying to get a handle on this fantasy. I believe I am entertaining the idea of remarriage only because Charlie has walked into my life, not because I am tired of being divorced or afraid my now-teenagey sons need a guy around the house or because I am worried about running out of money. At least that's what I tell myself. Then one lonely night, as I am cruising the Internet and sipping a brandy, I stumble across a website posting called Ten Reasons Not to Get Remarried. There at the top of the page is this: loneliness. "Don't get remarried because you are lonely, because lonely people will just end up being lonely in their remarriage," it says.

I have no idea who has compiled this list—some social seer, a wise elder, perhaps a psychopathic curmudgeon—but I find it unsettling. Along with loneliness, the list advises against remarrying for any of the other following reasons: love at first sight, rebounding, rebellion, obligation, financial advancement, sexual attraction, remarital pregancy, pressure, and escape.

So I am to remarry only if I have no hope of improving my financial status, which would be unlikely for any single mother not to want. I am to remarry only if I feel no pressure from society or family (as if that would ever happen). Only if I am not sexually attracted to the person, which raises the question of what I am supposed to feel instead. Only if I feel no sense of obligation, even if the person has become an important part of my life and I have become important to him. And I am not supposed to remarry to either escape or rebel against my lonely, on-the-fringe life (of course I am trying to escape being lonely and belonging to no one). As for love, I'm guilty there, too. It wasn't exactly love at first sight, but the attraction between us has been strong from the first smile. It was sort of love at about sixth sight.

I was doomed. I was deep into a remarriage fantasy, and for all the wrong reasons. I hated this list, because it suggested my heart was not pure enough. That by wanting to change my life, wanting love and sex and companionship, not to mention additional emotional and financial security, I was doing something suspect and indefensible. I might not be pregnant, but I was not doing much better than the girl who remarries to give her child a father's name. It was enough to make one go live in a cave.

So who are we, the many brides and grooms with previous experience, and how well do we know ourselves or understand the reasons we remarry? How well do we understand our own neuroses and what we can take in a partner? We range from those in their twenties seeking to recover from short, childless first marriages to seniors looking for a companion for their final years. We are the parents of babies, the parents of teens, empty nesters, people with complex lives and people with simple lives. Some are rich, some are stable, many are in crisis, and some are making do. But all, on some level, are lonely and filled with the hope of the second chance.

Americans, despite their high divorce rate, continue to believe strongly in marriage as an institution. Fully 75 percent of divorced people remarry, most within five years. Yet more remarriages fail than first marriages, and the more times you remarry, the more likely you are to redivorce. It's hard not to fear that failure will breed more failure.

Sociologists will tell you that second marriages are already at higher risk because they are made up of people willing to leave a marriage, people who are not allergic to divorce. Anybody with a strong personal or religious reason not to divorce will stay in their first marriage, whether they are happy or not. Sociologists will also tell you that the divorced are more likely to be people who were lousy at both communication and conflict resolution in their first marriages. They speak of traits that tend to show up in the divorced, especially the repeat offenders: irritability, impulsivity, failure to take responsibility for one's behavior, failure to learn from one's mistakes. If people fail to use their divorce to learn new relationship skills, they won't have much luck in their next sashay down the aisle.

One of my favorite divorce experts is E. Mavis Hetherington, the University of Virginia psychologist who has led a thirty-year study of divorcing and remarrying couples and their families. And in her new book, *For Better or for Worse,* Hetherington writes that divorce opens up something she calls a window of change. Divorce survivors who make good use of this window to, say, get more education, or pursue new job opportunities or develop new skills and more mature behavior are those who are more likely to remarry successfully. "People who seize the window of change often learn from the past, but people who ignore the window usually don't," she says. "They continue to engage in self-defeating, immature, or antisocial behavior, and to exhibit poor problem-solving skills. And unless something else in the new marriage differs markedly, the immaturity, the helplessness, the substance abuse and chronic depression that undermined the first marriage will eventually destroy the second."

Had I made the most of my window of change? Had I learned from my mistakes, taken responsibility for myself? Gotten rid of all that, ah, irritability? By the time I met Charlie, I was seven years out of my marriage, an older and wiser person than when I was married the first time. I was also a statistical anomaly. Most people remarry much sooner and faster, often within a year of meeting each other and usually within a few years of their divorce. In fact, the majority of remarriers move in together before remarrying, then sort of slide into marriage as their finances and lives intertwine. Which made me wonder if I was some kind of stick-in-the-mud girl unwilling to take a chance. Getting too comfortable in my singlehood, growing rigid with age and habit. Sometimes I thought I needed to remarry just to crank open the windows of my soul again. Remarriage as renewal.

My friend Danielle, who has married twice and divorced twice, joked to me one day over lunch that the first time she married someone like her mother, and the second time she married someone like her father. Engaged for a third time, she is approaching this marriage differently. "This time," she says, "I'm hoping to marry a husband."

Danielle admits she moved too quickly to marry her second husband in part because she was fighting a custody battle with her ex-husband, who had remarried and had another child, and she felt she needed to show the judge she could provide an equally stable household for her kids. She also felt uncomfortable being in a sexually active relationship outside marriage while also serving as minister of a local church.

"But it wasn't just that," she says. "I felt my second husband would provide such a loving way to do marriage, so different from my first marriage, and I wanted that opportunity. My first marriage had been too hard, and this marriage seemed so soft. What I didn't appreciate was that his softness wasn't going to be able to deal with my children."

After several years together, which culminated in a long depression for her husband and an inability of both of them to modify their own emotional styles, they split up. Danielle says her approach toward her third engagement is a direct result of what she learned from that failure. "I find I am much more protective of my children this time around, much more concerned with how this marriage and the children and family that come with it support my kids and support me. I'm engaged now because I love this man and because we work together really well. I have much better boundaries now."

When it comes down to it, why do people remarry? Is it about rings and property and security? Do we remarry to avoid a lonely or impoverished retirement? Do we remarry to escape boredom? Do we remarry to regain our position in society, our place at the domestic table? Do we remarry to get the kids we didn't get the first time around, or because the kids we have are just too hard to raise alone? Maybe, I think darkly, people marry so they will have a scapegoat in the family again, someone to blame for their problems rather than their rebellious children and vanishing ex-spouses. Every time I get irritated over one of Charlie's last-minute attempts to cram too many errands into a half hour, I wonder if that is my hidden goal. Maybe I was searching for my shadow more than my soul mate.

Those who remarry say it's all about love, but the psychologists and sociologists who study these things say remarriage is usually motivated by other, less conscious factors as well, factors that sometimes get obscured by the romance but drive people forward nonetheless. Professors Lawrence H. Ganong and Marilyn Coleman, a remarried team from the University of Missouri who study remarriage, say that people remarrying tend to have a rosy view of what they are doing, but mostly because they don't have the courage to "delve too deeply into potential difficulties," as the professors put it. Ganong refers to this as the tunnel vision of love. Many remarried women, particularly those left with primary custody for children, will admit they were looking for someone to "be the dad," as much as they were looking for love.

For my friend Renee, a single mom with full custody of a hyperactive five-year-old, remarrying was the fastest way to provide the discipline and security her son needed. "My husband had these three wonderful kids, all very well adjusted, and when Justin was with them he behaved much better than when he was alone with me," she tells me shortly after the wedding. "This marriage was all about the kids, and what would be best for them. Not everything is perfect, but Justin is doing much better in this family."

"Are you happy?" I ask her. "Are you glad you remarried?"

"Of course," she says, a bit evasive. "I'm happy that Justin is happy."

Remarrying can ease the child care burden for custodial and noncustodial divorced parents alike, but some potential partners are unwilling to take up that burden. Men are still far less likely than women to be custodial parents, although there are more and more divorced dads with significant time with their kids, from legal custody to expanded visitation schedules. Joint custody is still the exception, but increasingly less so. My ex-husband, a joint custody dad, tells me that many of his romances were quashed when the women discovered he had two little boys underfoot. "Even though I was capable of taking care of the kids, most of these women suspected I wanted a wife to take over," he tells me. "Most had grown children, and they just didn't want to start with little kids again."

Money is also a factor, the sociologists have found, particularly for women, though most would never admit that. Women have a stronger financial incentive to remarry than men because they tend to lose more wealth when they divorce. Divorce, it turns out, can push women who have lived a comfortable life out of the middle class and down into the range of the working poor. I met my friend Sherri when our kids were in school together, just two divorced moms waiting at the bus stop in a middle-class neighborhood. But while I owned my house, she was living with her parents again because her job as a grocery store checker didn't pay enough to support a house of her own in a good school district. Every morning she talked about the tension between her aging parents and her rowdy boys, and her desire to get out before the family imploded. A few years later I ran into her again. She had remarried and, with her new husband, now had a home of her own, with enough room for her teens and a new baby.

This isn't unusual, says Hetherington of the University of Virginia, who found that the fastest way for divorced women to improve their financial status was to remarry. There are—if you read between the lines of these studies—plenty of desperate women out there.

Women who are financially secure and well educated, however, as I was, tend to be choosier in selecting a second husband than those who live closer to the edge—simply because we can afford it. Still, even a woman with her own retirement account may find the tug of additional security nearly irresistible. Beyond a second income, most men bring additional resources, such as houses, pension plans, or medical insurance, as well as emotional and logistical support. Guys have been observed helping with everything from aging parents to broken-down cars. Who wouldn't want one of those, particularly if he had a good job?

The question, then, goes back to finding and recognizing the prince in the grass. Is the guy who looks so good from a distance going to turn out to be the real thing up close? Most of us doubt it, and it turns out we're right. There are fewer princes than frogs. Lots fewer.

Ganong and Coleman have found that most people looking for someone to remarry not only believe there are fewer options, but are in fact dating in a market with a poor selection of possible mates. (Sociologists must have been created to take care of the hope problem.) It turns out that people of lower socioeconomic status are more likely to divorce than those who are better off, so the pool of remarriageable people has a greater proportion of less educated people with marginal incomes who are stuck in unskilled jobs, which are less secure. If it looks like all the good people are already taken, that is not just a perception.

In my web searching, I found a report from the Centers for Disease Control and Prevention that said divorced women are significantly less likely to remarry today than they were a generation or two ago. In the 1950s, nearly two-thirds of divorced women remarried within five years. Now only half will do so in that same time period, and the odds of divorced women remarrying after five years of being divorced are slim indeed. Why? Because there are more than two eligible divorced women today for every divorced man. That alone explained a lot of what I knew about the world of divorced single moms, most of whom have little expectation of finding someone wonderful to remarry. I was beginning to understand why my friend warned me to grab Charlie quick before someone else snapped him up.

I have coffee one day with an old family friend, a man my father's age who, as he put it, married four times before he got it right. His first wife gave him two daughters but then took off, leaving the girls in his care. His second wife stepparented his children, but turned out to be an alcoholic, and he divorced her after ten years of problems. His third wife had two young boys, and the marriage lasted only a year. "In fact, it went bad the first day," Richard tells me, shaking his head. "It was the same mess."

By the time he met Abby, his fourth wife, the relationship that stuck, he had done some thinking about his previous failures and knew he wanted to do things differently. But his own family—his parents and brothers—were dead set against him marrying again.

"They looked at my history, and her, and her three kids and said oh no, don't do this," says Richard, laughing at the memory. "But she was so sweet, so different from the other women I had married, and I loved her so much I couldn't *not* marry her. It was out of my hands." He and Abby have now been married twenty-five years and appear as happy as any pair of grandparents in the world.

Out of his hands. It's so romantic, and it resonates in my own heart. But then the doubt returns. That's what he says, but maybe Richard just got lucky. This was his fourth wife, after all. Marriage by trial and error. When I asked what was different, Richard said he didn't feel like he needed to rescue Abby, or that she needed to rescue him. She was recently divorced, but doing quite well in her newfound independence. Richard's girls were mostly grown and gone. Neither one was looking for someone to pick up the pieces for them, which allowed them to come together more cooperatively, Richard said.

Then there's the rescue fantasy, the one my codependent self lives for. This one played big in my first marriage, and has been a snare in Charlie's life as well. When we first met, we assured each other and ourselves again and again that we didn't want to rescue each other. Charlie let me pay my way on dates (no financial rescue) and I respected his boundaries around his children, still fresh from their parents' separation (no surrogate mom rescue). But in point of fact, it is impossible to avoid getting hooked into believing a remarriage will bring both happiness and a better life for the beloved, no matter how independent he or she is. It may not be a high drama rescue, with somebody fighting off evicting landlords or abusive ex-boyfriends, but all love carries with it the promise of better times.

This hope that lies curled in my heart also goes against one of the rules of my post-divorce dating protocol, which was: Don't hope for change. If I didn't like the person as he was, I shouldn't hope to like him better after the wedding vows. The marriage gurus will tell you that's lesson one, but also that most people fail to appreciate how persistent this type of hope can be. Hope does spring eternal, and maybe that's how it triumphs over experience. It just keeps popping up.

But perhaps the hope that springs weedlike around second marriages is a function of the disorder and unhappiness of divorce. When I first met Charlie he was haggard with worry and that corrosive sense of failure that comes with all divorce. Yes, his life was chaotic, but mine had been in a similar state when I broke up with my ex-husband. In this light, it was hard not to hope or even expect that things would get better. And it was hard not to hope that the things I thought he really needed to change might actually change, such as learning to love well-organized closets. And from there, it was impossible not to hope for other things: that Charlie would persist as a prince

even as I got to know him better; that he would not leave me
after witnessing my frog-like moments; that he would not run
in the opposite direction the day I gifted him with a copy of
How to Organize Your Office. That the odds were in my favor
this time, even as every statistic and ounce of experience told
me to be realistic.

But when I shut the door on Charlie's closets and my own
fears, I would turn around and see this tall, handsome, smiling
guy who just wouldn't get out of my life. Not that I was really
trying to get rid of him. We had connected on such a deep level
that sometimes I just want to stop thinking and let life carry
me forward. As our early infatuation ripened into something
deeper, supported by a rich e-mail correspondence that kept us
connected all day long, I began to relax into the idea that I was
well on the road to remarrying. Ultimately I saw that it would
come down to trusting something deep inside me that would
know what was healthy and good. As I watched this man, I
could see patience and maturity and stability in nearly every
move he made, even as he was explaining why he would rather
not clean up his office.

And as I talked with more remarried people, I found there
was another set of stories, those from the fortunate couples who
remarried well, into a life that was challenging but ultimately
rewarding beyond measure. For the couples who made it, it was
the love and companionship that proved most valuable.

And it turns out, we all know this on some level. My
divorced friends, even the most cynical, all carried around a
remarriage fantasy that was about that kind of love, even as

they swore hell was more likely to freeze over before they stumbled into it.

For Kate, the dream was to have someone there when she got older, someone to go out with and share a glass of wine. "I'd like to meet someone in a situation other than a date, someone I could become friends with and have the relationship evolve gradually. It happens in books. I don't know if it happens in life," she tells me.

My friend Jeanne, who divorced her husband when her daughter was two, says she originally hoped to find a father for her child, but that her fantasy has changed as her daughter has grown up.

"Now it's about something different," Jeanne says. "It's going to be very hard for me when she goes off to college because our little dyad has been so strong. When I realized that, a few years ago, I knew I had to get a life. So I'm looking for a life." She tells me she dreams of finding a man who will let her read the newspaper from beginning to end without needing her to get up and get him something. Someone to share life's burdens and celebrate the things she enjoys. But sometimes, she admits, it is even simpler than that. "What do I want?" she says. "Really want? I want someone to take out the damn garbage. I don't need diamonds. I just need someone to take out the garbage."

When I talk to Suzanne again, she hits the nail on the head. "There is this wonderful sense of propulsion that comes from a strong relationship, this sense that someone believes in you, believes that you can do challenging things," she tells me. "And there is that intimacy where you can just glance up at a dinner party and meet his eyes and know what he is thinking. I'd like that again."

I nod, feeling more than a bit smug, thinking of the last dinner party and the looks Charlie and I shared over the candelabra. That's what I love best already.

CHAPTER FOUR

Baggage

THE SUMMER AFTER HIS FIRST year of business school, Charlie moved back to Washington to work for a dot-com start-up, and try to settle his complicated life a bit before diving back into his second year in Charlottesville. He and his soon-to-be ex-wife were still trying to finalize their divorce, going through the tough passage of dividing up real estate, household items, wedding presents, artwork, and heirlooms, while their boys struggled to figure out how and where everybody was going to end up in the post-divorce future. Charlie lived out of a large laundry basket stacked high with T-shirts, underwear, and divorce papers, which he schlepped from car to house and back to the car again whenever he moved camp. He stayed with me when my kids were with their dad or at friends, then relocated to his D.C. house when his children were there, and sometimes out to the farm in Virginia that he and his wife had bought as a second home. Between his work pressures, the divorce settlement, and needy kids, he found it almost worse than when he was away at school. We had lost our quiet Charlottesville togetherness now that he was back in town, and by summer's end I was feeling overwhelmed by the complications of his world.

As if to clear the air, Charlie invited me to go with him and his boys to Cape Cod in August, to stay at his mother's house in Eastham. Of course, I said. I love the Cape, especially at the end of the season, when the light in the early evening catches the edges of the sand flats exposed at low tide and makes the whole world rosy and soft. I saw us walking hand in hand through the shallows, sharing a lobster dinner for two in Orleans, hiking the cliffs over near Nauset Light. Many of my happiest childhood memories are from the Cape, and so too for my boys. I had already planned to split a week at my family's cabin in Brewster with my ex-husband, so I could fit that plan in with Charlie's trip. It would be a logistical challenge, but hey—the Cape was worth it.

By the time we got back, two weeks later, however, I wasn't so sure. If there was a low point in our romance, it was that vacation on the Cape. My ex-husband, Ron, drove up with my boys earlier in the week, and settled in at the cabin my family has owned for generations. Midweek, Charlie and I set out on the twelve-hour drive with his boys. It was the first real trip Charlie and I had taken together with them, and it understandably made them nervous. They were both cranky and difficult on the drive north, demanding stops at bookstores and fighting with each other in the backseat. They clearly had mixed feelings about sharing their grandmother and her house with my children and me, and didn't know what to make of the fact that I had been installed in the front seat of their dad's car, a symbol of power and position in their world. This shouldn't have surprised me. I had already noticed my own kids having the same problem sharing their grandparents with Charlie's kids, Adam and Matt, at an earlier holiday. There was something too close about this grandparent business, something the boys weren't ready for, but we didn't realize it at the time. All I knew was that I nearly bailed for the train in New York. When we got to the Cape, my children were upset to see me arrive with Charlie's family, as if I didn't belong to them anymore, and they got cranky and demanding too.

Ron was struggling, as well, with what Charlie might mean to our future. In the eight years since we separated, neither one of us had seriously considered remarrying until now. A remarriage would upset the delicate balance Ron and I had achieved in our post-divorce relationship, possibly crack open the potential for resentment or loyalty issues around the kids. This is not uncommon. Sociologists report that a remarriage of one divorced spouse usually sparks some deterioration in his or her relationship with the ex, and I had no reason to think I would be immune. Jesse, my youngest, picked up on his dad's unhappiness, and added that tension to his own distaste for change and for finding himself at the bottom of the pecking order when our boys were together. Charlie and I each stayed with our own children in our own family cottages, but met for daytime fun that often stretched into the evenings. The boys sparred over the Ping-Pong table and the remote control.

One day old friends of Charlie's, a couple that knew him from his married life, came to visit. They were both interested in meeting me and also uncomfortable, feeling caught between Charlie and his ex-wife, an old friend. I thought we had agreed to a beach picnic, but found them already eating lunch at the house when we arrived. I felt like an afterthought the rest of the day, rather than a treasured partner-to-be. Charlie and his friends joked about people they knew and their fun times together as young marrieds, while I sat watching the kids in the surf. The beach party finally disintegrated when splashing and name-calling broke out between our kids during a Wiffle ball game. The other family watched, grim-faced, as Charlie and I tried to corral our children and get the perpetrators to apologize. I was embarrassed and angry—embarrassed that we weren't doing better and angry that I didn't feel more support. I drove my boys back to our cabin and sat that evening watching the bats flitting over the lake in the twilight. Charlie had hardly had time to talk with me on this vacation, much less take long walks on the beach. He was busy on the phone with his divorce lawyer every morning, trying to finalize the settlement, and it felt like all his energy was still being funneled into his first mar-riage. His boys were still grieving over their parents' divorce, still too traumatized and conflicted. My kids were younger, weaker, easily pushed around. Charlie's friends would never want to know me if they all felt loyal to his ex. There was too much baggage. It all looked impossible.

Divorced people looking for a mate are like a spaceship soaring through space, a trail of trash and debris following close behind. No matter how perfect Charlie was for me and me for him, there was more to the story than our romance. And the minute we stopped long enough to smooch, the debris field came raining down on our heads.

Between the two of us we had four boys, four homes, three old cars, two incompatible pets, closets full of the detritus of our previous lives, books and papers stacked to the ceiling of the storage space, enough musical instruments for a band, enough furniture to outfit a boarding school, and enough lawn equipment to start a service. Aside from the very real baggage of our lives, we also carried a load of emotional baggage: bad habits from our first marriages, histories with other people, fears for our children. We also both had big, all-encompassing families, and large circles of friends with often divided loyalties. We had commitments to bar mitzvahs and graduations for years to come, grandparents who missed us, and numerous friends dropping by on conferences or trips. We also had what I thought of as our para-families, our ex-spouses and their kin, whose lives sometimes intertwined with ours and other times imposed on ours. It was enough to make any sane person think twice.

We hardly thought of the boys as baggage, but there they were nonetheless, hulking young men with their own perfectly appropriate teenage issues and growing suspicions about the intimacy between us. Whether they liked it or not, they were passengers on this journey—hostages, they might have said— who struggled to have a voice and who were capable of all-out mutiny if their concerns weren't heard. They weren't small children who could be expected just to fall into line. They were going to have their own opinions, and we would need to listen to those and accommodate them.

I had introduced Charlie to my boys first, a few months after we met, and he soon became a fixture at our Saturday-morning breakfast table. He and I would meet for a run in the park, then go back to my place for bagels or oatmeal while his boys slept in. David, my older boy, took to Charlie quickly, enjoying his wordplay and questions and relaxed, boy-focused manner. Jesse, my younger son, was more watchful, wondering what Charlie was up to. Jesse had never particularly liked the men I brought home, though he knew to be polite and often enjoyed outings with other families. These breakfasts struck Jesse as unusual, not the kind of date he had seen before, so he would sometimes join us at the table, sometimes not. Charlie could tell it would take time to win him over.

After about six months, having given his kids time to adjust to their parents' separation, I got to meet Charlie's boys. Adam was two years older than David, fifteen and intellectually precocious. We connected quickly because he was curious about my university life and liked hearing about campus controversies and issues. Matt, who fell between David and Jesse in age, was more private, more watchful, like Jesse. He seemed deep in his basketball and his friends, and I sensed that was the safest place for him, given the upheaval in his family. My own guys were in those same high intensity, middle school years when boys disappear into video games and their CD players and their Magic cards and their computers, instant messaging late into the night and talking about things that hold little interest for anyone else. I knew they would all emerge later, their brains curiously more developed, suddenly interested in the affairs of the world, and I was happy to wait for Matt to feel comfortable enough to come out of his shell.

Gradually we started doing things all together, usually scheduling something fun, like laser tag, and involving other families to act as buffers. Because they were boys, it was difficult to tell how everyone felt about being together. When asked, they would shrug and say, "I guess it's okay," or something equally vague. I noticed that Charlie's kids drew closer to each other when they were around my boys, squabbling less and looking to each other for solidarity. Sometimes they all seemed to enjoy the larger group, while other times disagreements over a chess game or a favored seat in the car would flare into something more, as the boys scuffled for advantage. When that happened, Adam would sometimes leap in to ease the tension, saying something goofy but to the point, and I was grateful for his ability to both acknowledge problems and disarm them. He led the way for all the boys, and over time they began to share jokes, learned to poke fun without being cruel and to share the jostling between sibling groups rather than just with their own brother. Being boys, or perhaps just being sweet kids who wanted their parents to be happy, they were forgiving while also keeping their protective distance. We knew that time would bring them closer but also that it wouldn't happen automatically. If we were going to merge these two different families into one large clan, we would have to be creative and careful, to balance needs and feelings.

As potential stepchildren, Adam and Matt looked pretty easy. They were generally good-natured guys who did well in school, had interesting things to say at the dinner table, and were already lining up their college applications. Well, at least Adam was. How hard could it be? But my friends who had taken on stepchildren, most of whom I knew to be charming, easy kids, still gave me sidelong looks and told me to stay tuned for future developments. After the trip to Cape Cod, I knew there would be other moments. I knew it would be a challenge to my patience and equilibrium to live with children over whom I had little authority and with whom, at first, I had not much of a bond.

We didn't even have a car big enough for all of us, other than Charlie's broken-down old Suburban, which smelled heavily of horse and dog. I was still driving the cheap compact car that had gotten me through the tight money years of my early divorce; it was now ten years old and lacked all modern safety features, like air bags. Charlie was horrified when he first saw it, saying he couldn't sleep at night thinking that the love of his life was driving around the Washington Beltway in a car offering little more protection than a paper bag. By the time Charlie was halfway through his second year of business school, we had been together nearly eighteen months and were only more serious about each other, so he helped me buy a van. It was the first thing we did together financially, and I would not have allowed it if I wasn't pretty sure the van would soon become our family car. We wrote a lien against the car for the money he lent me. If we split up, I'd pay it back. We gave my old car to a charity and vowed to sell the Suburban as soon as possible. I could already see that streamlining our life was going to be necessary for my long-term sanity.

By the time Charlie was studying for his last final exams, his divorce was finished and the goods divided. He would keep the old house in Washington, caught in mid-renovation and still fraught with problems. His ex-wife had purchased a new house in Silver Spring, not far away, and Charlie had been left with the farm in Virginia. It was a lovely spot and an enviable second home, but also another complication. When we were together we were either at my house in Kensington, Charlie's house in Washington, the farm in Virginia, or his apartment in Charlottesville. I had toothbrushes and underwear stashed in each house, but never had the right ingredients in any of the kitchens. I lived out of an old canvas boat bag and longed for the day we were down to two houses, if not just one.

By then, I knew that marrying Charlie wasn't just about marrying a particular man; it was about choosing a future: a lifestyle and an extended family and children and an ex-wife, on top of my ex-husband. It was about opening up to some possibilities and shutting off others. It would also mean adjustments in the relationships that already dominated my life, with my kids, my family, my workplace, my ex-spouse, and my friends. It would mean a significant shift in how I spent my time, what I worried about, what I thought about and enjoyed and experienced. Sometimes I wasn't sure if I wanted to experience everything in his life. He brought more things to the table, both good and bad, and he was still suffering through his divorce. He was still easily riled by his ex-spouse, for example, and sometimes I resented having to go back over terrain I had covered years earlier.

I had toiled a long time to build a stable working relationship with my ex-husband, so that we could co-parent our children without conflict. It took therapy and mediation and lots of practice at biting my tongue, but what we had was precious and hard won. Now, however, I worried that Charlie and his ex-wife would have trouble moving beyond their tension, and that I would get pulled into the kind of stress I had so carefully avoided with Ron. Many years earlier, when I was a young woman, a wise old man had told me: "Don't marry someone with more troubles than you." I forgot that advice when I married Ron, but I had thought about it a lot during my post-divorce years. Yet now I seemed headed into the same trap.

And as if to punctuate the case, our pets were firmly squared off in opposite corners. Snowy, my six-toed tomcat, stayed outside and downwind whenever Charlie's dog came to visit. The cat had swiped the dog across the nose a few times, but it didn't seem to stop Rex.

"He's just trying to say hi," Charlie would say as Rex took off across the lawn in pursuit of Snowy every time they came to visit.

"Hi, and you're dog meat," I would counter, turning to go in only after the cat was safely over the back fence. "At least the boys are trying to get along. These two are hopeless."

Maybe we were too old to marry, I sometimes thought, usually late at night huddled in my dark living room and sipping brandy again, this time to numb the occasional feeling of hopelessness. I couldn't figure out how this would ever work. I didn't doubt Charlie was the man for me. I just feared that I shouldn't be considering this remarriage thing at all. That I had missed my chance at happiness by failing to find Charlie when I was twenty-six. That to marry him now, with all these children and our complicated lives, was hopelessly late. Because I didn't know if we could ever find or make a home for us that would feel like my home, because our pets would never get along, because our boys would probably prefer not to have stepbrothers and stepparents, because our ex-spouses might make our lives miserable. That it would never work because these things didn't work. If three out of four remarriages with children failed, I was beginning to understand why.

My deepest fear, though, wasn't really about all the outside baggage. It was about my own emotional baggage, a dark suspicion that I didn't have what it took to pull off a marriage. That I didn't have it the first time and probably had less of it now—whatever it was.

For years I had a sign in the kitchen that said AIN'T NOBODY HAPPY IF MOMMA AIN'T HAPPY, and I believed that statement. My sons believed that. Now I was afraid that I was going to be the unhappy one, the one who couldn't compromise, who couldn't bend, who would lose her patience and possibly her mind. That the boys and Charlie would all be fine living in the testosterone-charged mess that life together would inevitably become, and I would be the one who couldn't hack it.

One day in the library I picked up Dalma Heyn's book *Marriage Shock,* because the title alone sent a jolt of recognition through my body. Within minutes I was cross-legged on the floor, mesmerized by her analysis of one of the more troubling cultural icons around marriage, that of the Victorian wife as the angel in the house. According to Heyn, the notion of the angel in the house developed as a moral model for women as they adapted from being industrious frontierswomen to more protected keepers of the parlor during the emergence of the middle class in Victorian America. Conduct books of the time, guides penned by men that dictated how new wives should behave, counseled women to think of themselves as the angel in the house: kind, cheerful, sympathetic, ladylike, punctual, sober, prudent, self-sacrificing, proper, delicate, virtuous, respected, and chaste.

"It's impossible to imagine what real person the authors of the conduct books are invoking, since her virtuousness and radiance, her utter lack of vanity, aggression and desire . . . do not illustrate a recognizable woman," says Heyn. "What begins to come through is a shadowy ideal, a sort of collective hallucination, part child, part angel, part domestic servant. It's as if an entire culture got together to fantasize about God's own helpmate, personified it and called it a Wife."

What most interests me, however, is that Heyn believes the myth is still alive and well. That as soon as they marry, women often feel compelled, on some subconscious level, to edit themselves—to tone down their behavior, clean up their story, make themselves more presentable.

"The dusty words and ruthless tone of the conduct books still echo in a new bride's ear, dictating the revision of behavior and feelings that we have seen, urging her toward a symbol, a stereotype, bringing with it as its shadow a darkening of mood," she says.

I read this and suddenly recognize one of my own neuroses: the need to be the perfect wife, the need to be strong and sensible while also being sexy and attractive, sort of like the perfect shoe. I may have thrown over the myth of the angel in the house by divorcing, but I wasn't really free of her, because I could feel her shadowy presence as I contemplated being a wife again. This myth, in fact, may be particularly loaded for those who feel they failed in their first marriage, and most of us who remarry believe, on some level, that we did not perform particularly well at the wife thing the first time around. If we had been a good wife, after all, we might still be married.

As I later learned, second wives feel an intense pressure to be not only a better wife than they were the first time, but also better than their husband's now-discarded first wife. One psychologist calls this the defective wife syndrome, the subconscious desire of the second wife to be the wonderful "corrective" to the bad first wife. When I heard Charlie talk about his ex, I stood those frustrations on their heads and adopted them as rules of conduct. But before long I found myself chaffing under these self-imposed guidelines and sometimes even identifying with Charlie's ex-wife. I wasn't sure I could live up to my own standards for appropriate wifely behavior, much less carry around the baggage from their marriage.

If tortured long enough, I probably would admit that I wasn't so sure about this wife business. I wanted love and companionship and emotional support, but I wasn't sure I wanted the responsibilities of a wife—keeping track of everyone's birthday, serving as the family laundress, supervising the housecleaning (or doing it myself), penning thank-you notes and making phone calls and ordering our lives. I'm no dummy—I was the woman in this relationship, and many tasks would fall into my lap simply because I would be the only one who would think of them. I was already pretty busy serving as the mother hen of my university department. (Technically, I was the department head, but who were we kidding?) I also usually took the lead with my children, making sure their doctor appointments were lined up, their school forms and lunch boxes and gym clothes ready for the trade-off between houses. I wasn't sure I wanted more executive responsibility.

While Charlie was facing his last set of final exams that next spring, I had lunch with my real estate agent, Mary Lee, who remained a good friend. I was curious to know how housing prices were doing in my neighborhood, and she was curious about my possible remarriage.

"So, let's say a person—we don't need to mention any names—was going to sell a house like mine in my neighborhood next summer," I say. "Let's say they bought two years ago. What kind of profit would they make? Any? Or would it be a total loss?"

"Oh, you'll do fine with that house, honey," she reassures me. "You were right about the market—it's done great in that area. You'll make money for sure; we just won't know how much until we sell it." She pauses for a moment. "But before we get into that, here's what I want to know. Who's going to do all the cooking?"

"All the cooking?"

"Yeah," she said. "The Sunday dinners and the weekday evenings and breakfasts, and let's not forget packing all those lunches." She can't help it. She's worried about me and sees me getting trapped in the kitchen, cooking for a parade of men. This is not an unreasonable assumption, despite years of feminist training and my mother's legacy of independence and scrappiness. Charlie is a reluctant cook at best, and even though we would have each set of teenagers only half the time, it would still be a lot of milk and burgers. Mary Lee understands that, perhaps better than I do—she grew up as the only daughter in a family of seven brothers.

"You may need a second mortgage just to cover groceries," she says, shaking her head. After a second glass of wine, she confesses that she remarried three times, and each time, she says, she got stuck cooking and cleaning for an ungrateful husband. She is single now, and determined to stay that way.

"There are other types of men, Mary Lee," I say.

"Are there?" she muses. "Does your fiancé actually cook?"

I think of Charlie's pork tenderloin with plum sauce and his signature meat loaf. He cooks those, sometimes in such rapid succession his sons beg for mercy—or at least Thai takeout.

"Some. Well, more than he used to. He's a great cleaner-upper," I say, searching for solid ground. "He knows his laundry soap."

But Mary Lee doesn't buy it. I make one last stab. "It's time the boys learned to cook, anyway."

This is my true remarriage fantasy—that life in our merged household will mean the boys all mutate overnight into perfect children. Helpful, supportive, tolerant kids who take out the garbage without prodding, refrain from arguing, and hang up their color-coded towels. And learn to cook.

"Yeah, I'm planning to lay down a schedule where I'm only responsible for meals a few nights a week," I say.

Mary Lee looks at me again over the top of her glasses. "Lots of luck."

A few weeks later, Charlie marched through graduation at the business school, while I snapped pictures of his kids trying on his master's hood and his parents standing misty-eyed under the arches. We packed up the apartment in Charlottesville, feeling nostalgic already for the quiet evenings in that honeymoon place. We would no longer have a place that was just for us, but I felt we didn't need Charlottesville anymore. Despite all my concerns about the inherent complexities in marrying Charlie, our union just felt more and more right. We had weathered a two-year separation, the surliness of our children's first exposure to one another, and the final settlement of his divorce, and had come out the other side stronger than ever. The time in Charlottesville had given us the chance to learn how to talk with each other to sort out the problems and thorns. After a long day of moving boxes into a rented truck, we drove Charlie's stuff back to Washington, stopping to drop a load of things at his farm in Virginia. He was back in my life again full-time, older, wiser, better educated, divorced, and a good bit happier than when I met him two years earlier. And employed. He would be working on the business side for a *Washington Post* subsidiary that published technology magazines.

A few months later, on the second anniversary of our very first lunch together, Charlie takes me to the same Thai restaurant in Bethesda, and we sit in the window again. Ironically, he seems more nervous than the day we met, so I begin to think something wonderful will happen that night. But I'm not sure. We had taken a three-day weekend earlier in the summer to go to the Berkshires in Massachusetts for music and hiking. I had thought then that he would pop the question on top of Mount Greylock, but I came back empty-fingered. I wasn't sure what he wanted.

We order dinner. Charlie says he had to run to the car, he's forgotten something. He comes back with a huge bouquet of flowers and hands them to me. "Happy anniversary," he says.

I look them over. "How lovely, thank you." Flowers. Beautiful, to be sure, but nothing unusual. No engagement ring tied into the ribbon.

We eat dinner. No engagement ring in my food. None in the conversation. When we are done, it is still light, so he suggests we take a walk in Rock Creek Park, as we did that first day together.

"Okay," I say, sure now that he will pop the question on the path. But as we drive north out of town, the sky darkens. To the west a purple cloud rises above the horizon.

"Sweetie, look over there," I say, pointing out the window.

"Oh, I think we'll be okay," he responds, pulling into the parking lot off the trail. We get out and walk a few steps. Suddenly lightning cracks through the hot air and big raindrops start to fall. We race back to the car.

"Let's go to my house," I say, which isn't far away. "I need to feed the cat, anyway."

We go in and sit on my sofa. I open the windows to listen to the storm, and we sit there in the dark enjoying the weather. After about an hour of gentle talking, I decide this cannot possibly be the night, so I suggest that maybe he needs to go home.

His kids are there alone, and it is dark now. They are probably wondering where he is. It is only then that he pulls out a tiny box. He opens it. Inside there is a small diamond ring.

"Wendy," he says, taking my hand, "I want to share my life with you, I want to share what I have with you." He pauses.

"So, what are you saying?" I ask, not trying to be coy but wanting to hear the exact words.

"Will you marry me?"

I wait for a minute, just to feel the deliciousness of it. I thought I would never hear those words again.

"Well? Why are you waiting?" he says, getting worried.

"It's so wonderful to hear that."

"So, will you?" He can't relax until I answer.

I look at this amazing person, the one made for me. "Of course I will," and I know as I say it that I will. No matter how crazy or complicated or challenging our life will be, I love him and I can't imagine the rest of my life without him.

He slips the ring on my finger. "This is just a placeholder," he says. "I want you to pick out the ring you want. In fact I didn't even insure this, so maybe you better not wear it. But I wanted to have something as a token."

It was lovely, but I agreed it was probably unwise to wear it. Also, we decided to wait to tell the boys. There was a lot to think about, and I wanted to get our ducks in a row before we included them in the planning. I put the ring back in its box and kissed Charlie good night.

After he left, I put on my nightgown and then, guiltily, opened the little box and slipped the ring back on, just to look at it and reassure myself it wasn't a dream. I sat for a long time trying to get used to the idea of a diamond on my finger. I hadn't needed a man to make my life work, and I was proud of that. But it turned out that maybe I needed a man to make my life grow. I thought of what my friend Suzanne said about wanting a partner that believes in you, that believes you can do hard things. I could already sense that this decision was the turning point, the day I busted out of the safe world of my post-divorce life and took on the challenges of the world in a new way. I had originally thought remarrying would feel like returning to a safe harbor, but I knew now that I was off on an adventure— possibly the biggest adventure of my life.

CHAPTER FIVE

Engaged

WE TRY TO KEEP OUR engagement a secret, but within days we admit to each other we can't keep it from our folks. It doesn't seem right to keep such happy news from them, and we both know how relieved they will be. My parents had been my strongest supporters during my post-divorce years, and there were countless times they worried about me as a single woman making her way in the world—driving around the Beltway late at night, moving trunks and furniture around by myself, supporting the boys on my thin academic salary. When I call to tell them the news, they are thrilled. My family instantly recognized Charlie as a prince among men when I first brought him home, and ever since have gently encouraged our relationship. Charlie's mom, who latched on to me early as a kindred spirit and a stabilizing force in Charlie's life, is also thrilled. I can hear the deep exhalation of long pent-up worry from all of them. Thank God. "You didn't deserve to be lonely," my dad says.

We tell a few other close friends and siblings, but then hold the line. We can't tell the kids for a few months, until we know more about what will happen, and we don't want them hearing it from anyone else. Still, the very fact that Charlie and I have agreed to marry changes everything. The planning machine starts rolling—will I sell my house, should we renovate Charlie's, what about schools—and within a few weeks I sink into irritability. Everything Charlie suggests makes me angry, and then I realize I am blaming him for upsetting our lives. Months later Jesse will ask, "He's a nice guy. Why did he ask you to marry him?" What he means, when I tease this apart, is that no nice person would do this to us—ask us to give up our home, our neighborhood, our life.

I try to explain this to Charlie: "I'm mad at you for wanting to marry me."

He looks at me, his worry lines deepening: "I'm trying to make you happy."

"I know," I say. "And it makes me mad as hell."

The first time I moved in with someone, it was easy. I broke my lease, rented a truck, and poof—three hours later I was living with my boyfriend. This time I feel like I'm launching a major military campaign. There's the question of housing, not just whether to live in his place or mine but in which jurisdiction, which school system, near which jobs and which ex-spouses. Will the children change schools, and if so, will the schools be good? If not, do we need to get them into private schools?

Would it better to keep one set of siblings stable in their home and neighborhood, or would it be better to disrupt everybody and put us all in a new space, as all the remarriage guides advise? And what about our finances? How will we sort out pensions, inheritance, property, and responsibilities? All of these issues are simultaneously practical, financial, and emotional. We weigh dollars and feelings.

Aside from these practical problems, there are the pesky identity issues: If we default to living in Charlie's house, will I be strong enough after ten years of separation to live two blocks from my ex-husband? What name will I use—the one from my first marriage, which I kept so people would know I was the mother of my children, or Charlie's name, which might make my kids feel I was divorcing them? Maybe, I think, I will just retreat to my maiden name and vow eternal allegiance to myself. Along with these questions come the complications of shifting my identity, such as getting a new driver's license, closing old bank accounts, rewriting my will. Underneath lurks the question of who I will be, and not just in name. For years I've reveled in the identity of scrappy single mom, with independence as my strong suit. I've fixed flat tires in the snow, argued with unpleasant landlords, battled large insects, and lived to tell the tale. Now, instead, I'm going to be a wife again. Someone cared for. Someone who could call her husband when she locked her keys in the car, instead of the locksmith. Someone who might get breakfast in bed on Mother's Day. Not scrappy but indulged. The thought is both unsettling and attractive. Charlie, who enjoys handling money, starts helping me with my investments, and offers to take over the bills and the medical insurance claims when we marry. The thought of not having to file my own medical forms makes me fall in love with him all over again, but then I panic.

"What if I forget how to write a check?"

"I think it's like riding a bike. You won't forget how to write a check."

"What if I don't know where any of the files are when you die in a car crash?"

"You will know where the files are. And I'm not going to die in a car crash."

But I do worry. I worry that if he takes over all the responsibilities, I will end up as the clueless wife, the one who sits lost at her husband's desk the day after his funeral, unable to find what she needs to run the house.

That second winter I go skiing in Canada with Charlie and his two boys, and Charlie offers to carry my passport for me with the others in his backpack. I look at him over the tops of my glasses.

"I am an adult and I will carry my own damn passport, thank you very much," I say, snatching it away. Adam, his oldest, looks up from his book to take in this interesting exchange. All my life I've sniffed at dependent women. My mother was a Navy wife, the type who moved the family, had babies, and managed everything all by herself while my father was at sea chasing Russian subs. When her girls grew into teenagers, she taught us how to change the oil in our cars and manage our checkbooks. Being scrappy and inventive kept me afloat during the long years after my divorce, and it feels like letting go of the life raft to give it up. But I also have to admit it is nice having

Charlie organize the trip to Canada and argue with the car rental agency. Can I be a wife without being dependent, without feeling like I have to be the angel in the house?

And beyond all this looms the wedding and the honeymoon. We have to figure out what kind of service to have, in a church or a garden; whether to invite just family or open it up to friends; whether to have a party or a picnic or a fancy reception. How much money can we spend, given all the other costs of this year, and how will we support the boys through these events? And where should we honeymoon? My instinct is to avoid places Charlie traveled with his ex-wife, which rules out much of Europe and the Caribbean. I know that vacation planning is supposed to be fun, but with everything else we barely have the energy to check websites and travel guides. The complexity of my life has already taken off in an exponential arc. I stack files by the phone in the kitchen: Kensington House Repairs and Sale; House Hunting; Renovation for D.C. House; Private School Applications; Wedding; Move; Honeymoon. Eloping never looked so good. If it weren't for the kids, who need to watch us get married publicly to fully understand it, we might just slip away.

After a couple of months of stealth planning, it is time to tell the boys. I take Ron out for coffee after back-to-school night and tell him Charlie and I are engaged. I've been worried that he might take the news badly, but instead, he seems genuinely pleased.

"This is good. Whatever help you need, let me know," he says. "It will be a good thing for the boys. I'm happy for you." He gives me a hug.

Charlie and I decide to each tell our own children on the same night, but to coordinate by phone. I tell Ron which night it will be and he offers to come over after I am done to talk with the boys, and I agree that is a good idea.

That evening I'm a bundle of nerves. Despite the fact that this is happy news, I feel the same sick weight in my stomach that I remember from that awful night years earlier when I had to explain to my little boys that their parents didn't love each other anymore and were getting divorced. The boys were so young, just three and five years old, that they were confused more than anything else. Jesse didn't even know what *divorce* meant, and David cried when I told him Daddy and I weren't going to live together anymore. But they had mostly just listened. They hadn't known what to ask.

This time it will be different, I know, but I can't really predict how they will take it. David is fourteen and Jesse is twelve, still caught in that bubble between childhood and adolescence. They are trusting kids, happy kids, boys who think they know what is going on. But they are also tucked away in their own worlds. I have no idea if they suspect anything. After dinner is cleared away, I ask the boys to come talk. They sit down at the kitchen table, tense but curious. I figure they must have some idea that Charlie and I are getting serious, but it turns out they don't.

I can't figure out any way to sugarcoat it, so I just blurt it out. "Guys, I know this may surprise you a bit, but Charlie and I have decided to get married."

Their mouths drop open. They are shocked speechless.

"What?" they say in unison. And then the cries: "No. You can't do this. This is a terrible idea. Will we have to move?

Where are we going to live?" Both of them burst into tears and entreat me to reconsider. I try to answer their questions, then go silent, figuring maybe I should just hold my ground. David, my quiet child, gets up and storms around the room. "You can't do this to us," he says. "You can't do this to Dad."

Despite the fact that Charlie and I have dated for two years, the news of our engagement feels to my children like the other shoe dropping out of an angry heaven. For them, this moment in the kitchen is the other painful half of my divorce. I suddenly see that I may have fully recovered, but my children have not.

The psychologists will tell you that many children watch their remarrying parents standing before the altar saying "I do" and mutter to themselves "I won't!" No matter how long it has been since their parents divorced, a remarriage feels like another chapter in the divorce story rather than a fresh start. Because when a parent remarries, it is the end of the secret dream that their mother and father might come to their senses and marry each other again.

By the time I'm engaged to Charlie, nearly ten years out of my marriage, I don't know if my children still carry that dream. I have talked with them about it for years, telling them that even though their father and I get along fine most of the time, there is no hope of us ever getting back together. The broken love that is a failed marriage is hard to explain to a child, and they see little evidence of it in our interactions. Sometimes I wonder if our low-conflict approach to divorce has actually made them more vulnerable to hoping. Just because we didn't act like we hated each other, maybe we didn't.

But that night the boys make clear it isn't just about me and

Ron. The boys are bereft at the thought of losing the tight, loving circle we've built together, just the three of us. I hadn't anticipated how much they would feel that.

I try to explain that my loving Charlie doesn't change my love for them. But grown-ups also needed other grown-ups to love and for companionship. I am lonely and want to live with a man again—specifically, I want to live with Charlie.

Jesse, sobbing, looks up at me. "Aren't we enough for you, Mom?" he asks.

"You guys have been everything to me," I say, crying now myself. "But you're getting older. You aren't going to want to be everything to me in the future. You're going to have girlfriends and go off to college, and by then I'll really be lonely."

"So wait until then."

While I am trying to think how to explain that love doesn't always wait around, David suddenly asks whether we will move and whether they will have to go to a new school.

"Yeah," says Jesse, fresh panic spreading across his face. "I'm not leaving my school!" I had hoped to talk about all that later, but I see now that they want to know the worst, want to understand the full sweep of this news. There will be no parsing it out over a couple of days. I admit that we probably will move, though I am not sure where, and that I don't know about schools.

"But you bought the house!" Jesse yells. "You promised we wouldn't move again!"

He is right. I did promise that, on that happy day we moved into the place. I wanted them to understand that the years of frequent moves were over, that this place would be their future.

It turns out my children took me at my word, had sunk their roots in the middle of the baseball diamond in the backyard and were loath to pull themselves out again. "I'm sorry I can't keep my promise," I told them. "But things change. When I bought our house I didn't expect to ever meet someone I wanted to marry, but I did. I think you will understand someday that I was lucky to meet Charlie.

"Besides, we might live in Charlie's house," I say, hoping that will help. "It's just two blocks from Dad's house. Wouldn't that be great, if you could walk between Dad's house and my house?"

"You mean we'll live with them?"

"You mean Charlie and Adam and Matt? Yes, that's what being married means."

"But it's their house."

"But if we moved there it would be ours, too," I say, trying to sound convincing. But they just look at me and shake their heads. Oh, what their elders would do.

Within an hour, Ron knocks on the door, then ushers the boys out for a walk, to give them a chance to talk alone. I feel a welling up of relief. Maybe with his help I can convince the boys this isn't the end of their world.

When they return an hour later, David has brightened a bit and seems more supportive. "I'm happy for you, Mom," he says. "Dad says this is good, so I think it is, too."

But Jesse is a tougher case. As I am putting him to bed I'm still trying to reassure him. "I know it sounds complicated, sweetie, but Daddy and Charlie and I are going to make sure this change is good for you. We're going to take care of everything. Trust me."

"But, Mom," he says, "it doesn't work that way. That's the whole point of chaos theory."

"Chaos theory?"

"The point is that no matter how much good planning you do, you can't control everything. That's chaos theory. You think you and Dad and Charlie can make everything turn out all right, but you can't. Things will go wrong, no matter how hard you try."

He has me stumped. Must have read *Jurassic Park* one time too many, is all I can think. I look down at his blond head on the pillow. He has a dark edge to him, a wise knowing that sometimes takes me by surprise and makes me wonder if he understands adults just a little too well. Still, I tell myself, he's a kid. He can't grasp the full impact of this, the steady good beneath the surface turbulence. But I'm worried. Is this the worst time to do this to him? I believe that if my children have to change schools, we need to do it soon, before David gets into high school, but that leaves Jesse struggling to keep up. Between my previous moves and being sent to a special magnet program for gifted kids, Jesse has already attended four different schools and he's only in sixth grade. Another shift just seems cruel.

He looks at me again. "It's not Charlie, Mom. I don't mind Charlie. I don't mind that you are going to marry him. But why do we all have to live together?"

"Because that's what being married is," I say, sounding pretty lame. But it's all I can think of to say.

After I get them to bed, I call Charlie. He reports similar howls from Matt, but Adam has reacted more positively. In fact, says Charlie, Adam wants to talk to me.

"Now?"

"Yeah, I'll put him on."

A minute later Adam picks up the phone. "Hey, congratulations," he says.

"Thanks." I'm stunned, but for the first time that night I begin to smile. "I promise we'll have fun together."

"Well, I think it's a good idea, so congratulations. Bye!"

I know that this kid will also have his issues. There will be days when he will probably think this was a terrible idea, one of the worst ever. There will be days when he resents the intruders in his house, the divided attention of his father, the unfamiliar rules of his new stepmom. But there will also be days when we stumble onto unexpected blessings, when surprising things happen and good things start to grow. No matter how bad it gets, I tell myself, believe in these surprise moments, these small but critical blessings. And hope that the next one is just around the corner.

In the following weeks, I find myself thinking about Jesse's chaos theory more and more. As much as I hate to admit it, I think he might be on to something. Aside from worrying about the tsunami of details involved in marrying and moving, I lie awake at night now desperately trying to figure out how on earth we will manage meals and computer use and chores after the family merger. I consider Jesse's *Jurassic Park* warning, and the image of dinosaurs crashing around a kitchen feels appropriate. He is right. It will be chaotic no matter what we do.

The planning machine also reveals other interesting things. As much as Charlie and I come from similar backgrounds, our marriages and our divorces have produced families with distinctly different habits. I start fretting not only about logistics but also now about the inevitable clash of family cultures. Individual lifestyles might cause a bit of friction the first time one marries, but at that point most of us are young and habits are flexible. By the time we are nearly fifty and bringing several children into a marriage, family habits are entrenched and well defined. In Charlie's house, for example, the kids go to bed late and wake up groggy. My kids and I work on the Ben Franklin model: lights out at ten, up at about six-thirty, even on weekends. When it comes to eating, Charlie's kids are nutritionally pure, while we shoulder an ice cream habit that has recently morphed into a root-beer-float addiction.

"Don't you worry about the kids' teeth?" Charlie asks.

"Ah, yeah," I say, feeling defensive. "But don't you worry about your kids' sleep deprivation?" We both worry about the future contents of the refrigerator and how we will get four boys showered, breakfasted, and out of the house by seven-fifteen on school mornings, considering that none of us are used to living in a crowd. I have visions of towels assigned by color, with matching toothbrushes, and insist on a wall of lockers to be built in the kitchen, one for each boy. Charlie listens to this and says, as patiently as possible, "I think we have to be careful with the kindergarten model. The boys will laugh at this."

Instead, the boys quickly develop their own idea for family harmony: Each kid gets a room of his own equipped with a refrigerator, a computer, and a TV. Adam suggests we throw in a food allowance, "so we can go out and get our own meals."

"No," I tell them, not knowing whether to laugh or cry,

"that's called college and you get to do that in a few years, but for now we're going to be a family. A family eats together and watches TV together."

"Okay," they say. "Who gets to hold the remote?"

At least the boys are trying, which is more than we can say for the pets.

"What are you going to do about Snowy?" asks my mother-in-law-to-be. She is very concerned about the cat, who, as I had anticipated, stands to lose the most in this whole enterprise. Charlie isn't enthusiastic about cats, to put it mildly. He often accuses them of nursing destructive grudges in their little feline hearts. He's afraid the cat will claw the new sofa or give everyone allergies or pee on the Orientals. I point out that his dog has destroyed one sofa already and peed on plenty of carpets, but it's no use. He's a dog guy. It's clear the dog will stay and the cat will have to adjust—or go live somewhere else.

"I don't know," I tell her. "Maybe we could drug him for the first month. Don't they have Prozac for pets now?"

"You mean a tranquilizer?"

"Whatever. He might not come out from under the sofa, but at least it would keep him from running away."

Just to make sure we aren't going to do our children irreparable harm, we check in with their counselors. Psychologists and psychiatrists are often little more than lukewarm about remarriage, and for good reason: They work every day with the remarried couples who don't make it. But we don't understand this yet; we're as green as new recruits. When we sit down with one of the doctors who knows our history, we're expecting to hear congratulations. Instead, he gasps when we announce our plans to marry and blend the boys.

"Oh, my God," he says, wincing, "have you thought about waiting until they all go off to college?"

We stare at him, not quite sure we have heard him clearly.

"Seriously, I mean it," he says. "Many couples do that."

"But that's seven years away," I say plaintively. "I don't want to wait that long to be married to Charlie."

What I want to say but don't is that it doesn't seem fair that other people get to be married and I don't. That you get only one chance for a happy marriage, and if you mess it up, too bad. I want a mate. I want a fuller life and a bigger family. Not because I feel incomplete, but because scrappy independence gets lonely.

But there's another reason: Just because the redivorce rates for couples remarrying with kids are so dismal, I don't think that means we should give up before we even try. I don't believe this is manifest destiny. When I first talked about getting divorced, everyone told me it would seriously damage my children. I was warned that kids of divorce do worse in school, tend toward addictions, are more likely to engage in risky sexual behavior. And they are more likely to divorce when they are adults. It was enough bad news to stop me in my tracks for several years, but eventually my marriage became untenable, and at that point I started questioning the dire predictions. I started talking back to the shadow that hangs over kids of divorce. I discovered in time that there were many reasons why my kids were less at risk than the average child growing up in divorce, and many other factors could soften the impact. I didn't accept that growing up divorced meant my kids had a sentence hanging over their heads, and I refuse to believe it about remarrying.

I talk with several other counselors, and some are more encouraging. "It may not be easy for the kids, but if you pay attention to their needs, they could benefit a lot," says the one who knows us best, and whom I trust most. "Kids need to learn to adapt to change, because that is what life is about these days. I don't think it helps them to pretend everything lasts forever. We need to get away from pathologizing stepfamilies. They can learn a lot about adjusting to others, being flexible, being more cooperative—all of which will stand them in good stead when they leave for college. Just like divorce, there are good ways to do it and bad ways. It doesn't have to be a disaster."

I start reading the guidebooks and talking with other merged families. As with divorce, there are ten horror stories for every success, but when I talk with real families, I find lots of support and help. Yes, it's hard, they all say, particularly the first two years, but it's not impossible. There are hundreds of factors in the equation, many things that we can control. The advantages that helped me through my divorce—a supportive extended family, steady employment and adequate financial resources, a solid education and a middle-class life—are still in place and give us more than a fighting chance to come out whole. We're reasonable people. None of our children come to this remarriage struggling with serious problems. The kids are already beginning to adjust to the idea of living together, even as they still circle each other warily. We've taught them to play Murder in the Dark, an old boarding school game that involves cards and a murderer and lots of bumping around in blackout conditions. It's more fun with a crowd and draws attention away from that tricky question about the remote. Aside from the cat, who may need a frontal lobotomy, we're in pretty good shape to set out on this adventure. Still, I try to make sure everyone's mental seat belts are buckled. No one said it would be smooth.

CHAPTER SIX

Of House and Hearth

By NOW I HAVE A small library of books of advice on remarriage and stepfamilies teetering on my bedside table. At night I flip
through them, scanning for solutions. One thing I notice: Every
single one says that remarrying couples merging families should
sell all their previously owned real estate and buy a new house, to
provide "neutral" territory for the newly created family.

Sort of like a demilitarized zone, I think to myself. A patch of
earth without booby traps or land mines. As if that is humanly
possible. I find these books both helpful and maddening, because
they regularly remind me of all the ways we are doing things
badly. As useful as this advice might be in the abstract, it bears
no relation to reality. First, it makes almost no sense in the Washington area real estate market. One of us already owns the perfect house for us, Charlie's rambling Victorian in a leafy, in-town

neighborhood of like-minded people, just two blocks from my ex-husband's house and two miles from my university. It is one of those houses other Washingtonians drive by and say, "Gee, I wish I had bought that thing back in the eighties, when I could have afforded it." And that was the point. We were lucky to have it.

I tell Charlie about the neutral territory idea, and so we dutifully go out house hunting in neighborhoods like ours, stealthily, without telling the kids. In one afternoon we confirm what we already suspect: that all the houses like ours are more than twice what we can afford, and there's only a spotty selection. We could theoretically sell Charlie's house and purchase a new one, but we would end up in a smaller, pricier house that might not fit our needs very well—and we would enrich several real estate agents in the process. The only other alternative, besides staying in Charlie's house, is to buy some brand spanking new, cheaply constructed monolith halfway to Pennsylvania, and spend the rest of our life sitting in traffic. The boys would mutiny.

Beyond the financial considerations, Charlie's house was, well, Charlie's house. His kids had lived there for most of their conscious years and they knew everyone on the block. My kids had lived just two blocks away with their dad since they were born. I knew many people in the neighborhood and had always loved the location—close to the Metro, walking distance from shops and theaters, a quick bike ride away from Rock Creek Park. The area was a bit haunted for me, as it echoed with the pain of my pre-divorce years, those unhappy days I pushed the boys' stroller around those streets and wondered if my marriage would last. The house was similarly haunted by Charlie's ex-wife, who left her decorating touch in every room, including an enormous hand-painted dragon on the wall of the boys' bathroom. But it was still a great house, the kind of house I had always wanted—big and airy, with high ceilings and tall windows. It had a beautiful wraparound porch and a side yard. It was all a bit dilapidated and overgrown, but with work it could be a grand place. If we lived there, we wouldn't have to uproot Adam and Matt at all, and David and Jesse would only lose the neighborhood and home they had shared with me in Maryland.

Part of the problem was that we needed lots of space. We would soon look more like one of those big families from the fifties than the more typical two-kid model of our generation. The boys were old enough to need their own rooms, and Charlie and I both needed home offices. That meant seven bedrooms, unless Charlie and I doubled up into one study. I eyed the stacks of papers and books in his office and wondered if I could work in such an environment. Whenever I raised this issue he would jokingly clear the stack of mail off the straight-backed chair by the door, push the piles away from the edge of the desk, and say, "Here. You can work here. I'd love to share my office with you."

"Maybe I'll just fix up my study at the university," I tell him, "and hole up there. I might even put in a cot!"

There was never any serious discussion of staying in my relatively charmless split level—too small for all of us and not nearly as convenient. Except, of course, that it was our home and I knew we would miss it. The house represented for me the final chapter in my effort to recover from the damage of my divorce. When I bought it I felt like I had achieved something substantial for myself—a good home in one of the better neighborhoods in the Washington area, paid for without anyone's help, through my own sweat and blood. It was more than just a house—it was a monument to my effort to remake a good life for me and my boys. The kids immediately settled in, establishing routines and carving out their space. They played Wiffle ball in the backyard every afternoon, while the cat patrolled the perimeter, keeping the other neighborhood cats at bay.

Life at our house had a certain predictable simplicity. I had a tiny kitchen, so seldom gave dinner parties or hosted family get-togethers. We had one computer and one bathroom, so there was lots of sharing and the feel of a slumber party half the time. Our bedrooms were all grouped together, just off the living room and kitchen. I could go lie down and read for a few minutes while waiting for the spaghetti to cook. When the boys talked in their sleep, I could hear them and turn it into a funny story at breakfast the next day. There was a huge sunny recreation room in the basement that absorbed all the boy energy in the house, the perfect place for sleepovers, birthday parties, science experiments. We had pared our life down to the essentials, and I liked it that way.

Compared with Charlie's life, ours didn't have as much complexity, but it also didn't have as much gravity, and I wondered if their world would overtake ours if we moved into their house. They had more stuff and lived bigger than we did, by a good bit. They did more exciting things, took more trips, had wider horizons, but also spent more time dealing with logistics and planning. Their house had few cozy spots, and all the upheaval in the family had left the place a jumble of odd furniture and boxes filled with dusty knickknacks. I worried sometimes that the life David and Jesse and I shared was like a small livable planet that was going to be sucked into the orbit of something overwhelming and possibly toxic, like Jupiter, just because we had a smaller critical mass. Worse than that, I worried that I would wake up one day and be surrounded by good things—a bigger and better house, a sweet husband, more kids—but resent it all because it would feel like a stranger's world.

One day I was talking with my friend Karen, a local psychologist, and she mentioned a stepfamily she counsels that was in real trouble.

"The big problem is that the second wife moved into the husband's house, where he lived with his first wife, and the children just can't take it. They have all these associations of good times with their mom in this space, and now the second wife is there. Everyone's a mess." She pauses. "So what are you and Charlie going to do after you get married?"

"I'm going to move into his house, where he lived with his first wife and his kids have lots of associations of good times with their mom," I say, looking away so I don't have to see her expression.

She nearly gags on her coffee. "Oops," she says, "I'm sorry. I didn't mean that it couldn't work, but oh boy. That's a lot."

Picking a house to live in after remarriage—and negotiating how to live in that space—looms as a central issue for everyone who tries to remarry. And it's about more than whose house you choose. Territoriality issues crop up on all levels for remarried families, from the macro-world of city and neighborhood down to the micro-world of drawers and chairs and who gets served first at dinner. Do the neighbors stop and say hello or cross to the other side of the street out of loyalty to the ex-spouse? Do the resident children give up their regular spots in front of the TV because someone needs to make room for the pesky little stepbrother? Territoriality issues often feel juvenile, but the psychologists will tell you they trigger deep emotions and often reveal the fault lines in newly merged families. Territoriality can erupt over anything from closet space to use of the car, and it often serves as a proxy battleground for other, less tangible resources, such as attention from parents and family status. The kid who feels demoted because he is no longer the oldest or the only may scramble for the best computer because it is too hard to ask for what is really missing, his former position as Mom or Dad's confidant and support.

When I wasn't reading advice books, I scrolled through stepfamily websites looking for alternative opinions, and one day I ran across some sage thoughts by a D.C. family therapist, Dorree Lynn. I called her the next day and introduced myself. She warmed up quickly, sensing my discomfort around the growing problem of how Charlie and I were going to mesh two very different families in a house that belonged to one faction . . . that is, family.

"The territoriality issues are monumental for a blended family," she tells me. "And that's because they are really wars of definition, of defining who you will be as a family and how the pecking order will go."

"Sometimes it drives me nuts when I go over to Charlie's, because no one with my kind of obsessive cleanliness has wiped the counters," I tell her. "Is this going to doom us as a family?"

"I don't think so, but I do think you need to sort it out. The house issues are largely about who you will be. It's about whether you are a family that puts the lids on the jars tightly or not, about whether everything falls out when you open the refrigerator door. Some people live very happily with sticky counters, but you may not be able to do that."

Lynn cautions me that it will take a lot of sensitivity about small things to keep these territorial issues from spilling over into conflict. "I call them the bathroom wars, and I've seen them over and over in stepfamilies," she says. "It's common for kids of divorce to feel like they have the right to be in their parent's bathroom and bedroom. But the minute Mom gets remarried, there's a strange man in her space. The child feels pushed out and ends up resentful."

I think of my own boys, who have only recently stopped climbing into my bed for a morning snuggle. I am glad they have outgrown that, but know they may still feel unfairly blocked from my bedroom once I'm married. I know that Adam and Matt have their own habits, their own sacred spaces in the house—the favorite TV couch, their dad's office computer. It is clear many things will shift.

I ask Lynn if she thinks we're crazy to merge families in Charlie's house.

"Not crazy, because sometimes that's the best you can do," she says. Despite believing in the neutral territory principle, she herself ended up having her second husband move into the house she shared with her twelve-year-old daughter when she remarried, and says now that a new house might have spared them a lot of stress. "My husband needed space in the house for his study, so he ended up taking over most of the space my daughter considered her playroom," she tells me. "Even though we tried to set up other play space for her right outside her bedroom, she always felt as if something had been taken away and she never forgave him. We should have added on to the house or built an addition to the garage for his study, if we were unable to move to a new house. Anything would have been better. It made the first few years quite tense."

Her daughter never forgave him? No wonder I'm nervous. Maybe this isn't just about some initial hard feelings, which I figure we could weather. Maybe this house decision will haunt us forever.

Houses and other private spaces contain more than our furniture. They are a safe haven in a difficult world, the boundaries people draw around their lives. Houses also give people an identity, especially those who have grown up in a particular house, or those who may identify strongly with their bedroom or particular bed or chair at the dining room table.

Houses also contain our stuff, the accumulated debris of a life fully lived, and therefore contain memories and traditions that may feel alien to half the blended family. Apart from the things the resident family holds dear, houses may hold the stuff left behind by a former spouse, stuff that serves as a daily reminder that someone else was once queen of the space. I didn't feel at home in Charlie's house in the beginning, in part because every time I opened a cupboard, I found more things from his earlier life with his ex-wife. Bags of shoe polish, old photos, old clothes, shoes, and Halloween costumes, Christmas decorations, and half-finished craft projects came tumbling out. It felt like she had just gone out visiting and would be back any moment.

I had read an article once by a woman who fell in love with one of her professors, a man who was married. She soon became his second wife, but only after a messy divorce from his first wife. The woman moved into her husband's home just months after the first wife left, and was haunted for years by the sense that she took the wife's place while "the seat was still warm."

While attending a conference in Chicago, I meet Louisa Smithfield, a single mom who moved into an enormous Victorian mansion on the banks of Lake Michigan when she married her second husband, Robert. The house, she says, is like something from another era. There is room for a dozen children, and space for entertaining on the ground floor that could accommodate a prince. She shows me pictures, and this place is something else. The house has sweeping staircases, a huge garden, and at the point she moved in, a kitchen that Robert's ex-wife had recently spent over a year renovating and repainting. This is the kind of house neighbors talk about, the kind that would be on a garden tour. And suddenly Louisa, who had previously lived in a small ranch house, had to try and make it hers.

"I came in and essentially had to piss on every corner," she tells me. "It took a year and a lot of money, but I had to make that house mine. I took it apart—redid every room to some degree, refinishing either the woodwork or the floors, and recovering every piece of furniture. Fortunately, we could afford it. Otherwise I never could have lived here. His ex-wife was just too present in everything about the house."

I wasn't going to be able to redo every room, but Charlie and I decide to go ahead with plans to modernize and cozy up the kitchen, as well as finish off the cement-floor basement and put in a bedroom and bath for Adam next to the family room. We also had to finish the work Charlie had stopped during his divorce—fixing up the master bedroom, resanding the upstairs flooring, and painting the interior. We meet with the architect and talk about family dynamics, desires, hopes, and concerns. I'm hoping the renovation will give me the chance to put my mark on the house, while Charlie is hoping to solve age-old problems. Together we struggle a bit to define our style— what do we like, and can we find common ground? Charlie loves the look of old kitchens, the kind that had plenty of servants in them. I like the look but am wary of the inconvenience inherent in having side pantries for dishes and refrigerators. There was a reason those kitchens had a brigade of scullery maids. The house is old, but the kitchen is more modern, added on later. The architect tells us we need a style that bridges both periods. We flip through magazines and books on remodeling, settling finally on a look that is old in tone but modern in execution—an arts-and-crafts look with clean lines and warm woods.

Before the renovation can begin, however, we need to empty Charlie's basement, a task that becomes a testament to both my devotion and Charlie's willingness to change. We tell the architect, an old friend who knows Charlie well, that we will have it done in two weeks. Having been down there measuring the area and wading through the stuff, he scoffs. "Right," he says in disbelief. "You guys call me when you're done." That weekend we go to work. Charlie, it turns out, is a collector, the type of person who believes everything might have another use someday. As a consequence of his divorce, he's been left behind in the family home with a mountain of dubious possessions, including his sons' baby clothes, old furniture handed down from elderly relatives, kitchenware that dates back to his first apartment, stacks of craft and sewing materials, a gallery of obsolete appliances, piles of old computer games, and enough boxes to build a fortress. No one's quite sure what is in them. We put on the radio and work through the weekend, breaking only for meals or to lie on the floor to rest our backs. It's like archaeology. Every hour we reveal a new layer, unleashing a cascade of memories for Charlie. He holds up a child's raincoat. "I remember when Matt went off to preschool in this thing." Next he picks up a tiny sweater that was Adam's, choking up at the passage of time.

After a few more baby clothes come out of the box, I move in. "Sweetheart, why don't you pick a couple of things to put in the boys' memorabilia boxes, and the rest we can give to a charity. There are real children who could use a lot of this stuff right now."

He nods, knowing I'm right, but it's still hard. In one tough weekend he is facing the loss of his kids' childhood, the closing of the era that was his first marriage. I went through a similar process years earlier with my ex-husband, helping clean out the house we had shared, mourning the loss of the good times even while I closed the door on old memories. A few minutes later he stumbles across old family photos, long since forgotten. "Boy, I didn't even know we had these." With each discovery I give him a few minutes of nostalgia, then take over, prioritizing, asking him if I can just put all the items in a box together for him to go through later, moving what looks like trash into garbage bags stealthily but with determination.

I operate under the dictum that everything in the house should be either beautiful or useful or meaningful, though I'm flexible. It's easy for me because this is not my stuff, and I have a strong need to clear some space in this house for my own small mountain of possessions. With every decision, I'm pushing Charlie a bit to make room for my children and me. We are also defining how the future will be once we live together. We fill a box with things to help the boys furnish their first apartments, laughing at how the stuff will have aged into valuable collectibles by the time they open the box. We fill a trunk with old clothes for making home movies, which the boys enjoy. We keep the best of the children's toys for visiting nieces and nephews. We keep some things just because they matter too much to somebody to give up. We lug everything we want to save upstairs, then sort the rest into piles headed for a garage sale, charity, or dump. Gradually the floor emerges.

By the time the architect returns, we're done. He looks around the empty space, astonished. "Boy, somebody must be a slave driver." He looks at me with new respect. "Congratulations."

Meanwhile, Charlie's kids are getting nervous. Workmen are dismantling nearly half their house to do the renovation, leaving them with unrecognizable spaces and few places to curl up with a book. The living room is stacked with boxes and furniture pushed out of the spaces we are clearing. Both kids are worried about their things migrating around the house and possibly ending up in the trash, as Charlie and I sort through box after box of old videos, kids' games, books, more old videos, half-finished art projects, last year's school binders, and dusty magazines. They can feel the coming invasion. Now it's just a matter of time.

The territoriality issues aren't just about space; they also touch on a host of intangibles, such as loyalty to the past, taste, values, priorities. We sit down one day to figure out where all the furniture will go, and I begin to feel irritated that my stuff seems slated to go out to the farm Charlie owns in Virginia. I feel especially protective of my lovely antique dining room table, which is actually an old library table from my great-grandmother's house in Michigan.

"You're dissing my table," I tell Charlie, looking over the list.

"I'm not trying to disrespect your table, honey. It's just that it goes better out at the farm. It's smaller than mine and fits better in that space."

"It's certainly more valuable than your dining room set," I say petulantly. "Yours isn't even an antique. It just looks like one."

"Do you want yours here in Washington?" he says, giving up on reason. "If you feel that strongly, we can switch them."

Now I relent. He's right, from a practical perspective. It

makes more sense for my table to go to the farm, since it fits there and we need to move it anyway, and to leave his larger one here in Washington, where all the other furniture in the dining room is the same style. But something in me doesn't want to be practical. I want to live with my table every day, not just when we are visiting the farm. I want my stuff around me, not warehoused somewhere else because Charlie's is already here. I can almost feel myself elbowing for room.

Artwork is another problem area. Everything has been pulled off the walls in Charlie's house, because the whole place is getting fresh paint, and mine will have to be integrated in. The art that Charlie and his ex-wife bought together is valuable, much of it is wonderful, and all of it is emotionally loaded. I dearly want to define a style for Charlie and me that is different from the style they shared, and yet Charlie has preferences that still reflect her vision. Will we put their artwork over the mantelpiece, as he hopes, or bury it in the bottom of some closet, which is sometimes my secret wish? I feel defensive about the quality of my wall hangings, offended if Charlie suggests I hang certain items in my university office. We quickly discover hidden assumptions and unspoken prejudices, and begin the process of working through the thousands of minute negotiations we will have to make to live together.

So we compromise. We make some decisions based on practicality and others based on feelings. Charlie says again and again, "I don't want you to be unhappy. I want you to feel like this is your house."

I'm already glad we are redoing the entire kitchen. In fact we're moving it from a smaller room in the house into space where we'll be able to get all four boys around the table and have plenty of room for making lunches and big family dinners. I help Charlie clean out and pack up his existing kitchen, gleefully tossing out old boxes of cereal and spice jars gummy with the enthusiasms of the previous cook. Kitchens and bathrooms, in particular, are intimate spaces, and they are usually the first places new wives try to make their mark in a home. My own mother struggles not to rearrange my kitchen drawers when she comes to visit, and I struggle not to rearrange hers. Many women find moving into someone else's kitchen as nerve-racking as trying to establish yourself in a haunted house.

"I think women connect with their nests, and they can feel the presence of the former wife," says Laura, one of my college friends and a veteran of remarriage. I talk with her late one night on the phone when I'm feeling overwhelmed by it all. "When I feel angry at my stepkids' mom, you know what I do? I throw out another old kitchen utensil of hers. It's silly, but it makes me feel better."

Laura also cautions me to watch out for hauntings in the master bedroom. The room that will be our master bedroom was renovated just as Charlie's ex-wife moved out, so she never really lived in it the way it looks today. My remarriage guidebooks say the bedroom is the place where the newly remarried do the most redecorating and rearranging. Few people want to sleep in the same bed where their new husband or wife slept with their previous spouse. Many buy new beds or at least new mattresses, and nearly all buy new linens. Because bedrooms are the innermost sanctum, the decisions involving them are often critical to maintaining a good marriage.

Laura tells me that she was once startled to find her husband's ex-wife, who had come over to talk with Laura's stepdaughter, in their master bedroom stretched out on their bed while she used the phone. "I couldn't believe it," Laura says, still angry after several years. "The gall. There she was, with her head on my pillow. It really pissed me off, because it showed how thoughtless she was about what she was doing. It used to be her bedroom, so she just walked in."

I go back to my own house when things at Charlie's get too overwhelming, but it isn't much of a break. If I am to get it on the market this spring, it needs to be painted and other things repaired. Mary Lee comes over and walks through it with me. "Get rid of all the personal knickknacks," she says. "The photos of the kids, the stuff on the refrigerator, the school papers— all that has to go. Then move out as many of the smaller pieces of furniture as possible, so you can make it seem bigger. Also, you need to get the carpets cleaned." I call Mike, my philosophical lawn service guy who doubles as a handyman. He's a single dad with custody of three kids, and he's been in love himself recently, though he broke off the relationship after his girlfriend's children misbehaved one time too many.

"Are you sure you want to go through with this?" he asks me as I go over all the things that I need him to repair in the house.

"Oh, yeah," I say.

"Well, maybe it's easy for you. Maybe all your kids are good."

"They're pretty good," I tell him. "Also, though, I think I'm ready."

"Ready?" He smiles. "You think I'm not ready?"

"That's right. When you are ready, the right person will show up."

He shakes his head, laughing at me. "You say that because it happened to you. I just don't meet too many women."

"That's because you aren't ready. Get ready to remarry, and then I predict that it'll happen to you, too."

"I'm not sure I'll ever be ready to marry someone with disrespectful children," says Mike.

"You don't have to. When you're ready, you won't care how her children behave."

Now he looks at me hard. "Okay, you win. I'm not ready. Are you satisfied? Now, what is it you want me to fix?"

Over the next few weeks I tend to the details at my place, packing away the china and books and piano music, getting a head start on moving. I pack up the AIN'T NOBODY HAPPY IF MOMMA AIN'T HAPPY sign and all the goofy photos on the fridge, wondering if I'll put them up in my new kitchen. The place starts to look as impersonal as Mary Lee wants it, and it makes me feel like I'm losing my home. The boys register that this is happening, and they get nervous. It's the first concrete evidence that things are beginning to change. On the weekends, Charlie and I drive loads of my stuff out to the farm in Virginia, then stay to fix things up there. We're considering getting married in the garden of the farm, and will need to do a lot of work on the place to make it sparkle.

Of all the loaded territorial issues for us, the most difficult is the question of what to do with Charlie's farm. My friends and family tell me it sounds wonderful. A farm out in horse country, in the beautiful foothills of the Shenandoahs. How lucky could a girl be? Not only is Charlie a great guy, he is a great guy with a lovely second home. When I grumble about loading up my boat bag and going out there for a weekend of weeding the garden, my friends ask pointedly if I'm menopausal or just stupid. I often felt like a heel for complaining, but the farm is an even bigger symbol of the life Charlie lived with his ex-wife, and it feels like the biggest piece of baggage for me. It had been old and run-down when they bought it, and they both poured a lot of effort into fixing it up and making it theirs. I wasn't even sure I wanted a second home, but I knew that if I did, I wouldn't have chosen a farm in Virginia. Having grown up in a sailing family I have always wanted a small place on the Chesapeake. It wouldn't need to be fancy—just big enough to keep a canoe in the backyard and with access to water, possibly with a small sailboat. A place where you could watch the waterfowl and the storms out on the bay.

But the truth was, I had spent so many years packing and unpacking my boat bag, I was ready to settle in one place and live without any second or third homes. Simplifying my life had been one of the most compelling lessons I'd learned from my divorce, and was my secret for sane living. As a Navy brat, I had grown up appreciating the lightness of being generated by regular moves. Whenever I was sad at leaving a house or old toys behind, my mother would tell me: "They're just things, sweetie. They aren't what make us a family." My boys and I had carried on that tradition, shedding old possessions like too-tight skins every time we packed up again. If I was going to marry Charlie, I had to accept that he came bearing many more possessions and complications than I did. Some were wonderful, but they all came at a cost, and I was worried the farm would feel like some sort of enchanted albatross—magical but full of problems needing attention and pulling me under.

One night I was having dinner with a friend from graduate school, Nancy. She is recently divorced from her second husband, and trying to make sense of a life scaled down from the years as the wife of a wealthy lawyer. She doesn't tut-tut at me when I mention my love-hate relationship with the farm. She and her second husband moved into her house for their primary residence, but she inherited her husband's vacation home from his previous marriage, a cabin in the Maine woods redolent with memories of his earlier life with his first wife.

"I know just what you mean," Nancy says. "The place always felt like her home, even after I spent several years trying to make it mine. There were these three little watercolors she painted still hanging in the living room that I didn't have the courage to move. I have no idea why she didn't take them with her when she cleared it out. She said they belonged with the cabin—they were scenes from the front porch. I don't know. I just hated living with her artwork, but I didn't want to take them down because his kids would resent that. I wonder now if I should have just told them tough luck, or packed them up to give to them later in life. All I can say is that I'm glad I no longer have to live with her work staring down at me."

Charlie and I talk about the farm's problems and its benefits. The land is appreciating in value, so one way to think of it is as an investment that's also a nice place to visit. We spend more time out there, trying to help me connect with the land and the hills. Working in the garden helps, makes me feel like I'm not just a visitor. In the summer the place is abuzz with hummingbirds and flowers, and feels like the Vermont hills where I spent many childhood summers. We pick peaches in the nearby orchard and get the boys to help us make jam in big vats. In this pretty place we can escape the media-saturated world of our Washington homes, get the boys out from behind their computer screens, make them talk to us. We stay up late playing cards, pull out the board games and puzzles. I rearrange the kitchen so it suits me better, clean out the freezer. In time it starts to feel like a place where my soul can be at home. We don't know if we will keep it in the long run. The cow pond does not count as waterfront, I tell Charlie. I still harbor a secret wish for a little house on the bay. But for now, I'm counting this as a blessing.

CHAPTER SEVEN

Prenuptials and Money

NOT LONG AFTER WE ARE engaged, Charlie comes up to me one day looking a bit nervous.

"I hate to ask you to do this, but we're going to have to write a prenuptial agreement," he says, looking down at his hands. "With the boys and everything, we just need one." He looks tense and unhappy, but also determined.

I'm not really surprised, though I am taken aback. I had hoped that it wouldn't be necessary. That maybe our wills would address all the necessary issues. That he would trust me to be aboveboard and honest, that he wouldn't be worried about being taken to the cleaners in another divorce—both because we weren't going to get divorced and because I wasn't like that. Prenuptials are considered, as one money adviser puts it, the "serpent in the Eden of love." They are what wealthy athletes or actors require of their girlfriends or boyfriends, the ones they don't intend to stay married to. They represent all that can come up and bite you in a remarriage. Prenuptials, with lawyers hired on both sides, feel unnervingly like the divorce process. You and your loved one squared off in opposite corners, negotiating over money and property. It's not a pretty picture.

"Oh, I figured that," I respond, trying to smile. "Don't worry about it. We can do that." I'm trying to collect myself, but it flashes through my mind that his first wife wasn't asked to sign a prenuptial. Why did she get a free pass when I don't? He says he loves me, and yet . . . But then I return to reason. She was the *first* wife, Wendy. First wives always get the free pass. I'm the second wife. The wife that will probably not be the mother of any of his children. He already has commitments to his boys by virtue of being their dad. But already I can sense the quicksand under my feet, the unpleasant questions a prenuptial raises. It reaffirms the unavoidable fact that I'm second, that I will never get treated the same way as the first wife. It also reaffirms the unavoidable fact that my children are also second somehow, not as worthy as his. But I remind myself that I knew all this and fell in love with Charlie despite it. That we are lucky because there is plenty of money to support us all, and that if his children inherit more than mine, that's the luck of the draw. It doesn't make me and my children second-class citizens. It just makes us second.

He's looking down at me and seems relieved. "Really? You don't mind?"

"Well, I don't know what it will say yet, but I trust you to be who you are—somebody kind and generous," I answer. I don't answer the question of whether I mind. Best not to raise that. "I think we'll be okay."

I sensed something dangerous on that day, but I wasn't sure what it was as yet. When we started talking about a prenuptial, I thought it would be about deciding what would happen if we got divorced, which wasn't going to happen. I knew it wouldn't happen with a sureness that I didn't feel the first time I married. I would never have agreed to marry Charlie if I thought there was any chance the marriage wouldn't last. So I thought a prenuptial would be about something that wasn't going to happen, in which case I didn't need to think about it much or argue over the terms. Aside from dealing with the division of assets in the event of a divorce, the prenup would outline how we would manage and hand down our money, which we had already discussed. We planned to share current salaries in a household account but keep our individual inheritances separate, each pot to be handed down to our own children.

But before I knew it, the money issues raised by the prenuptial discussion quickly morphed into something far more complex. Financial issues may look dry on paper, but—make no mistake—they have emotional taproots deep in our psyches. This wasn't just about what we do in case of a divorce, a concern any pragmatic woman should take seriously. It was also about how we would carry out our lives, what we would value, how we would share, what our children would grow up to expect and—possibly toughest—how we continued to be linked to our first spouses. When the money issues finally get put on the table, they strip away the romantic haze in a hurry, because they reveal people for who they are and why they are remarrying—their values, their character, their fears, and their unspoken hopes.

Most remarrying couples, not surprisingly, avoid the topic completely. Relatively few remarried couples hire lawyers and write prenuptial agreements, and only a handful more sit down together and plan for college tuition, retirement, savings, and home ownership. Remarrying couples are much more likely to just slide into financial arrangements, through convenience more than anything else. Most of those remarrying, the sociologists have found, move in together first. Before they know it, they quickly begin to merge their financial stakes—split the rent, share income, help each other out with unexpected costs. They do this haphazardly, without planning, because they don't want their love tainted by financial discussions. By the time they marry, it's all one financial knot.

My friends the Schumers are typical. They barely discussed money when they married twelve years ago. "We didn't think about it at all," Mimi tells me when I ask how they handled financial arrangements. "Neither of us had that much, and we just put together what we earned and ran the household on that. It worked fine until we started thinking about college and buying a house. Then the old system sort of fell apart." This couple has a strong second marriage, the kind that endures and deepens over the years. They've raised their two daughters, one from each side, in an atmosphere of love and respect, and their kids have thrived. This veteran couple—who have survived the death of a parent, wars with ex-spouses, numerous employment ups and downs, as well as their daughters' teenage years—are affectionate and supportive of each other. But ask them about their money issues, and within minutes they are in a heated debate. Veterans, yes, but when it comes to money, unresolved conflicts fester just below the surface, especially when it comes to issues such as college tuition, inheritances, and retirement.

Money is power, even in a marriage, and he who has the bigger wallet has a subtle advantage in calling the shots, particularly when it comes to opening the wallet and buying something. As a single mother, I had resisted letting boyfriends buy me much of anything, because I didn't want to be indebted to people I didn't want to fold into my life. One of my single-mom friends in Texas let her boyfriend buy her a new car, then hesitated to break up with him when she outgrew the relationship, mostly because of the car. I relented a bit with Charlie, because I knew I was going to marry him, letting him help me buy my van, but it still made both of us a bit nervous. That independent pioneer girl in me didn't want to be taken care of because I wasn't quite sure who I would be if I ended up as a pampered wife. But the tired, sick-of-worrying-about-it me couldn't believe my good luck. By getting engaged to Charlie I had wandered into the land of enough, if not the land of plenty, and I would have had to have been a fool not to want to live there.

When Charlie and I finally sat down and started talking about what our prenup would look like, it became clear why so many remarrying people avoid the topic entirely. To start with, the complications are legion. Couples in traditional nuclear families usually don't worry who is paying the mortgage and grocery bills—they get paid out of the family account. But remarrying couples often say they need to differentiate between his expenses and hers, if just to keep things fair, particularly if there are children. You might think the solution would be easy: Set up a joint household account and pay for joint expenses out of that pot. But what do you do with child support payments intended for specific children? Add them to the general mix, where they might get used to help support other children, or put them exclusively toward the needs of the kids they are intended for?

And who contributes what percentage or amount to a general household account? All of one's income, or are partners allowed to retain a portion for their own savings, money that might go for a child's education or perhaps an inheritance for their kids? What if someone quits a job and is living off investments or credit cards? Is dividend money income or should it be treated differently, like an inheritance? How do you calculate fairness if one spouse is still paying alimony and child support to another household? What if one set of kids is resident in the house and the other only visits? How about if one spouse brings debts from the first marriage into the second? Who pays those? What about the family home, particularly if it is held in the name of one spouse? Does the mortgage get paid out of the joint household account or a separate savings account? Do you rewrite the deed, and how does that change future funds for kids? What about college funds invested with one child in mind, or inheritances that come down one side of the family? Do those get shared or kept separate?

. . .

Then there are the unspoken expectations that people bring to remarriage, the dreams, the hopes, the subconscious longings—what therapists call the unspoken contracts. Many of these issues remain unspoken because it's too threatening to discuss them openly. Most people headed for remarriage are coming out of divorces, and many feel gun-shy, at the very least, about financial issues. Others are desperate—either they don't want to ever be in a position of feeling fleeced again or they are desperate about their unsteady financial future and don't want those needs coming too close to the surface.

Maybe one partner is hoping the remarriage will mean he or she can quit the job they hate. Maybe it means someone can pay off a nagging debt or buy a bigger house. Maybe it means someone can stop asking for cash infusions from parents. Maybe it means one or the other can go back to graduate school or buy a boat or help an aging mother. These expectations, especially when they are not shared, can make financial decisions doubly difficult.

Money, and the power struggles and dependencies around it, is often cited by remarried couples as the single most difficult issue after parenting conflicts, in part because concerns about money evolve, over time, and need to be renegotiated regularly as circumstances change. Remarriage is always haunted by the divorce experience, and if that experience is one of loss and broken trust, you may find it hard to go into a remarriage believing that this time the financial story will be different. Even if you have a good understanding of how you will split money and costs, arrangements that worked fine when kids were little or while someone held a good job can change overnight when circumstances shift.

When I talk with the Schumers, it is clear there is lingering resentment over whether John should ask his ex-wife to contribute to the hefty college expenses for their daughter. Mimi and John have had full custody of her since she was seven, and they have never asked John's ex-spouse to contribute to her care, because they didn't want the ex-wife interfering in their life. But now the child is eighteen, and Mimi is concerned that there won't be enough money for her own daughter, who will start college next year.

"There's no reason Jennie's mom can't be asked to contribute something," says Mimi. "We're scraping the bottom of the barrel here for her books and all. I admit I've resented it all these years that she didn't help pay her daughter's costs, and now I don't see why we can't push the issue."

The situation is complicated by the fact that Mimi's ex-husband has shared expenses for her daughter, although his "contribution" has come with considerable stress and tension. The interference that they worried about was real indeed. But in Mimi's eyes, John's unwillingness to go to his ex-spouse feels like him protecting her, and that hurts, Mimi says. "I'm his wife, and I've done the hard work of helping him raise Jen. I love her deeply, but it wasn't easy, and I don't understand why he can't support me in this. Why is his ex-wife more important than me?"

What the experts will tell you is that money smokes out the demons in a remarriage. People often bring complex feelings about money to a remarriage—fears of hooking up with a gambler or an addict or a wild spender, fears of unwittingly taking on someone else's debts or full responsibility for someone else's children, or the fear of losing everything in another divorce. At the same time, money also smokes out the deep needs people bring to remarriage: the need to feel reassured, the aching need to ensure that their children will be provided for, the need to feel valued even if one doesn't bring much to the table, the need to feel like the queen of the house—even if it isn't your house.

When faced with the idea of remarriage, with questions about prenups and wills and first wives and pension plans, other people sometimes asked why Charlie and I were even bothering to make it official. Why not just live together?

Anyone who has been through the agony and expense of a protracted divorce would give this serious consideration. My parents reported a growing number of elderly friends who were coupling up without actually marrying. The Census Bureau recently reported that the fastest growing type of household in the United States is unmarried partners, up 72 percent in the last decade. Why not just go for the romance?

It sounds tempting—so simple, so seamless—but for me, the kids change the equation. If I am going to bring children into the partnership, there needs to be an underlying foundation, a commitment. Otherwise, the situation feels unfair. It is unfair to ask children to open their hearts to a stepparent and new siblings if it isn't for real and for good. I want my relationship with Charlie to be hard to get out of. I want the bonds of marriage to hold us together in times of stress. I want us to build a vessel that can withstand a storm, so my instinct is to plan for flexibility but lash it all up pretty tight.

Charlie's lawyer, however, has other ideas. Having just helped Charlie out of one marriage, he would like to dig a big moat around Charlie's resources and keep me out. I wonder if he is worried about the fact that I'm the only person Charlie dated post-divorce and sees his role as one of protecting Charlie from an inevitable second divorce. Maybe he examines my relatively modest dowry and questions my motives. Maybe he's just doing his job—being a good lawyer to Charlie.

I knew Charlie would bring more to the marriage than I did, but suddenly the wealth I had managed to squirrel away as a single mother looked paltry, dwarfed by what Charlie put on the table. I was proud of what I had managed to do—winning tenure at my university, building my retirement fund, buying a house in a rapidly appreciating neighborhood—but now I worried about the disparity. I worried that his family would think I was marrying him for his money. I worried that having more money for household things would spoil my children. I worried that if he was the one financing a winter vacation, we would always do what he wanted. And I worried about whether I deserved this stroke of fortune. If marrying him was going to mean that I didn't have to worry about my retirement as much, then I was going to have to earn that. I was going to have to be one hell of a wife.

I was also worried that these financial issues would upset my relationship with my ex-husband. Ron and I co-parented our children with relatively little conflict, in part because we had worked hard at building a supportive relationship, but also because we had about the same amount of money.

With nearly equal salaries, equal debts, and equal individual wealth, we really didn't have a whole lot to fight over. When we divorced we split our assets fifty-fifty, the way we split the time with our kids, though we did do some creative horse-trading between accounts to meet each of our individual needs. A bit more retirement here, a bit more for a house down payment there. When the dust cleared, we both felt financially whole, stabilized, able to support our children. There wasn't a lot for amenities or the college fund, but there was enough for each of us to own a home and build our retirement accounts. We rarely dickered over little items anymore—we just tried to keep things even in an informal way, and that worked for us. Neither of us felt cheated, mostly because we didn't think the other would try to cheat us. We had rebuilt our trust in each other around money issues, and both of us knew that what we had went to the kids, so it wasn't about us that much anyway. The two households felt equal to our boys, and that balance mattered to them.

But when Charlie asked me to marry him, I knew that the financial balance between me and my ex-husband could easily get disrupted. Inevitably, just because I would have another salary to help support my household, not to mention retirement accounts and savings, things would be easier for me. And I worried that this would make my ex-husband jealous or nervous or unhappy.

So between shopping for a wedding dress and testing out caterers and talking about cakes and flowers and honeymoons, Charlie and I talk furtively about the prenuptial, where the children can't hear. Charlie agrees that his lawyer is being too conservative in his approach, and suggests I hire my own lawyer.

He generously offers to pay the fee. "I don't want you to feel like you got run over," he says. "I want you to feel like it is a fair document for both of us."

The lawyer I hire, an older man with a gentle sense of humor, quickly helps us see that there are several scenarios to consider in writing this prenuptial. The first is what will happen if the marriage doesn't make it and breaks up fairly quickly, within the first few years. The second is a scenario based on what happens if the marriage breaks up after a longer time— say, five or seven years. A third scenario is what happens if the marriage never breaks up. According to my lawyer, we should each have different rights and responsibilities under the different scenarios. This approach feels more equitable and allows us to keep the divorce demon at bay. If we divorce after just a few years, I agree that I have little right to share in his wealth. If I help him finish raising his kids and am a loving wife who gets dumped years down the road, then maybe I have earned something more.

But other areas are more complicated. We aren't sure how to handle the kids, from allowances to private school costs to college and graduate school expenses and to their future inheritances, if there is anything left after all that education. We can tell that our feelings about sharing assets with the children will probably change as relationships develop over time, but we're not sure how to state things now. We also have to think about life insurance policies, retirement accounts, and real estate assets. None of it seems easy, in part, because there are few social models to use as guidelines.

Emotional shoals lie just under the surface of the discussion and often force us to alter course. As soon as Charlie and I start discussing the terms of our agreement, the first emotion that rises to the surface in me is my strong need to feel like an owner of my home. I know real estate to be a good investment, particularly in our metropolitan area, and I don't want to be cut out of the opportunity to use it to increase the value of the estate I will eventually leave my sons. But mostly I don't want to live and care for a home that doesn't feel like mine.

"I'm not going to get down on my hands and knees and scrub the bathroom molding with a toothbrush if I'm not an owner in the house," I tell Charlie one day, to the amusement of his lawyer. "I'm not going to feel free to argue about the color of the walls or whether we should splurge on expensive countertops in the kitchen. I'm just not going to feel like it is my house. I'll feel like a guest."

I hadn't really known I was going to feel that strongly about owning the house I lived in, except that it was quite difficult for me to think of giving up my own house. If I was to move into Charlie's house, which raised all the obvious territoriality issues, I was going to need to be a co-owner if I was to settle in as the mistress of the hearth.

But Charlie's house is valuable, especially after the renovation. Should he just sign half the equity over to me the day of the wedding, or is something else more appropriate? This is where the differing scenarios prove helpful. After some discussion, we agree on a plan where my share starts small but increases each year after that until it reaches 50 percent.

A second strong conviction that emerges is my desire to continue working and providing my share of the household income, if only for the satisfaction of being an equal provider. My self-esteem, it turns out, is closely knitted to my job and my financial independence, and I'm not ready to give that up. It feels important to keep my own support systems in place, even if I am marrying Charlie, because I don't really know what will happen. I call this the Cute Secretary scenario, the one where Charlie dumps me for someone much younger, buys a yacht, and sails for Fiji. I know in my heart he wouldn't do that, but a girl needs to be practical.

"Let's call it the 'Charlie gets Alzheimer's and runs off with a cute secretary' scenario," he says. "Because I'd have to lose my mind to do something that stupid."

"Okay," I say. "What do we do with the house if that happens?"

Charlie and I started the prenuptial process early in our yearlong engagement, mostly because I didn't want it clouding the weeks leading up to the wedding. But like everything else that year, it takes longer than anticipated, and there we are, just days away from the ceremony, signing our agreement. The emotional process of the work proves draining and difficult. I feel like a heel arguing for certain rights, then the next moment irritated that I even have to fight my way out of certain corners. In the end, though, I am glad to be getting the decisions on paper. It means less negotiating on the fly, once we merge families, when the emotions will be even higher and the stress worse.

I could already tell the first few years of this remarriage were going to feel like a trial by fire. By the time we were calmly discussing how we would divide assets if we divorced, I was fully aware that most second marriages with children end up back in family court. I had joined the Stepfamily Association of America and regularly scrolled through their website, and I mentally filed all the advice I could find. In short order, I ran across articles on financial issues by their president, Margorie Engle, so I decided to go to the source and give her a call.

Engle, it turns out, is a font of wisdom on the topic of remarriage and money. She has both a Ph.D. in law and an MBA in finance. She also is the veteran of remarriage herself, having merged five teenaged daughters into a stepfamily with her second husband. Whenever she can, she tries to talk about finances with remarrying couples, because she knows how easy it is for them to avoid this conversation.

"When you get engaged to remarry, you are loath to discuss these issues, because you love each other to pieces and you don't want to ruin or lose that," Engle tells me. "You also hear, every morning over the breakfast table, how that bitch, the ex-wife, raked your fiancé over the coals financially. So it's no wonder that you aren't going to be the first one to ask, 'Well, am I the beneficiary of your life insurance policy?'"

Engle pauses for breath and I make a mental note: Ask Charlie about his life insurance policy. "The truth is," Engle continues, "divorce is a time of real or perceived financial hardship for most women, but they don't want to be perceived as materialistic or greedy, so they don't say much of anything at all. But trust me—it's much better to speak up."

Engle says couples do best when they deal with the emotional side of these money issues up front. Quite often, she says, the partner with less money or fewer assets feels undervalued in the relationship. And in most cases, she adds, there need to be protections in the distribution of property, income, and wealth to avoid building resentments over time, particularly if there are limited resources for helping college-age children or grown children who may need to borrow money for the down payment on a house or for other needs.

"What is difficult about a prenuptial," says Engle, "is that it is based on the idea of divorce, and most remarrying couples don't want to think about that." Most couples, she says, don't realize that the state will dictate how money is divided if people don't have any other legal document, either a prenuptial or a postnuptial. "They already have a prenuptial—the one based on state requirements," she says. "Most people don't know that. Not every family will go to the trouble to hire lawyers, but you can have a conversation, write up an agreement, maybe even get it notarized, which gives it more legal force. It at least gets some of the issues on paper."

One of the challenges, she agrees, is trying to gauge future financial needs or even future feelings. Some prenuptials include a clause that says if the parties are still married after ten years, they will tear up the document. It can be difficult to tell, at the time of the marriage, how a stepparent might feel about using some of his or her retirement money to help a grown stepchild buy a house. By the time the stepparent and the child have lived together for years, such generosity might feel like the natural thing to do. Or, she says, sometimes additional children are born to the couple, rendering prenuptial arrangements outdated or unfair.

One of the thorniest money problems for many remarried couples is how to deal with financial obligations to ex-spouses or with financial support to children whose other parent isn't providing support. Will an ex-spouse have enough money by the time the kids start college to actually help with tuition, as stipulated in the divorce decree, or will the stepparent have to come up with more cash to keep the child in school? Should a new husband have the right to demand that his wife go back to her ex-husband and renegotiate child support? Does a remarried husband still protect his former spouse (and his kids) by helping with bills or rent, even beyond what he is required to do by law? And what about the stepdad who feels that most of his money goes to support his second wife's kids at the expense of the children he had by his first wife, who live with their mother?

None of these are easy issues, and many remarrying couples just sweep them under the rug. "When James and I got together, he said, 'Let's use whoever's money is available, and when we run out of one pot, we'll take from the other,' " says my friend Mary Dimmesdale, who remembers haphazard arrangements for buying things for their kids in the beginning of her second marriage. Both of them brought kids from their first marriages, but they also brought quite different income levels. "I knew instinctively that we were going to run out of my money long before we ran out of his," says Mary.

The Dimmesdales eventually worked out a more organized system, partly through the use of a postmarital contract, which is another way to address unforeseen changes, such as surprise inheritances or unanticipated financial demands from kids, says Engle. She also suggests that remarried couples revisit their financial plans and legal documents on a regular basis, in order to keep them current. "Most couples say their financial plans are still a work in progress."

A host of financial issues for remarrying couples are obscured by varying state laws or institutional practices. Taxes can be a nightmare, particularly for those who move to a new state or change residency in the process. Institutions often seem to have little understanding of the pressures on stepfamilies. Colleges, for example, often ask for the financial data on a stepparent's income and factor that information into financial aid decisions, even though stepparents are not obligated under the law to support their stepchildren. Like all adults, remarried couples need carefully written wills to accurately reflect their wishes in case of death. Inheritances, life insurance policies, real estate holdings, and other assets need to be accounted for to prevent nasty fights between former spouses and different sets of children.

Charlie and I agree to rewrite our wills, to make them conform to the prenuptial. Until we can get around to that, though, we promise to be careful while crossing streets and to keep risky driving to a minimum. Many remarried couples say that the financial conflicts eventually ease, particularly after the kids are through college and off on their own. For couples who have been together for more than seven years, the early divisions between yours and mine often fade.

"I don't have anyone else to leave my money to other than Maggie's children," says my friend Jim Caine, who remarried a woman with two grown teens twelve years ago and long since gave up keeping separate accounts. "I'm an only child and have no kids of my own. So it doesn't really matter that it has all merged by now. I would want them to have what we can leave behind. They are my kids and my grandkids, in my heart. That's what matters."

I envy Jim's sense of partnership with Maggie, that sense that they are a team that forges ahead together, sharing everything with each other, in part because Jim and Maggie remind me more of my parents' enduring partnership than this cobbled-together alliance Charlie and I are building. But I trust that in time, Charlie and I will make more financial decisions together. For now, I need to be content in the generosity of our good fortune.

CHAPTER EIGHT

Premarital Counseling

I'M STANDING IN FRONT OF a mirror in a lacy silk dress, wondering why someone my age would ever walk down an aisle. I do not look like a bride. I am not young or virginal or fresh, not at age forty-six. I'm what the bridal magazines delicately call an "encore" bride: someone who's got a history; someone who, instead of starting out, is trying desperately to start over. Someone who looks more like a mom than a bride.

"Aren't you supposed to wear white?" Jesse asks. The dress I'm trying on is actually a bridesmaid's dress because I can't bring myself to try on more traditional dresses, those big puffy things. I've brought it home, but I can see now that it's not right. Not because it isn't white, but probably because it's too jeune fille, as my dad would say.

"White is for virgins," David says.

"Oh, jeez," says Jesse. "That's a problem."

That's me, the problem bride. Too old to be naive, too young to give up hope.

By spring, the renovation of Charlie's house is under way, my house is almost ready for sale, the school issue is nearly settled. The wedding and honeymoon plans are in place. Things are moving along nicely. And I'm depressed.

I go to see my therapist. "I'm the weak link," I tell him. "I don't think I can do it. I'm going to crack, and it will all come apart."

"Weak link," he muses. "That's an interesting term. But I would ask you this: Why are you the only link? Why does it all fall apart if you break? Why do you see it as a chain instead of a fabric? Isn't there anyone else holding it together? Like Charlie, for example?"

I've been functioning as the single executive of my life for so long that I have trouble imagining another model. I have both the arrogance and the exhaustion of one who thinks she holds the world together. "Are we talking about my autonomy issues?" I ask. "I know I'm used to doing everything myself. Is that the problem?"

"Well, I would actually call it a control issue," he says drily. "You need to examine whether you are willing to let Charlie share the power in your life."

"Share the power?" I'm almost squeaking with tension. "You mean, let him in on decisions about my boys? Stuff like that?"

"You are planning to marry him, right?" my patient therapist says. "Most successful marriages operate as teams, with power roughly equally distributed. Sometimes, people split responsibilities—she's in charge of the kids, he's in charge of the money. Other couples share in most decisions. But few couples make it who keep two separate family systems operating. At some point, you two will have to become one family, and until you do, you will be exhausted from trying to keep these two worlds from crashing into each other."

I go out with my friend Suzanne, who is now engaged to remarry as well. We're supposed to be wedding dress shopping, but we've given up and are sharing a salad at a sidewalk café. She is another scrappy independent. She too can think of a million ways in which blending households with her fiancé is going to challenge how she manages her life and her daughter's.

"I'm having a problem with this team issue," I tell Suzanne. "I feel like some two-bit Eastern European country trying to join the European Union. You would think I would be grateful, because I want in on the party, but I'm terrified of being overwhelmed, of losing my familiar life and identity. I don't want to give up my currency."

She laughs. "Yeah, I feel like Yugoslavia all the time. The problem, as I see it, is that surviving a divorce gives you this tremendous sense of accomplishment. You get through these hard things by yourself and end up with this sense that you can handle anything." She forks her salad around. "But you know what? There's a liability to this—that you end up wondering if you can trust anyone else to do it as well. Or that it will take too much explaining to bring someone else into the process."

Too much explaining, like why I allow my children to drink

root beer floats every evening. That's my problem. It isn't that I don't trust Charlie to be wise and thoughtful, because he usually is. It's that I don't have the energy sometimes to explain all the complex reasons behind the ice cream habit. That maybe I don't want to be the perfect mother all the time. That sometimes I want my children to love me just for being indulgent. That sometimes I'm tired of telling them no. That I don't believe soda pop is evil, as Charlie does. That no matter what he says about the soda pop problem, I will probably never consider it evil, but that I'm also unwilling to admit that. That I wish I could be a better mother, but some days it's just too hard.

My best friend, Sandy, calls me up one day to check on me. She has noticed that I'm having trouble finding a wedding dress and thinks maybe it's related to cold feet. She and her wonderful husband nursed me through the worst of the post-divorce years, including me in their family dinners, letting me come over on Saturday nights for movies and popcorn. I've sat on their sofa and cried and talked and worried, while folding a raft of the socks generated by their athletic brood. She and her husband have kept their marriage alive and vital by fighting, loving, forgiving, and helping each other through illnesses and broken bones, all the while staying fully engaged—sort of lovingly in each other's face, as I think of them. I've learned a lot from them.

"I saw a couple of dresses you might want to consider," she says. "I was out shopping with the girls. I could go pick them up and bring them by for you to look at."

"Oh, I don't want you to go to that kind of trouble," I tell her. "Really, I'll buy a dress soon. It's just not a priority at the moment, because there's still so much else to deal with."

"At the rate you're going, you'll be getting married in your bathrobe," she protests. "You're still engaged, right?"

"Yes."

"And you're getting married June twenty-second, right?"

I look at the calendar. My God, it's nearly the end of March. "I'm going to go out looking this week, promise." She's quiet on the other end of the line. "If it makes you any happier, I'll get my robe dry-cleaned, just in case," I tell her.

"Maybe we can just get you a big corsage. Then no one will notice you're in your robe."

The first time I married, at twenty-six, I wore my mother's candlelight satin gown, along with the Belgian lace veil that stretched four feet behind me as I walked down the aisle. It had been worn by almost every woman in my mother's family, but I was the first of those married under it to be divorced. There was no wearing that veil this time, or any other veil. Whatever it represented had long since been ripped away. I wasn't sure what a second wife was supposed to wear. My sister Anne wore a beautiful brightly colored shawl over a simple cotton dress at her California remarriage. It was a lovely idea, and she looked terrific in the simple setting of a friend's backyard. But she's the arty one. I didn't have that kind of creative vision, or even any vision of myself getting married again. Maybe that's what Sandy was worried about.

Anne, who is an ordained minister, has agreed to officiate at our garden wedding, but she sets one condition: She will marry us only if we go through several sessions of marriage counseling with a pastoral counselor. This isn't because she distrusts our commitment; she requires this of all couples she marries, and says it is particularly important for older, second-time brides and grooms. "Those who," she says as delicately as possible, "think they already know all the answers." She has a lot of experience in remarriage, it turns out, perhaps because she practices in California, land of the divorced. She usually does this counseling herself, but she's too far away, and besides, she's my sister. We promise to find someone here in Washington and let her know how it goes.

But finding a pastoral counselor willing to talk with us for a few sessions proves daunting, and it takes several weeks of referrals and canceled appointments before Charlie and I find ourselves in the office of a local minister. She is slightly older than us, a gregarious and blustery woman who sits munching her sandwich while she throws out loaded questions. We perch on her couch, giving curt, cryptic answers. We are more than a bit resistant, in part because we've done so much soul-searching already and this seems like old ground. We've consulted with several different psychologists and psychiatrists on the children and our own individual issues. We don't feel like revealing ourselves again just to get this stamp on our passport. In fact, we are behaving just as my sister predicted: We think we know all the answers. But within minutes the minister starts to get at issues that make us squirm in our seats.

She asks us first to list our values, the values we want in this new marriage and that we will consciously and unconsciously try to build into the family structure. I've long thought Charlie and I shared all the important values, and we do share the big ones, like honesty and trust, but we have some differences when it comes to where boundary lines get drawn, particularly around the kids, and we have different approaches to developing independence among the boys. We start to open up more, and the discussion bumps along, with old issues from both previous marriages surfacing as we try to articulate what we mean.

Charlie says the marriage should be built on honesty, with no lying. I say it needs to be a place where it is safe to tell the truth. We also believe strongly in mutual trust, but the need to be able to trust each other's judgment comes with the shadow requirement that everyone's judgment must then be dead-on in every case. We talk about the different family cultures around money issues, and how that could create challenges in the future. We talk about disciplining the boys, doing the laundry, and hogging the remote. We promise that we will listen to each other, and then also try to forgive and let go of old angers, particularly if someone's judgment just didn't quite turn out to be so solid after all.

We leave exhausted. Within just fifty minutes, this complete stranger has raised an army of potential demons, and I'm not sure how to get them back in the box. As we go out the door, she suggests we think about any myths or social expectations we may subconsciously be carrying into this remarriage. And can we think of any good models of stepfamilies? We can take those up during the next session.

I sit down and go to work sifting through a lifetime of cultural and social conditioning, searching for models of and myths about stepfamilies. Growing up in the fifties and sixties, I had very few such families on my social horizon. But there was one on TV, and I watched it religiously: the Brady Bunch, the most insidious of the modern social fairy tales about blending families. Nearly every time I mentioned that my fiancé and I were planning to merge two sets of boys, people smiled and said something like "Oh, a boy Brady Bunch." After hearing this a hundred times, I went back to look up old episodes of the show, to figure out what was so compelling about this image of stepfamilies.

After sitting through several hours of the irritatingly happy antics of this family, I can suddenly see what the attraction is. What works so well about the Brady Bunch is that they function just like an idealized nuclear family. They have fun, they have barbecues, they have little problems that are easily solved. Their children are talented and successful, every last one. This blended family, in fact, operates better than most intact families. The Bradys have modern conflicts, but they resolve them with old-fashioned values, those usually associated with nuclear families—trust, understanding, the bonds of love, and familiarity. And that is where the myth became so powerful. *The Brady Bunch* set a standard for stepfamilies that the psychologists will tell you is pretty much a pipe dream. Two lonely adults, young and still attractive, find love and support by merging their tribes of kids, with little trouble beyond the occasional sibling squabble and growing pains of typical families. There is also a subtle sexual pairing between the three daughters of the mom on one side and the three boys of the father on the other. Sort of like a mass wedding, as if to say that this second marriage worked on all levels, not just for the grown-ups.

But when you go back to the shows, you'll notice that the

Brady Bunch worked precisely because most of the stress associated with remarriage and stepfamilies had been airbrushed away by the TV writers. First off, the parents are widowed, not divorced, because there's no evidence of ex-spouses—a huge difference between them and most stepfamilies. No other parent lurks out there making demands or tugging on the children. There is no lingering bitterness over earlier failed marriages. The kids don't move between houses or have to deal with conflicting loyalties. Also, they have a housekeeper who makes dinner, oversees homework, and doubles as the resident shrink. Mom Brady doesn't work, and in fact, thanks to the housekeeper, is usually found reading a magazine in the spotless living room. She's not cleaning up a bathroom that her stepsons left looking like a locker room, or even cooking for this monstrous-sized clan. It's much easier to be patient and available for your children when you run neither the house nor a company.

There is also something about the Brady Bunch, and all stepfamilies, that is appealing because it is both bizarre and a little dangerous, a glimpse of life outside the norm. It's like a high-wire act: Everyone watches to see if they will fall. I'm just as curious as the next person. As soon as I thought I might remarry someone with children, I started asking those who had merged families thousands of questions. Do you discipline each other's children? Do you call yourself a family? How is little Lucy or Emily or Jacob actually doing?

Now I'm exhibit A. As soon as I mention I'm remarrying, friend after friend circles in with a loaded question. "How are the boys handling this?" "Have you told your ex-husband?"

"What are Charlie's kids like?" "How do the boys get along?"

It feels as if I have wandered off into unknown terrain, and people want to hear the travelogue. Every family who has done this says it feels like being a pioneer, in part because there are few maps, few models, and precious little to go on. *The Brady Bunch*, for most of us, proves a worthless guide.

The next time Charlie and I meet with the minister, I have plenty to say. We talk about the Brady Bunch and the angel in the house, who seems suspiciously like Mom Brady. What has worried me throughout—the feeling that I'm just not woman or angel or kind or tolerant enough to hack it—now seems laughably obvious. Yet here I sit, preparing for my marriage.

"I know I wasn't patient enough or mature enough in my first marriage," I tell Charlie and the minister. "And now it looks even harder, with all these kids and everything. If I remarry, I want to do it right. I cannot live through another failure. I'm afraid I have to be perfect at this or it won't work."

What I'm unearthing during this process are the many unspoken expectations I have about myself, my new marriage, my new husband, and my new life. And it's a bit overwhelming. No wonder we were resistant to talking about this.

It turns out, though, that this is common. In fact, Charlie and I are right on schedule. In my quest to understand this better, I find a study by psychologist James Bray of Houston, who with support from the National Institutes of Health spent ten years studying stepfamilies in Texas. Bray found that most remarrying couples carry unrealistic expectations into the chapel. The most pervasive is the nuclear family myth, that remarrying will magically heal the damage of divorce and restore the broken families to wholeness, as it appeared to do for the Brady Bunch. Some remarried spouses even believe that if they can escape their former spouses, by gaining full custody of their children or abandoning them, then they can re-create a nuclear family in their second marriage.

Many families also suffer from the expectation that love will occur instantly and naturally between children and stepparents, as long as the stepparent is friendly and supportive. In actuality, most children are hard to win over, and open up only when bonds develop between them and their stepparent. Other families, says Bray, have a rescue fantasy, the hope that their new marriage will redeem them from the failure of their first by being better. Another common rescue fantasy is the hope that they can save their new spouse from the hassles and indignities of single parenting or the mistreatment of an abusive ex-husband, or possibly even rescue their own children from the clutches of an angry ex-spouse. Other families enter remarriage with the expectation of an egalitarian world, Bray says, where everyone will be an equal member with equal status and power—democracy in action. This is the one that Charlie and I seem to be ascribing to. What most families discover, in the first few months, is that parents don't want to cede equal voting rights to kids, and that stepfamilies can easily split into factions that make it difficult to keep the household in balance.

And the children of people remarrying, it turns out, often have a fantasy about the reunification of their own biological parents, hoping against hope—no matter what their age—that their parents will wake up some morning, come to their senses, and go home. Everything can then go back to how it used to be.

These expectations, Bray says, are often unconscious. He found that even the most realistic couples subconsciously expect the new stepfamily to function like a nuclear family. This happens in part, he believes, because there are so few maps for how stepfamilies really work, and because remarrying couples need to dream and engage in a certain denial—or they won't ever have the courage to make the leap.

But the key to finding sanity on the other side of the wedding, according to Bray's research, is to let go of the expectations and plan for chaos and the unexpected, exactly as my son Jesse suggested. To help us through, the minister suggests we draft some practical systems for managing our household, so that neither of us needs to be perfect stepparents or superhuman family executives. She particularly urges us to consider family meetings, where the boys get to air their grievances and help us work out solutions. Charlie and I look over at each other, dubious. We both envision the same fractious scene: four boys yelling, someone stomping out, nobody listening much, and me and Charlie in the middle, buffaloed, mute, unable to explain why we ever thought this would be a good idea. The university professor in me, in particular, questions the value of letting the mob get a chance to air their disputes publicly. I've seen it happen in the classroom, that nasty gang effect. I'm not sure I want to sit through it in my living room. But we nod and take notes. Maybe it's worth a try.

As I ponder whether we will ever be able to live up to this model of good stepfamily management and hold a meeting that is anything other than a rout of the adults, the minister suggests another important tool: humor. "Maybe you could stash a witch's hat in the broom closet, and when you need to ask your stepsons to pick up their dirty socks, put on the hat and do it in a funny way," she says. "That can really lessen the sting."

I'm sure she's right, but when I'm making dinner after coming home from an exhausting day at work, worrying about the homework that still needs managing, the laundry that sits in an aromatic heap in the hallway, I doubt I'll have the energy to be the evenhanded, never annoyed, humorous, playful, witty stepmom. Sometimes I'm just going to want to ask them to pick up their socks, without having to get into costume. What normal mother is expected to entertain whenever she has a simple request?

By the third session, the minister helps us get at the core of many of these concerns, the issue of roles. The hardest thing about creating a stepfamily, she says, is that the new roles involved aren't spelled out, and they will probably be different from the roles everyone held before the remarriage. My younger son, who has long been the dominant child of my pair, will suddenly be the youngest of four, and unable to wield the same influence in the house. Charlie's oldest will need to make room for three pesky younger brothers rather than just one. My oldest and Charlie's youngest now become middle children, those kids who end up as diplomats and problem-solvers. We could use a few of these, no doubt, but will our kids be able to learn this new role at their relatively advanced ages? Will they want this role?

The biggest question for us as the adults in the household, particularly with four teenagers, is the problem of authority and responsibility. With these kids nearly grown and ex-spouses on both sides still operating as active parents, we will have relatively little room to be stepparents in any significant parental way. We wonder whether we should even call ourselves a family. Maybe we are just a community of people who care about each other. Housemates. Charlie and I look at each other. No, that's not quite right, either. A two-sided family? A multiheaded dragon?

After the third session with the minister, she pronounces us ready to marry and Charlie and I, chastened, slink back to our normal life closer to the surface of things. Many of the hurdles of making this move are nearly done. My boys have been accepted into a small Catholic Benedictine school in Washington, a place known as a relaxed, friendly community of serious students. It's a blessing to have both boys accepted into the school that was their first choice, and an enormous relief to know we have a place for them. They are still sad about leaving their friends, but both can see the advantages of their new school, and that allows them to let go. We've decided not to send them to the school Adam and Matt go to, despite the logistical advantages of having them all in one place. Too much togetherness, I figure. We don't need to have them facing off in math class as well as over the dinner table.

My house in Maryland sells the first weekend it's on the market. When Charlie hears of the profit I'll make at settlement, he whistles. "From now on you are in charge of all future

real estate investments," he tells me. I'm just happy to be bringing more to the table.

But even though the pieces are falling into place, I still lie
awake at night, staring at the ceiling, worrying about—on top
of everything else—how haggard I'm going to look at the wedding if I don't start sleeping. If I spend too much time thinking
about how hard this is all going to be, I'm not going to be able
to do it. Nobody suffering from the tunnel vision of love here.

Believing in the god of good communication, we spend hours
talking out our fears and concerns. Finally, because I still seem
to be depressed, we go back to see my therapist, this time
together.

"After all these years of counseling couples and of being married myself," he says, "I'm now convinced that the single most
important thing to making a marriage work is . . ." He pauses for
dramatic effect. Charlie and I inch to the edge of our seats.

"Communication?" I ask.

"Well, all that stuff is important, and it doesn't hurt, but
this is what it comes down to—the ability of each party to tol-
erate the neuroses of the other."

We look at each other. It's not necessarily about autonomy?
It's about neuroses?

"That's right. It's about whether you can stand the fact that
he has some irritating habits," my therapist says. I look sidelong
at my sweet fiancé. He does have this really annoying belief that
God will strike him down if he ever returns a video late, and he
is almost deathly afraid of bank service fees. No crosstown
ATMs for this guy. You go to the bank you belong to so you
don't get hit with any of those charges.

I can see that Charlie is pondering my flaws.

"Yep. If you're going to make it for the long haul, you're going to have to learn to live with those neuroses. In fact, you're going to have to learn to embrace them."

Jesus. Nobody said this was going to be easy.

CHAPTER NINE

Tying the Knot

SIX WEEKS BEFORE THE WEDDING I'm still struggling with my house, the move, wedding plans, honeymoon plans, the kids' summer schedules, not to mention the emotional roller coaster of doubts and fears—but the only thing people ask about is what I'm going to wear for the wedding.

"At the risk of sounding like a broken record, what *are* you going to wear?" asks my colleague Pat.

"My bathrobe and a big sign that reads: 'I Couldn't Find a Dress.'"

She laughs. "Well, if you like the bedroom look, I'll lend you the white silk pajamas I wore to my wedding fifteen years ago."

"That's sweet, but no thanks," I tell her. "I'm not exactly your size."

"Well, they're there, and they're loose," she says. "In case you get desperate."

I *am* desperate, but I don't want to admit that. All this interest in what I'm going to wear makes me think there is something heavily symbolic about wedding dresses. I mention this to my therapist one day, and he nearly falls out of his chair laughing.

"Okay, the woman is wearing white and is heavily veiled and on her father's arm," he says. "And you wonder if it is symbolic?" He's been helping me see that my fears about becoming a wife again aren't just some reactionary twitch. They are legitimate, healthy concerns. "Go back and reread your feminist literature from college," he suggests. "You have a right to be nervous. There are lots of things about marriage, particularly traditional marriage, that feel oppressive to women. You aren't crazy. But I do think you can have a very different kind of marriage with Charlie, based on what I've seen of him. The societal expectations may say one thing, but I think you two can figure out what you want between yourselves."

I go over to Charlie's. "My therapist thinks we can negotiate a marriage that won't be oppressive to me," I tell him.

He looks at me, puzzled. "Well, sure, sweetie. Are you really worried about that? Am I oppressive to you?"

"No, not at all." I'm not quite sure why I'm talking about this, because he isn't. But I'm afraid that after the wedding, things will matter more. And then I'll feel the pressure to be better than I am as a girlfriend. As a girlfriend, I can go home to have a meltdown or pull into my shell or punch a pillow. I can present my best face, then slink back into hiding when I need to retreat. As a wife, I won't be able to get away with this. I'll be under the spotlight all the time. "I'm just, well, I seem to be nervous about being a wife again. Maybe that's why I can't find a dress."

"Just tell me if I'm doing something oppressive and I'll stop," he says, trying to reassure me before I dig myself into a hole. "We're partners here. I think you know that I respect your judgment and intelligence and so many other things. I need you as my equal or this will never work." He looks at me. "Okay?"

"Okay."

"If you want me to come shopping with you, I will."

"No, that's okay. I'll do it."

"Gee, you sound like you're off to a funeral."

"Sorry." I shake myself. "Okay, I'll be fine. Don't worry about me."

As I shuffle off, I realize that I'm still lugging around a lot of baggage from my first marriage, which I really need to put away before I marry Charlie. I still operate under some of the old habits—being evasive rather than direct if I think Charlie might disagree with me about something; hesitating to ask for what I need, then resenting that he can't read my mind. What I love about him, though, is that he is usually direct back. He doesn't let resentments build. When he feels me slipping into a dark space, he sits me down and asks what is wrong.

An old friend once told me that on her wedding night her husband made her promise that she wouldn't hold grudges. He had been married before and knew what could happen. "He told me to let him know if I was unhappy so that we could deal with things while they were still little, still manageable," she told me. "His fear was that if we let things simmer, the problems would build until there was this big tangled ball of resentment, and then, he said, it would be impossible to set things straight." Their marriage has lasted twenty years and is as strong as ever. I have never mentioned this philosophy to Charlie, but he seemed to have learned it for himself. Sometimes I squirm under his questions, not wanting to tell him hard things, but we are always better when problems are out on the table. He tells me again and again that I don't have to hold back, that he can handle whatever I need to tell him. I am beginning to believe it.

To help myself through the dress dilemma, I buy a copy of *Bride Again* magazine, which I find tucked in the rack behind the regular bride magazines. I can't flip through those other magazines for more than a minute without feeling hopelessly outclassed and old. Even though *Bride Again* is a magazine for second (or third or fourth) brides, I still expect lots of photos of elegant dresses, and those luscious flower arrangements and elegant cake displays. Instead, I find articles that tell me things are different this time, just in case I hadn't already figured that out. There are some lovely flowers, but mostly the models are older and the dresses understated. The magazine is distinctly realistic, almost painfully honest with these remarrying brides, lest they marry in a romantic haze. The magazine has articles that range from "Coping with His Ex" to "Etiquette for the Encore Wedding" and "Radiant Wedding Smiles: The Latest in Teeth Whitening." Compared to the approach of *Bride* magazine, the readers of which generally don't worry about whitening their teeth, *Bride Again*'s focus is less on china, crystal, and expensive dresses and more on making your marriage work. When I look closely, I realize the magazine is filled with diamond rings—plenty of platinum and sparkle. We second wives must be a practical bunch. We know what lasts. Maybe the lesson from *Bride Again,* I finally conclude, is that if you get a big enough ring, no one will question your dress.

Sandy takes me out dress shopping, and we riffle through dozens of displays in a mall full of stores. It's actually quite difficult to find the right tone. Mexican things look silly on me, particularly since we are getting married in Virginia, and the really romantic stuff feels too Victorian. Too angel in the house. I want something simple. Simple but elegant.

"Do you want white?" Sandy asks, pulling out things that look like prom dresses. They *are* prom dresses.

"Maybe, but maybe off-white would be best."

"Okay, how about this?"

It's a lovely oriental thing—the kind of dress that looks great on really tall, skinny women with no hips. That's not me.

"Sandy, look at that dress. Is there any chance that is going to work for me?"

"Oh, right. But what about the concept?"

"I don't see myself as Chinese."

"Okay. Concept's bad."

It goes like this. When I tell saleswomen I need something for a wedding, they assume my daughter is the bride and pull out things that are hopelessly matronly. Tea gowns are nice, but many are too froufrou. I'm not a bridesmaid or a typical bride. After a few hours, we finally give up.

"I can see now why you're having trouble," Sandy says, sitting down wearily. "Apparently, nobody our age gets married."

"Maybe they all just elope."

My sister Anne, who is going to officiate at our wedding, calls to review the premarital counseling and talk about our plans for the service.

"We're good to go, Annie," I tell her. "Yep, got this stamp right here on my forehead: Ready to Marry!"

"Well, that's a relief," she says. "Got a dress yet?"

"Let's not talk about that." Instead, we talk about some of the points the minister raised, and Anne's particularly interested in the discussions about the values we want our family to have. She says it will help the boys if we articulate the kind of family we want to create as part of the service, rather than just assuming everyone's on the same page. She's done scores of second marriages and has several good suggestions for the wedding service.

"I think you want it to be serious, because you want the kids to get that you are really doing this, but you also want it to be relaxed, not too formal," she says. "Many couples with kids decide to keep the wedding private so that the kids don't feel too exposed. You have to be prepared for the fact that they are probably not going to be real happy about this."

Charlie and I had already decided that a big public wedding would be unbearable for our boys. When we ask the kids for advice, all they can really say is that they want to wear their Hawaiian shirts. I get visions of us standing in front of the minister looking like refugees from a luau. Maybe I should just get a grass skirt.

Charlie and I decide that what is most important to us is to bring our two extended families together—our siblings and their spouses, our parents, and our many wonderful nieces and nephews—and give them a chance to get to know each other. We plan a weekend together, with picnics and a canoeing expedition on the Shenandoah River. We hope that our sons will feel the strong web of family support and feel buoyed by it. That if one of them feels as if he just can't sit through the ceremony, he will have a loving uncle who will follow him out and serve as a supportive shoulder.

We schedule a late-afternoon wedding in the garden, dressed up but not too formal, and a lovely post-wedding dinner at an old colonial manor house nearby. The day after the wedding we'll have a barbecue picnic with the larger circle of our friends. The guys can wear their Hawaiian shirts then.

A few months before the wedding, Annie comes east from California for a conference and joins me for a weekend out at the farm to help me look over the place. The house is still thick with knickknacks Charlie's ex-wife picked up at flea markets and antique stores but decided she didn't want. As we go through the house, Anne suggests I box up this stuff and bring some of my own things out from Washington.

"You want this place to reflect you, not Charlie's ex," she says. "It's going to be hard to get married here if it feels like her house."

We work hard all weekend, cleaning and dusting and assessing what more we need to do to get the place ready. After all the other house-related sorting and packing and fixing up

Charlie and I have been doing, I'm losing steam, but Annie putters around the farm making lists and suggestions. I add it all to the staggering list of to-dos in the reporter's notebook I still carry with me in my purse. When I got married the first time, my mother served as general for the endless wedding tasks, and I resisted her interference almost as much as I appreciated her help. This time, my mother is AWOL, completely hands off. "Just tell us when to be there, and we'll be there!" she says merrily. I guess if you are pushing fifty, people figure you can run your own life.

In the weeks leading up to the wedding, life seems to crescendo. Charlie, who has been doing market research for a technology publisher, gets caught up in organizing a major financial conference, and dashes around Washington enlisting speakers and setting up programs. He's under a lot of pressure, yet still manages to keep track of many of the wedding details. In between work and kids, we run around deciding on light fixtures and bathroom knobs for the renovation. There are a thousand decisions, and my tolerance flags long before his. I'm also fielding questions from family members about the wedding weekend and making preparations for it, including ordering the food for our first family picnic. My friend Connie goes out to the farm with me one day to help hang curtains and move things around. We drape a beautiful red and white quilt on the wall above the living room, then arrange dried flowers in the empty fireplaces and corners of the house.

With just a few weeks to spare, I finally find myself in a dress department that seems to have options appropriate for a middle-aged bride. I select a simple linen sheath in ivory with bands of netting at the waist and hem. It's elegant and under-stated. It doesn't make me look skinny or young or virginal, but it makes me happy. I call Sandy, who is so relieved she suggests we insure it.

There I am, standing on the brink, in love and nervous and excited and scared, when my editor in New York calls up and suggests I write a book about all this—remarriage, the inside perspective. She knows I've already done a lot of reading and nosing around. Surely there must be people out there who have some of the answers to the questions that still worry me. Like, what kind of stepmom should you be when you inherit teens, already formed and well down the road of rebellion? What kind of family can you knit together from two preexisting fam-ilies? What can we expect in the future, as the boys move off into adulthood? Who will we be then? Maybe writing about it will lead me to clarity and answer questions for others as well. So some time between signing the contract to sell my house and signing our prenuptial, I sign a book contract. As I put pen to paper, though, doubt flickers at the edge of my mind: Do I dare? This is our life I'll be writing about. Do I really want to try and capture it, pin us all to paper? But I have Charlie's sup-port, and I already know people are interested because so many stop me to ask about different aspects of this enterprise. I just pray I know what I'm doing.

Suddenly it all starts happening, and I can feel my heart start to lift. The day before the wedding, our families convene, connecting quickly and finding ties and commonalities through lots of chat. There are thirty-two members of our combined families, and it's a happy crowd. Charlie's nephew Nick has put together a beautiful book of individually penned biographies and photos of everyone. Our four boys have been tense in the weeks before, but once their cousins show up they start to relax. Everyone enjoys the canoeing, and we have fun swimming and picnicking together. The morning of the ceremony, the women shower me with little gifties—chocolates, bath soaps, advice, and support. My brother, as a joke, gives me a copy of a hackneyed poem about the perfect wife.

"Oh my God," I tell him, "have you ever heard of the angel in the house?"

"The what?"

"Well, never mind, but this is my nightmare."

"Hey, I bet Charlie would love it!"

"Exactly."

An hour before the wedding, Anne takes me and Charlie aside.

"I think we need to change the service slightly," she says. We've included a section where the boys stand up with us and we ask them if they will live with us under a family covenant of respect and support. We've dodged the love issue, because these boys don't seem ready to love each other much, but Anne still thinks asking them to affirm this covenant is risky.

"I think you should just tell them this is what you are going to do," she says firmly. "If we ask for their agreement, you might be met by a deafening silence. You don't want that in the middle of your wedding."

She's right, of course, which is why we hired an experienced professional.

Charlie has a beautiful dark blue jacket, and my nieces have made me a bundle of irises to carry. I have picked out nice ties for the boys and ordered yellow boutonnieres for their dress shirts. We push them into the showers, and by the time they get dressed up and slick their hair back, they take my breath away.

Minutes before the private family service is to start, a thunderstorm slices through the garden. Everybody dashes for the house, and we huddle for half an hour, listening to the rain, joking, everyone doing what they can to ease the obvious tension among our boys. They've all gotten increasingly stiff and awkward as the day has wound up to its emotional climax, but they are still with us, determined not to ruin our day. Soon the sky clears and the birds start to sing. We go out into the garden, say our vows to each other, promise the four children we will build them a family life of love and support, and poof—we are married.

The minute it is over, as we are toasting our future together, the boys come back to life. Adam offers a toast to my courage in taking on the challenge of his dad. Jesse, the man of the chaos theory, toasts the four boys "who have to live together!" Everyone whoops. We go out into the garden, get some pictures of everyone all together, then break for dinner at the inn.

After an elegant meal, complete with a dessert bar that undoes the kids, my brother takes most of the teens down to a guesthouse for Murder in the Dark, while the grandparents and adults listen to my brother-in-law Chris play Dixieland and Celtic tunes on the piano while Nick, Charlie's nephew, follows along on his fiddle. My father turns to me: "Thank God the divorce years are over." I haven't seen him this happy in years. Charlie and I have trouble tearing ourselves away from this wonderful scene to go off and have a wedding night, but finally we do.

The next day our friends stream out from Washington and we have a big barbecue at the farm, with Irish music and volleyball and kids running around in bathing suits. It's wild and relaxed and I'm finally beginning to believe this is all real. We cut into the wedding cake tower of flowers and fruit, and I gleefully toss my bouquet from the upstairs bedroom window, with my sisters at my side. We string up a piñata Annie brought from California, and all the kids take turns. Finally the party breaks up. Our four boys are headed off for camps the next day, so Charlie rounds them up for the drive back to Washington. I dash around for a bit, trying to help Adam find his CDs and Matt find his shoes, then take a moment alone with Jesse and David upstairs.

"You guys have been terrific this weekend, just amazing," I tell them. "I know this wasn't easy. You've been helpful and sweet. I'm so proud of you."

"It's okay, Mom," they say, leaning against me for a moment in that teenage way that passes for full hugs. "We love you, Mom," Jesse says. "I'm glad you're going to be happy," David says. And then they are gone, whisked away. I won't see them for two weeks. But I can feel that they will be all right.

A day later, Charlie and I are on a flight to Stockholm. My head is still spinning from the wedding and I can barely believe it is over. We arrive in the middle of the midsummer festival, and the city is filled with people sunning themselves in the plazas and lingering in sidewalk cafés as the twilight goes on for hours. It never gets dark—but between eleven and two the sun finally dips down below the horizon for a bit. We wander through the medieval streets, poking into shops, taking in museums, watching the busy harbor. One night we take a ferry out through the archipelago of islands that runs north up the coast. It's the regular ferry that services these remote granite rocks, not one of the party boats, and we watch as families come down to the docks to greet friends and relatives. On the way back, we sit in the beautiful oak-paneled dining room and share a salmon supper while watching the lights of the distant city appear in the radiant twilight.

"Do I get lots of Swallow points for this one?" Charlie asks. That's our joke about all things nautical, which I was raised on and still love. He has already earned a bundle of Swallow points for going with me to the ship museum and climbing around several four-riggers docked in the harbor. Charlie and I, like twins, sometimes talk almost in code, referring back to old jokes, shared stories, silly memories.

"Yep. This is worth a lot of Swallow points."

"We have to go back to our life soon, you know."

"I know. But not tonight. Let me just be here with you."

When we get back to Washington, I'm not sure which house to return to, but I'm married now, so I go with Charlie to his. The next morning, my first as the resident wife, as we are relaxing in bed, Charlie turns to me and says, "For breakfast I would like scrambled eggs, pancakes, a fruit salad, and . . ."

This is supposed to be a joke because the house is still

under renovation and we do not have a working kitchen. Still, I narrow my eyes. "So this was all about getting a cook, an angel in the house?"

"You're not laughing."

"Well, my friend Mary Lee warned me about this."

"Sweetie," he says, "if I wanted a cook, I would have found a cheaper way to get one."

We go down and have cereal.

A few days later Jesse breaks a finger at baseball camp and my first reaction is to jump in my car and deal with the emergency myself. But Charlie says no, he'll come too, even though it isn't his crisis. He drives so I can focus on my boy. Charlie jokes with Jesse and gets him Doritos from the vending machine while we wait for the doctor. I could have done this all on my own, but it's easier with a partner. That night I realize that I can relax into this married life, and that it feels like falling into a deep down pillow.

I had no idea I was so tired.

CHAPTER TEN

Reality Hits

THE TRUTH WAS, I MIGHT have gotten married, but after the first few days, I went back to my own house.

My friend Susan, curious about the honeymoon, called Charlie's house one morning, assuming, naturally, that I lived there. When she got him and the news that I was still at my old place, she quickly dialed that number.

"What are you doing?" she yells. "You're supposed to be living with your husband, you remember that guy? The one with the big house in D.C.? What is the matter with you?"

I had to laugh, because a friend of ours did the same thing: married, then returned to her own condo after the honeymoon and resisted moving in with her husband for several months, until we shamed her into it.

"I'm packing," I say defensively. "The move is next week,

and the house closing the next day. I just couldn't face all this before the wedding."

"You swear?"

"Yes, really. You can come over and help, if you don't believe me."

She relents. "Okay. Just remember, I'm going to test you. I'm going to call Charlie's next week, and I expect you to answer the phone."

What I didn't tell Susan was that I popped the worst case of hives I had ever had the week I packed up my house. At the time I figured I was allergic to something in the dust and dirt of the move, but deep down I knew my body was probably trying to send me a message. I was allergic to moving itself, not just the disturbed grit. It was painful to dismantle the house I had worked hard to decorate and furnish, and I didn't look forward to trying to make a home for myself in Charlie's place, still a chaotic mess. I could also sense that the move was going to be harder on my boys than the wedding had been, because this was the real change, the seismic shift they knew was coming.

It was a tense week all around, and the worst moment came when I was hurrying the kids out the door to catch a plane to California to join their dad, gathered with the rest of his family by the bed of his brother, who was critically ill with cancer. As we tossed their duffels in the back of the van, I realized this was their only chance to say good-bye to the house. It would be sold by the time they returned.

"This is it, guys! Say good-bye," I yell.

Halfway in the car, they freeze, then look back at the house in dismay. There isn't time for Jesse to go jump on the rope swing in the backyard, or for David to climb up into the tree house their dad built for them.

David waves awkwardly, then gets in the car. Jesse mouths a farewell, then climbs in the back. "I really hate this, Mom," he says.

"I know, honey. I know this is hard."

I didn't know quite what to tell him. Giving up this house, I knew, meant that the tight, intimate, and loving knot that had been my life with my children would have to loosen. The summer was filled with grown-up moments for them, from the painful good-byes at the end of the school year, to the wedding, to this move, to the loss of their uncle in California. They were holding up remarkably well, but I worried, knowing that kids have their limits. Just boarding the flight to California by themselves on this sad mission, they seemed weighed down with loss. At the airport, I told them to stick close together and gave them extra money, which they stuffed into the pockets of their cargo pants. They disappeared down the skyway, elbowing each other with pent-up tension. I prayed they wouldn't get lost in the Oakland airport before their dad found them.

So, I went home, packed my boxes, daubed calamine on my hives, and wept into the crumpled newspaper. I felt like my life had shifted into high gear, with things changing in every direction, and that I could barely maintain control of my existence. I wasn't sure who we were going to be in our new life. My boys weren't quite old enough to give up their childish toys—not because they still played with them but because these were the icons of their childhood, and the new house wouldn't feel like home if their old stuff wasn't stacked in their bookshelves. So I packed all the toys, even the ones I knew we could pass on to younger cousins. I was determined to set up their attic space at Charlie's to look as similar to their old rooms as possible, right down to the color of the carpet. The house still felt like alien territory to me, and I was the grown-up. How would I ever make all of us feel at home?

As moving day approached, Adam and Matt left for a vacation with their mother. We didn't plan it that way, but I was glad none of the boys were there to witness the actual disruption. This, of course, violated one of the cardinal rules of merging families: Get everyone involved! But I could already see the practicality of doing things ourselves and presenting the kids with a fait accompli. Sometimes that was just easier.

After the movers unloaded everything into Charlie's house, there was barely space for us to walk between the stacks of boxes and the furniture. Half the main floor was still in mid-renovation, including the kitchen, which was hopelessly late. Adam's basement room would be finished by the time school started in September, but until then he had to sleep on the living room sofa, because David and Jesse had moved into his old room in the attic. Our kitchen consisted of a microwave on top of the dryer in the laundry room. We ate out of plastic bowls and washed dishes in the bathroom sink.

When school started, the real pandemonium hit. The boys and I were suddenly back on the academic roller coaster, off to school every morning and fretting about papers and assignments. One morning the building contractor watched us trying to get sandwiches made and all four boys fed and hustled out the door, colliding over the microwave and fussing with the camping cookware, and finally took pity on us. He disappeared, then returned a few hours later with a section of kitchen counter consisting of a sink and a range. With these he was able to set up a temporary kitchen for me in the corner of the empty shell, to get us through the next few months. It would be Thanksgiving before the kitchen was complete.

That fall the boys circled around the house trying to figure out where they could settle their things and their spirits. The younger boys complained that Adam had his own living room, because his room opened onto the newly refurbished recreation room in the basement, complete with television and sofa. We tried to explain that the rec room was for everyone, but it didn't feel that way to them. Hostilities would break out over the question of the remote and everything remotely like it, such as preferred seats in the car, places at the table, the leftover brownies, even chores and privileges.

We struggled in part with just being such a large group. We couldn't indulge four boys the way we had each indulged—and thereby managed—two, so consequently wrangled over everything from choosing a movie to sitting down at the table. Even if a family is trying desperately to make everyone feel equal and equally entitled to the family goods, kids are different and have different needs. It may be better to give a particular child his own room or to give someone else the front seat—especially if it means they are less likely to throw up. Chores need to be calibrated according to ability, age, and availability—whether the kid is home from baseball practice early enough to help with dinner.

It didn't help that they were all nearly the same age: thirteen, fourteen, fifteen, and seventeen. This made it harder to allocate privileges according to age and ability, because the boys were pretty similar, except for Adam, who already had several advantages. All were tall and wanted the seat with the most legroom in the car. I suddenly felt like midget woman. I was also beginning to sense that living with five men was something new. Two boys had felt manageable. Now the evidence of testosterone was everywhere, from the dinner table conversations that degenerated into sparring over algebra problems to the competitive jostling for the best rake, the largest milk shake, the spot in the front of the line. And that's not even mentioning the jokes.

It's not that things were bad, not really. The boys were trying their best to be openhearted about the merging of families, but there were rough spots, difficult moments for all of them. We had trouble with the idea that we were a stepfamily. No one referred to anyone else as step-anything, except Jesse, who seemed to feel we should just go ahead and make this leap and get it over with. Charlie and I struggled to manage a household of six people—the grocery shopping, the food issues, the Matterhorn of laundry that accumulated in the hall every week. There were workmen hammering at seven each morning and the doorbell and phone seemed to ring incessantly. We gave the kids keys, and they promptly lost them. They grumbled when they didn't like what was served for dinner or we ran out of milk or cereal, which we did daily. None of us could quite believe how much milk and cereal we really needed.

We proceeded as gently as possibly, serving family dinners together but insisting on little other togetherness. The boys huddled mostly in their own bedrooms, occasionally bumping into each other in front of the television or over the ice cream container. There were very clear family differences, and the two sets of brothers were on different schedules, which made any family activity—like shared chores or outings—a particular challenge. We asked for politeness and forbearance, but for the time being didn't expect much else.

My boys liked their attic space, which felt private and familiar to them because it was furnished with all that was theirs, but they were hesitant about using other rooms in the house. "We could put in one of those little refrigerators up here," suggested Jesse, "and then we wouldn't even have to go downstairs for food." Adam, I knew, would have loved a similar system in the basement, and Matt would have been happy living at school, in the basketball gym.

As the workmen painted and sawed, Charlie struggled to work through the noise and mayhem. He had left his job after a year and was trying to establish himself as a communications consultant for several different companies, but often had to break away to deal with the next construction crisis: the flood in the basement, the AWOL cabinet-maker, the wrong paint or the wrong tile or the wrong knobs.

As I got caught up in my academic pressures once again, I quickly began to feel overwhelmed. As much as I didn't want to admit it, being married again and living with this large group in this chaotic house was not turning out as happily as I had imagined. I loved Charlie, but I was having a hell of a time getting my feet under me. Whenever I had lunch with a close friend, she would buy me a glass of wine and then ask: "So, how is it, really?" And that would set me off. My friend Kate, who thinks about remarriage sometimes, listened to me nattering away over my wine one day and finally raised her hand, as if to stop the flood. "You need to talk with my friend Barbara," she said. "Barbara sounds just like this."

Barbara, it turned out, also remarried recently, merging her set of residential kids with her husband's two, who visit every other weekend and for the summer, riding the train down from Baltimore. On top of that, they had just had a new baby. "You guys need to talk," Kate says. "This will all feel very familiar to her."

As soon as I get home, I call Barbara, and we connect quickly over the phone, brushing aside the formalities and bonding like long-lost twins. A few days later we meet for lunch. We've both cleared our schedules so we have the afternoon free, sensing that this conversation could go on for hours.

When I finally confide that I love being married again but I'm not sure I can take all that this seems to involve, Barbara nods.

"Do you remember marriage being this much, well, work?" I ask her.

"Remarriage is exhausting," says Barbara. "No two ways about it. I've never been so tired. At first I thought it was having a new baby, but that isn't it. It's the constantly shifting household, my kids leaving for their dad's, Robert's kids arriving for the weekend. But I'll be honest. The hardest part is all the negotiating that seems to be necessary.

"The other day I wanted to get broadband service to the

house so that I could work more from home and be with the baby," she continues. "When I was single, I would have just done it. Now I have to lay out all the details so that my husband can check to make sure I'm making the right decision. I appreciate the help, but frankly, I also feel like I'm getting picked to death. He and I wrangle over control all the time. I'm used to my independence, and he's a man with set routines. It's a challenge to try and work with him on some of these."

I nod sympathetically because this story feels so familiar. Charlie and I recently spent a good hour one Saturday morning arguing over how to do laundry. I'm shocked to discover a man who actually does laundry more carefully than any woman I've ever met, but his system of reading tags and following every line of instruction hamstrings my system of lights to the left, darks to the right. I don't have time for all this precision. It's just laundry, after all.

"I thought it would be good to marry a man who does laundry," I tell her. "But now I have to change how I do laundry. I'm forty-seven! I'm not interested in changing how I do laundry."

Barbara laughs. "That's it, exactly. I had all my systems in place, and I've had to rearrange nearly everything."

I thought I was nuts to be irritated by these little things, but over the course of the summer we got married, I had to renegotiate everything from how to load the dishwasher to what kind of mouthwash to use to where to store the toilet paper. Outside the house I had to switch banks; find a new drive-through ATM, which wasn't nearly as convenient as the old one; find a new cleaners, drugstore, grocery, and liquor store; learn new supermarket layouts; figure out a new pattern to the day so that I could run errands efficiently; figure out the mysterious culture of my sons' new school; find new routes through the city so I could get everywhere I needed to go; learn about my stepsons' lives; and make room in my busy schedule for a husband who occasionally wanted love and attention. The only thing that held constant was my job. At least I had that.

Then one day I find Charlie shelving the books in our newly renovated den. He is doing it in a complicated, two-tiered system: by genre and country, and within that, alphabetically by author. I would have done it by size, with perhaps some rough subject groupings. But mostly I would have just emptied the boxes, tidied up the rows of books, and shut off the light.

When I protest, Charlie says, "Please. This will work great. We'll actually be able to find what we want. Let me do this. I'm not asking you to do it. Let me, though."

I realize it is time to back off. "Okay," I say. "You get the library, but I get to organize the kitchen the way I want."

"Deal."

A few days later my older sister sends me an interesting book for our collection. It's about two book lovers who married later in life and found a whole world of psychology and conflict and negotiating in how they managed their piles of books. "I thought this might resonate for you," Annie writes in the card. "Happy organizing!"

If I had nurtured dreams of bringing order to Charlie's life, I quickly abandoned them. Every effort to keep the house from subsiding into chaos seems to be met by a tide of problems or indifference. While Charlie may have enjoyed sorting the books in the library, much of the rest of the house was still a haphazard jumble of boxes stuffed in closets and items pushed under beds. It was difficult to find things, and I began to wonder if some items from my old house had just disappeared, possibly into the trash. I bought the three younger boys individual baskets for their toiletries (color-coded, I'll admit it), because they are sharing a bathroom and don't like the idea of cross-family toothpaste sharing. Fine, I tell them. I get them all their own stuff— shaving cream, razor, face soap, and acne cream—and tell them to keep it in their baskets. But over the course of the week it all migrates out onto the counter, and then the housekeeper just throws things into the baskets willy-nilly. Maybe we need to label everything, as if we are all living in some big summer camp.

Every family has its own preferred or tolerated level of mess, and those established limits rarely mesh perfectly in a newly blended family. I find it hard enough living with my own teenagers; it sometimes seems doubly trying to live with the dirt and irresponsibility of someone else's teenagers. All parents know that a teen's room serves as a petri dish of passive-aggressive behavior, and those resentments are often exacerbated by the presence of a stepparent.

"We're just not used to living like this," Adam complains one afternoon when I'm asking if the boys can wipe the kitchen counters after they've had a snack. The truth is, my boys aren't used to living like this either. I'm not sure why I've become a clean-counter Nazi since moving in with Charlie, but it seems to matter more. Maybe because the amount of kitchen traffic just means there is more stuff on the counters. Maybe I have a hidden threshold for kitchen-counter cleanliness, which has been crossed.

Most people don't like to admit to either a high level of tolerance for mess or a compulsive attention to dust and dirt. It is not uncommon, says my therapist friend Dorree Lynn, for a parent who has slipped into messy habits as a consequence of divorce to remarry someone who promises to get the house (and kids) in order. "That's a very common scenario, but the problem is that the kids and the parent are now used to the chaos, and they often resist when a stepparent suggests they do things differently."

More than just the explicit rules have changed for the boys; so have many of the unstated ones. As the only woman in a family with five men, I sometimes feel like I'm living in a fraternity house, with bathroom doors left ajar or half open when I'd really prefer they be shut. I stomp through the hall, hoping they will hear me coming. We've also put a lock on our bedroom door, after David stumbled in there one night sleepwalking.

Privacy is a huge issue for blended families, especially for teens, conflicted with their own burgeoning sexuality. Adolescents themselves barely know who they are or what they are doing, and are trying desperately to establish some autonomy for themselves, as well as an identity different from that of their family or parents, and possibly from their siblings. When parents go and remarry, their identity often shifts, making it even more difficult for the teen to figure out what he is trying to distinguish himself from.

As my younger son said to me once, "I want a normal family. I want a mom who doesn't date." It reminded me of a moment in a *Seinfeld* episode when George, who dates sporadically with little success, has lunch with his mother after she has recently separated from his father. She says she is going in for a face-lift because she is planning to start dating, which horrifies George. "You can't date," he yells at her. "You can't be out there, because I'm out there!" When parents do something as unparent-like as fall in love and marry, with all the thinly veiled sexual innuendo of weddings nights and white gowns, teenagers confused about their own dawning sexuality usually cringe in response.

"Most teens don't like the idea of this strange man or woman sleeping in their parent's bed," says Dorree Lynn. "They don't like to think of their parents as sexual at all. Their reaction is *yuck*." My reaction to thinking about them thinking about me as sexual is *yuck* as well.

What seems to happen naturally is that the house quickly separates into public spaces—the living room, library, kitchen, rec room—and the private spaces of bedrooms and studies. We seem to have an unspoken deal that no one goes rummaging around in someone else's bedroom or study without asking, or unless you are that person's biological parent and need to find something. While the kids resent this a bit in the beginning, sometimes showing up in our bedroom to watch TV or to get special pampering when they are sick, they mostly adapt.

At the center of this craziness is Charlie, putting in another load of laundry, trying to keep the family afloat, and asking about dinner. He is beginning to get work he likes, and says he enjoys working from the house. It turns out to be a great boon to our life to have one parent at home during the day, particularly with the house still in so much disorder. When David gets sick at school one day, Charlie runs over and picks him up, because I'm in the middle of a lecture and Ron is stuck in a meeting. Charlie is there for the stream of visits from electricians, plumbers, carpet guys, and painters. Charlie is there when I realize I forgot to put the meat out to defrost. Sometimes I cozy up to him and say, "Boy, I didn't know what a great house-husband you were going to turn out to be."

But while I'm deeply glad to be married to Charlie, I am often astonished by the thousands of adjustments needed to mesh my decision-making style and priorities and schedule with his. While it is nice to have a husband at home, it also means I never get any time alone in the house. As someone who loved her solitary Sundays puttering around, I find this loss registers big. Sometimes I feel like we're two people lost in a labyrinth of daily demands, with different internal maps and instincts. We lurch from trying to be available for our kids to resenting it when the other is being overly available for his or her kids and unavailable for us. We work overtime trying to build a family out of these disparate parts, but it often feels as if I have Legos and he is working with wooden blocks. The two systems are fine on their own, but it is almost impossible to build a family that blends both.

When a couple marries for the first time, here is what they get: plenty of time to develop a strong couple bond before children are added in; clear boundaries around the family unit—whoever lives in the house is in the family; symmetrical ties between parents and children; common activities and history, based largely on living together all the time; and clear roles and relationships that evolve gradually as children mature, rather than shifting overnight. In nuclear families, marital happiness starts out high and often tails off a bit later, particularly as the children grow up.

When a couple marries and forms a stepfamily, here is what they get: no time to develop a strong couple bond beyond the dating period; fuzzy boundaries around the family unit—all kinds of people have a say in how the family operates, including ex-spouses, new spouses of ex-spouses, older stepchildren who may not live at home, and others; ties between parents and children that are so asymmetrical the household sometimes splits into warring camps; little shared history and spotty common experience, even if they are living together some of the time; and roles and relationships with no clear models that take years to figure out and which can shift on a regular basis. Sociologists have found that people who remarry with children tend to have a different happiness trajectory from those in first-time marriages: marital happiness tends to start out low, despite how much they love each other. Only after a few years does marital happiness rise, after everyone adjusts and the kids relax. I guess one just has to have faith.

I wonder again about my fantasies going into this marriage, though I'm not sure what I thought would be different. Maybe that I would feel at home in this house, maybe that there would be more fun times, certainly that the boys would be easier to talk with and mobilize for assistance, certainly that it wouldn't be quite this much work. Maybe I don't know what my role is, particularly my role as a stepmom. Am I a parent or a mentor? An ally or an obstacle? The house mother or Mother Superior? Maybe I'm just Dad's companion or maybe, I think blackly, I'm the maid.

It doesn't help that I thought I would do better than this: be more flexible, resilient, patient, forgiving, upbeat. Jesse hates seeing me down, and occasionally says "I wish we were back in our old house, when you were happy." I sigh more than my kids can stand to hear. When I do it too much, Jesse darts me a warning look.

"I am happy," I tell him. "It just doesn't look like it."

I'm still technically a bride the day I walk into my doctor's office for a regular checkup and, when he asks how life is going, burst into tears.

"It's good." I hiccup. "Actually, good." I cry harder.

"Really?" he asks, looking at me over his glasses.

I hadn't planned to get into it with anyone, since I've been struggling for weeks to ignore it myself. It didn't seem, well, appropriate to be so down. Everyone is still congratulating me, my friends still misty-eyed over my good fortune. I smile when people ask how we are doing, say, "Oh yes, it's wonderful, we're great"—then go home and cry.

Now I'm crying in my internist's office.

He leans forward, concerned and curious. He's known me for years. I've never seemed rattled by much. "There's just been a lot of change in my life," I say by way of explanation, hiccuping and trying to stop.

"Tell me," he says.

"Well, I got remarried this summer, sold my house, moved into my husband's house. We've merged two sets of teenage boys, the house is under renovation, and we still don't have a kitchen. My boys changed schools and I'm terrified they're going to flunk out, and then my husband decided to work at home. Oh, and my dad seems to have an aggressive form of prostate cancer. On top of all this, I'm supposed to be writing a book about my remarriage, and I can't even imagine where to start."

He calmly writes this all down, then asks, "Are you crying a lot?"

Yeah, you could say that. "I'm really irritable, too. And I hate that. I seem to have two choices: be irritable or cry. Usually I cry."

"If you add up these stresses, you've pretty much topped the list here," he says.

"But most of these are good stresses," I say. "Except, of course, the cancer."

"Even good stresses are stress," he says. "What you are trying to do is hard. There's just no getting around that."

I go home that day with a prescription for antidepressants. It takes me a few days to even tell my sweet husband, who is trying harder than anyone to make our life work. He looks at me, sad beyond words. "You need antidepressants? Because you married me?"

Sometimes I daydream about my old life, the quiet of my house, the solitude I had when my boys were with their dad, the ease of routines and expectations settled years ago. And when I catch myself doing that, I force myself to remember the lonely moments, the days I had to go to the grocery just to find a human to talk to, the bad times when the washer overflowed or the car wouldn't start and there wasn't another adult around to help. It's true—I should be happy, this is progress. I try to count my blessings, but the big house and the passel of kids, and the hubbub in the kitchen and the dog that needs to be walked and the food that needs to be cooked—all these blessings sometimes feel like stones around my neck.

I've had periods of moderate depression in my life before, and I know that this time it is grief, however inappropriate that may seem. I waited to get remarried until I fell in love, not when I desperately needed someone to rescue me. I had a good life, a nice life I built all by myself. That probably means I married for the right reasons, but the downside is that I left a life I loved and now I'm mourning my losses. I've traded quiet, solitude, and control for a husband, more kids, more chaos, and more mess. I've chosen life, I've chosen risk, I've chosen challenge and adventure. And now that I'm here in the middle of it, I'm not sure I have the heart for it.

CHAPTER ELEVEN

Kids in the Blender

ONE DAY DAVID COMES HOME from school and says he has to film a video for his visual media class and needs a good subject. Before I think about what I'm saying, I suggest he set up the camera in our kitchen and interview his brother and stepbrothers about what it is like to live in a stepfamily. Two of the other boys are in the room when I make this suggestion, and they all stop and give me that classic teenage "she's off her rocker" sort of look, then slide their eyes around the room to see how the others are reacting.

"Really," I say, flush with the idea. "This could be a groundbreaking personal video. I don't think anyone's done this yet. You could send it to film festivals and win prizes. It might get you into college!"

They are all still staring at me. This happens a lot in our

house. I get excited about something and everyone else thinks I'm nuts. Finally David shakes his head, as if fighting off a headache. "Mom, that's a bad idea," he says. "Let's not go there."

Let's not go there. Let's not disturb the peace, ruffle the waters. Let's not look too deep.

Over one million American children watch a parent get remarried every year, and by the time they are eighteen, one out of every three kids will be part of a stepfamily. That's a staggering number, considering how marginalized stepfamilies often feel in American society. But despite these numbers, nothing feels normal about becoming a stepfamily. Most kids, the therapists will tell you, find living in a stepfamily challenging as well as vaguely embarrassing. "It's just weird," says Jesse in the beginning. It's the thing that sets him apart from the normal kids—those from intact families. He's like most children whose families have broken from the norm and wandered off into that land of other—he justs want to find some comfort and get on with his real job of being a teenager.

When Charlie and I married, our "blended" household mixed together about as well as oil and water, splitting into two factions more often than not—related but not really operating as one family. More like housemates. I sometimes wondered if what we had was more commune than anything else. Charlie and I split the household chores, like cooking, bills, groceries, and laundry, but we individually took care of most of the needs of our own children—chauffeuring, doctors' appointments, Latin drills, and studying for the PSAT. I had little extra time or energy after tending to my own kids and my job, and I was wary of being swept into the vortex of tending to Charlie and his kids as if they were my primary responsibility. Still, we each monitored the other's kids. We usually knew where they were and what was happening in their lives, who their friends were, and how they were doing in school. We didn't go to each other's parent-teacher conferences, but we shared what we learned at them and talked endlessly about how our boys were doing. We had a short list of household rules and expectations, but when a kid stepped over the line, the infraction got dealt with by that child's parent.

My instinct in the beginning was not to push the boys into anything that smacked of a traditional nuclear family. They might not have wanted to admit being a stepfamily, but it was worse if people mistook us for blood relatives. The boys in particular didn't quite know how to feel about their new stepbrothers. Every interaction seemed loaded, and I constantly monitored the dynamic in the kitchen and rec room to make sure everyone was, well, okay, if not exactly happy. Not getting elbowed out of a game, not being unfairly dissed or kicked off the sofa or made to feel too lonely. I knew that if our children were not happy in their new life, that Charlie and I could never be happy. It wasn't that we didn't expect a period of adjustment—we weren't *that* naive. It was that we knew we had to make it work for them, make it worthwhile.

Many children in stepfamilies come through the transition and adjust to life quite well, but others struggle for years to regain what they lost when their parent remarried. At the point that Charlie and I moved in together, I was unsure how the boys would adjust. There was so much bad news about kids in stepfamilies, it was a challenge just to see past the statistics and think about the reality of our situation. Kids in stepfamilies tend to exhibit more behavior problems, leave home earlier, engage in risky sexual behavior, do more drugs, do worse in school, etc. When I read those statistics I immediately recognized this list: It was the same set of purported tendencies exhibited by children of divorce! So maybe it was a function of divorce, rather than remarriage. Maybe I didn't have to feel so guilty about asking my children to live in a stepfamily. Maybe being in a stepfamily would help.

Psychologist E. Mavis Hetherington has found that children in well-functioning stepfamilies do better statistically than kids in single-parent homes because there is another adult to provide financial and emotional stability. In her study of over 450 families, she also found that 80 percent of children in remarriages do as well on all measures of childhood happiness—academic, behavioral, social—as 90 percent of children in nuclear families, after an initial period of adjustment.

But not all kids end up in well-functioning stepfamilies. Many of the children who have trouble in a stepfamily are kids who did not adjust well to divorce, often because their parents had adjusted poorly. She has seen cases of parents who modeled risky sexual behavior after their divorce only to discover their young teenagers engaged in similarly risky sex. Or parents who remarry and divorce repeatedly, weakening their children's ability to attach to adults, either their parents or their changing stepparents. Or parents who fail to improve their lives after divorce and, instead, sink into poverty or addiction. Again, stepfamily living exists in the shadow of divorce.

In first marriages, sociologists have found, happiness flows from the parents to the kids. If the parents are happy, the children tend to be happy. But in remarriage, it's the other way around: Happiness flows from the kids to the parents. If the kids are happy in their new family, couples tend to be happier. Unhappy children, in fact, are the biggest risk factor in whether a stepfamily makes it or not.

How could I make sure our kids would come through this well adjusted so that Charlie and I have a shot at a twentieth wedding anniversary? I had already read much of the advice in the field, but now I needed to look deeper. Not just to inform my writing, but to answer the more fundamental questions. I'm looking now for the real evidence, rather than just advice. I want to know what the science of stepfamily dynamics can tell me. My instinct is to read everything I can find, mull over the statistical evidence, and then try to craft a world for my kids that will give them the best chance. I go to the university library and take out about twenty books, lugging them home and piling them in my office. If there are answers in the remarriage literature, I'm damn well going to find them.

One of the first things I discover is the reassuring news that Charlie and I have created one of the most complicated forms of stepfamily, what stepfamily expert Taube Kaufman calls the complex-combined family. It reminds me of those multiclause sentences that my college writing coach said were just too complicated to be clear.

Too complicated to be clear is indeed how the world reads us. When she calls, my best friend always asks, "Who do you have tonight?" The grandparents tend to ask the same thing. The house is a never-ending rotation of small meals, huge meals, packing up boat bags with those teenage accoutrements—CD player, headphones, textbooks, gym shoes—then unpacking dirty laundry, trying to locate belts and ties and hairbrushes. Personal items become important in a family with this much flux—probably because it is harder to establish territory within the shared house, particularly as they come and go.

"Not everyone wants to be there," says Kaufman, describing complex stepfamilies like ours in her book *The Combined Family*. "And not everyone who is there wants the same thing." That's putting it mildly. I have a hell of a time just finding enough different dinner menus to satisfy the majority—and often find myself cooking various options until the table looks like one of those Pennsylvania Dutch restaurants with mashed potatoes and noodles and ham and turkey and green beans and five other vegetables.

There really aren't that many complex-combined families, so if we feel like pioneers lost in uncharted terrain, there's a reason for that. The statistics on stepfamilies in the United States are notoriously fuzzy, but roughly 9.8 percent of American kids under eighteen live in a complex-combined stepfamily, what we would call a blended family, although in most cases only one set of kids considers the family their primary home. The other set usually only visits. Since our boys are here 50 percent of their time, neither residential all the time nor just visiting, our stepfamily configuration is one that rarely shows up in the sociological literature. I read the studies and try to extrapolate.

Kaufman also points out something interesting, something I hadn't considered when I remarried: that the individuals in stepfamilies often find themselves in very different life stages, which creates another venue for conflict. One teen may be ready for real autonomy—control of his own schedule and money— while another (perhaps almost the same age) still forgets his backpack every other day. On top of that, each original family unit is in a different stage of family development. My children had nearly ten years of living as a three-person family unit with me half the week and then with their dad the other half. It may have seemed a little odd to the outside world, but they were used to it. Charlie and his kids, however, were much more recently out of their original family, and were still trying to find their balance when we entered the picture. On top of that is the overall life cycle of the stepfamily (that complex-combined thing), which differs in life stage as well from my relationship with Charlie—the thing that started it all.

I also discover that young adolescents are the hardest group to merge.

"If you're thinking of remarrying someone with kids in early adolescence, forget it," Hetherington jokes, discussing her research at a stepfamily conference. I haven't attended the conference, but I order the tapes of the sessions and sit in my office listening to them late at night. "Older adolescents, who are already thinking about leaving home, are easier, as are younger children, who are more likely to make the adjustment. It's those young teens that are hard because they are dealing with that burgeoning sexuality and all those intimacy questions, which get very confusing for them when their parents remarry."

Great, I think, snapping off the tape player. Just great.

The big challenge for most remarriages today, Hetherington says, is that couples and their children are still dealing with significant emotional, financial, and social losses from their divorces at the point that they pledge themselves to each other. The remarriage may boost the adults out of their grief, but for kids the remarriage often feels like a new set of losses. Some kids lose the private bond they've shared with their biological parent, now that the adults are wandering around in romantic bliss. Many kids report they feel like a fifth wheel after their parents remarry, rather than the treasured companion or confidant of before. They may have lost space in the house, a favored position in the household, or their spot in the pecking order. The oldest may become a middle child. The indulged baby may become an older sibling. The center of gravity among the kids can shift down several years, and a kid who used to feel like top dog may suddenly find himself the outlier, the one who doesn't fit in with the others. Many kids, like mine, lose a home and neighborhood and school. If the remarriage triggers increased tension with an ex-spouse, which is often the case, kids may feel sorry for their other parent and also resentful that the truce has been jeopardized. Loyalty issues loom large for these kids.

Kids also say they worry that their relationship with their parent will have to change under pressure from the new member of the household, the stepparent, who may lay down new rules and have different expectations. From the children's point of view, someone unwanted has infiltrated the inner fortress of the family, banishing their father (or their dream of him) and stealing their mother's heart. It's a conflict as old as Hamlet, who, let us not forget, came home from college and discovered he was a stepchild.

"Do you realize that Hamlet is a stepchild?" I say to David one day as we are talking about Shakespeare. He read the play last year in school, and we talked about it quite a bit at the time, but we've never discussed it in these terms. But suddenly, when I make this connection, the play jolts into bold relief.

"Whoa," says David. "I guess that's right." I can see him considering this. We talk about Hamlet's unsettled feelings about being pushed aside, about his anger at his mother, about his rage that his father has been murdered and replaced. He comes home from college and discovers that he, the former "sweet prince," is now persona non grata in the kingdom, in his own castle. So he sets out on a destructive path. Reflecting his new contempt for marriage, he tells Ophelia to get herself to the nunnery, triggering her descent into depression and suicide. He sees enemies everywhere, and in his own depressive rage pulls everyone into his death. The play is powerful and unnerving and captures the intense undercurrent that rumbles beneath every stepfamily.

David doesn't quite know what to make of all this. "Don't worry about it, sweetheart," I tell him. "Forget I mentioned it. It's just a story, a myth."

"It's one of the most important plays ever written."

"Yeah, well, it is unsettling, but so is all of Shakespeare. It doesn't have to be our script."

Hamlet's abandonment by his remaining biological parent—his mother—is a fear lurking in the heart of every kid going through a remarriage, and yet psychologists say it is often completely undetected by adults, who usually see the remarriage as a chance to add an adult to the child's life rather than lose one. But kids often read the process quite differently. Unless kids can build a bond to their new stepparent and retain a strong relationship with their biological parent, they will feel displaced by the remarriage, counselors say. And when that happens, they start to act out.

When stepfamilies come in to talk with the therapists, the hottest topic is usually discipline: the discipline the kids do not seem to have, and the discipline the parents struggle to hand out in measured, even ways. Are kids of divorce different from kids living in intact families, and does that affect stepfamily life? While many therapists would call this a gross generalization, they say that kids of divorce often seem to have been raised by guilt-ridden parents, and consequently are more likely to be overindulged and less strictly disciplined. Single parents rarely have the same clear authority as a team of parents, and often say they have such limited time with their kids that they don't push discipline because they don't want to spend their precious hours fighting. Kids of divorce are often adept at managing their parents and may resent someone, like a new stepparent, getting in the middle and messing with the balance of power. Some kids of divorce, often girls, have served as trusted confidantes for their single parents and may suspect that they will lose this role when their parent remarries. Most kids of divorce, say the experts, are usually overempowered and can be more difficult to manage.

"We've moved from a very authoritarian style of parenting to a permissive style," says family therapist Ron Huxley, of Clovis, California. "Kids who have gone through divorce are seen by adults as hurt, and the parents often end up with a style that gives these kids a sense of entitlement. The parents are constantly trying to make up for something that can't be made up, and in the process, they give in to their children too much." Huxley also says that many parents who remarry either consciously or subconsciously seek a partner who will help them gain control of their children, but such a wish often sets up the stepparent for major trouble.

"The most common problem that brings stepfamilies into my office is a crisis where the stepkids won't listen and the parents disagree about how to manage them," says Huxley. "When you put overentitled kids together with remarried parents who can't agree on how to run the family, you've got real trouble."

Do Charlie and I have overempowered kids? When they tromp into the kitchen at dinnertime complaining that they don't eat chicken or carrots or potatoes or whatever it is we are having, I sometimes wonder. Usually I tell them to sit down, eat what they can from what is served, and fix themselves a sandwich if they don't like it. Certainly our kids have been indulged through the years, though I'm not sure they are worse than some of the children I know from intact families. Mostly, Charlie and I seem to have kids who are empowered differently. Charlie has always allowed his kids to operate more independently, and they are consequently more independent. Mine have been held to a shorter leash, but also often need help keeping track of all they have to do.

Every time I say to my kids something like "Let's look at your homework schedule and figure out what we have to do," Charlie grimaces.

"It's going to be awfully quiet around here when you and David go off to college together," he says pointedly. "I think you could drop the royal *we* when discussing their homework."

"I'm a mother," I tell him. "I can't rest until all their homework is done."

"Be a mother, and tell them they shouldn't rest until all their homework is done."

He has a point, I think to myself, and go up into the attic to lay out the new rules to my kids. "Okay, I'm not going to ask about your homework, but you guys have to do it and finish by ten-thirty, with lights out by eleven. If I find out from your teachers that work is missing, we'll take the network cards out of your computers." That should put the fear of God into them.

But at eleven-thirty, when I'm trying to go to bed, I find that everyone is still up, banging around the house getting late-night snacks, printing out documents in Charlie's office, looking for clean clothes, taking showers, and generally behaving like college students.

"Okay, honey," I tell Charlie as we try to fall asleep amid the noise. "They're independent now. Happy?"

As much as I sometimes bewailed my status as the mother of boys, I had to agree that it was better than trying to blend four girls. "Oh, yeah, four girls would be a challenge," say my friends with daughters, rolling their eyes. Our boys generally aren't offended by much and are pretty comfortable ribbing each other about household infractions. Girls, on the other hand, read more into small gestures and interpersonal subtleties. Even a mature woman like me often reads too much into small gestures and interpersonal subtleties, and I can only imagine what I was like as an adolescent. ("Let's not go there," my mother says, shaking her head.) Margorie Engle, president of the Stepfamily Association of America, ended up with a household of teenage girls when she remarried fifteen years ago. "It was a challenge," Engle says. "You can't even imagine. Boys would have been much easier."

It turns out that this is not just an impression: Sociologists have discovered that girls often have a harder time in stepfamilies. Because most stepfamilies consist of mothers with their biological children and a stepfather, most girls in stepfamilies are living with stepdads, who can sometimes feel like a sexual threat to young girls, particularly if their mother and stepdad have an unhappy relationship. They often struggle to accept stepparents, research shows, in part because they have been empowered through the divorce of their parents to assume a more authoritative role in the household. Even if they have not become "little mothers," girls left in the custody of their mothers as a consequence of divorce often form strong ties with their mom, and find sharing their mother with a stepfather and possibly new stepsiblings quite disruptive to their happiness.

On the other hand, "boys have a lot to gain when a stepfather enters the family," says Hetherington. Teenage boys who have lived exclusively with their mothers since their parents' divorce often find the presence of a stepdad reassuring rather than sexually threatening, as girls sometimes do, because the older male provides a buffer to the oedipal love they may hold for their mother. Stepdads say that sports can provide an easy venue for building ties with stepsons, and stepdads can provide much needed emotional stability for boys, who suffer more than girls do when their biological fathers disappear from their lives, as often happens in divorce. Even though my kids have a strong relationship with their dad, they also seem to enjoy getting to know Charlie, as long as he doesn't try to discipline them too much. He is different from their dad, provides another model of how to be a grown-up guy. And he provides a balance to my overmothering. As long as we have plenty of electronics in the house, the boys seem pretty contented.

One of the more interesting controversies in stepfamily dynamics is the idea of togetherness. Many people asked Charlie and me if we were going to take the boys with us on our honeymoon, an idea that left me speechless even after I'd heard it several times. Who would want kids—*any* kids, as much as you love them—on your honeymoon? Yet *The Wall Street Journal* recently reported that "familymoons" are the newest trend in stepfamily togetherness. Fortunately, I didn't see that article before Charlie and I planned our private, romantic honeymoon alone, because I would have hated feeling guilty for escaping together. We had planned several family trips later in the summer, and I'm glad it never occurred to us to drag the boys with us on our post-wedding vacation.

Besides, togetherness isn't always a great thing. Australian psychologist Margaret Newman says that each family has a particular togetherness force, and that this force can sometimes be too much for a new stepfamily.

Newman says that remarried couples often push children into unnatural togetherness in an effort to fulfill their own private dream of an instantly happy family. "Parents try artificially to create togetherness and closeness," says Newman. "Rarely, however, do such strategies work. In fact, they are more likely to inhibit the coming-together process."

Newman says that togetherness, while generally a fine goal for a stepfamily, has to be given time to develop slowly for genuine good feelings to grow among everyone. Charlie and I decided early on that dinner would be our togetherness focus of the day, in part because our boys love good meals and enjoy the give-and-take of dinner table discussions. Not everyone is there every night, but we try to eat together and require the boys to settle down for at least a half hour, even though some of them ask to be excused after the first ten minutes. We try to keep the conversation topics general enough so everyone can join in, and the ribbing to a minimum.

We encourage the boys to attend one another's important events—plays, championship games, recitals—though that isn't always easy. We don't pressure them to do things together, but we do ask that they be polite, give each other a present or card for holidays, include one another as often as is comfortable when they are doing something special. We vacation together several times a year, and find those weeks away from home and school are often the times that bring us together for card games and sports.

Togetherness pressures that are uncomfortable for newly blended families, says Newman, are things like insisting that children play together and love each other, bunking stepsiblings together, dressing kids alike, or encouraging sameness in other ways—either in opinions or activities. Our boys sometimes rebelled against plans (many of them mine) that bunched them together as "the kids," particularly the eldest, who felt different from the younger boys and uncomfortable when that difference was not honored. In time, we learned to let their individual differences shine through and to try to accommodate each of them on his own terms, as most parents of larger families figure out. Newman says that all people in stepfamilies struggle with the need to be an autonomous individual and the family's gravitational pull to bring them together. Sometimes a kid's behavior can be explained in just that light: as an effort to establish that he is different, when all around him he feels the pressure to blend.

The experts have lots of advice for remarrying families, which I discover in my reading. Most of it is useful, I guess, if in fact it can be implemented. But that's the problem. To me, a lot of it seemed unworkable or just plain phony.

Here is what we should have done, according to the experts: moved to a new house, despite the cost or uprooting involved (neutral terrain is always best); created as many new traditions and family patterns as possible, despite the years of disparate history and habits; held family meetings from the get-go, so the boys could sort out their feelings for one another, even if this feels like something that would work only for the Brady Bunch; avoided triangulating with anyone, which means that if you have issues with someone, go directly to him rather than parent or brother, despite any offputting hostility; and given the boys lots more choices in how to live their lives. Maybe we should have set them up with their own TV and refrigerator and food allowances. Well, it would have cut down on the cooking.

Here is the advice that seemed to work: Post a short but firm list of house rules so everyone knows what is expected, then let kids be disciplined by their own parents. Stepparents should wait several years, until they have formed a strong bond with their stepchildren, to move into positions of authority, particularly if their stepchild has two active bioparents in their life. Kids need plenty of attention from their own parent in the remarriage, particularly in the beginning, when they are most concerned about being pushed out of their mom or dad's heart by the new members of the family.

As for living together in this rambling house, we've tried to base our rules on issues of respect and community: quiet by 11 P.M. so everyone can sleep; clean up the bathroom so it doesn't gross out the next guy; pitch in with kitchen and laundry and yard work so the parents don't get surly; rotate the privileges, from best seats in the car to holding the remote.

To stay bonded with my kids, I often hang out in their attic space, just reading or grading papers while they do their homework. We try to bond as a larger family over the TV, watching basketball and one particular adventure thriller that gives us a dinner table topic if the school news gets old. The boys haven't managed to mutate into perfect children yet, but we're working on them. Sometimes I ask someone to help me make dinner or a special dessert, and that's as much togetherness as they want. I try to let my stepkids know they matter to me by choosing Christmas presents they either need or will like or by suggesting activities they will enjoy or by making foods they appreciate. I try to reflect back to them what I've learned about them, so they will know I'm paying attention.

We've also learned the hard way that it's critical to avoid comparing kids or judging them based on the behavior of other kids, particularly that of stepsiblings, who will be trying to gauge their place in the family and wind up feeling extra sensitive to such comparisons. The experts say it is common for stepkids to ignore each other in the beginning and instead invest more in their relationships with their own blood siblings. In time, particularly if given a chance to work out their issues on their own without parental interference, stepsiblings often find an easy balance—not too involved but also not too competitive. Some kids will find merging households easier than others— some will act out, some will aim their hostility at the new stepparent, while others will ignore or tease their stepsiblings—but that doesn't mean they aren't all trying.

Going for professional help when things get out of hand is also a sign of a strong stepfamily, I remind myself. I keep the therapist's number handy.

And then there was Charleen. The little girl we might have had. We caught glimpses of her sometimes. Once, while we were skiing in Canada, I spotted an older couple, like us, with a tiny daughter clad in red, complete with an adorable little red ski helmet. She buzzed around after them like a ladybug, zipping between them, her skis in a perpetual snowplow, arms flailing to help her balance. She must have been about five and had little trouble keeping up with her older parents. I could have kidnapped her.

But stealing someone else's little girl was not the point. What ached inside me was the idea of having Charlie's daughter. The dream of creating a child with the spouse you love is powerful indeed, and society seems to view children as a necessary glue for a marriage. Many people asked Charlie and me if we would have a child together, despite the fact that we were in our late forties when we married. My friend Sandy, in particular, was convinced that a fifth child—a girl—was the icing on the cake that would make our family complete.

Her name, when we talked about her, was Charleen, because she would be Charlie's girl. He loves talking to kids, often dropping to the floor and into their mental goof zone to commune with them on their level. He is a man who could have had ten children, who asks if he can rock babies to sleep, who loves nothing better than reading a kid a book or putting shoes on his ears to amuse them or giving them laugh-out-loud nicknames. When I first met him, I figured he would make a swell grandfather, but after Charlie complained several times that using birth control amounted to a Charleen holocaust, I sat him down for a serious discussion.

"Are you crazy?" I said. "I just turned forty-seven, we have four children already and they are getting ready to go to college. In a few years we'll be free."

"I know," he said, getting that hangdog look. "You're right, as usual."

But maybe he didn't want to be free. Sometimes even I had this odd sense that I wasn't done raising children. Here we were, veteran parents, good parents, with a big house and roomy kitchen. In six years, we would be rattling around in this place. Maybe we weren't done.

I had always thought of her as Elizabeth, the daughter I would have tried for if I had stayed in my first marriage. I was raised in a strongly matriarchal family, with two sisters, and I missed having girl energy around me, particularly now that I was so heavily outnumbered by boys. My parents had a fourth child later in life, my amazing younger sister, who ended up being everyone's favorite. At the time, people thought my mother was nuts to have a child at age thirty-nine, with three approaching middle school. But despite the additional work-load for everyone, my sister's birth proved an elixir for my folks—keeping them young, giving them a companion for their later years. None of us could imagine our family without her.

"Okay, I'm willing to entertain this notion for about ten minutes," I told him. "Convince me we should try for another child."

"You're on the older side for this, but you're in good shape," he said. "You're not in menopause yet."

"I'm in good shape now, but I probably wouldn't be after having another baby."

"We might get lucky and have a Charleen, a Penny."

"We might get lucky and have another boy," I told him. "In fact, I think God's decided we are a boy family, so the odds are probably very high that we would have another boy. We would be back into T-ball and peeing contests before we knew it."

About half of people remarrying have a "mutual" child with their new spouse, usually within the first few years, a child intended to cement the relationship who provides a buffer to divorce for at least ten years, according to census data.

Anne C. Bernstein, the author of *Yours, Mine, and Ours,* says: "The baby born into a stepfamily is related to everyone, whether or not they feel related to one another. The promise of having 'one that is ours' is that he will tie together fragments of two families and make them one, symbolizing by his very existence their hopes for unity and renewal. Part of his job description, from birth, is to make it 'one big, happy family,' and like most occupations, this one colors who he will become."

In many stepfamilies, the birth of a baby can help develop closeness among stepsiblings and bring parents together as a team. "Everybody loves that baby," says my new comrade in arms Barbara, the one who remarried and formed a stepfamily and then added a baby boy. "When my older son gets home from school he just plops on the floor and plays with him," she says. "When my stepchildren are here with us, the baby is what draws us together."

Barbara admits to me she did not plan to have more kids, but quickly realized that her husband had other ideas. "His two kids are adopted and he had been very cut off from raising them by the divorce, so he still had this dream about having a biological child he could raise," she tells me. "He said he pictured himself sitting on a lawn surrounded by kids, and I realized he was ready to have more. And frankly, I was bowled over that he wanted to have kids with me in a conscious way. He's a very interested dad, very involved. It's been really fun.

Even though I run myself ragged, taking care of everyone, I've never regretted it."

It is not uncommon, Bernstein says, for remarried parents to see a "love child" as an opportunity to do it right, and to have children that do not have to go spend time with an ex-spouse. She cautions, however, that parents should consider how another child will impact existing kids, especially children still adjusting to the stress of remarriage. Sometimes, she says, stepmoms who do not have their own kids lobby hard to have children, because they subconsciously feel it will give them more authority in the family and with their husband in parenting and financial issues.

Having a mutual child can also disrupt family power dynamics, experts say. Miranda Evans, a West Virginia mother I met at a stepfamily conference, had two daughters from her first marriage and a baby boy from her second. While it was great at first, being a father suddenly seemed to empower her second husband to be more authoritative with her daughters. The new baby totally changed the family dynamic.

"The girls can see that he thinks that baby hung the moon, and they know he doesn't feel that way about them," says Miranda. "Sometimes it makes me very defensive for them. With the girls, he's the stern stepdad. With Aaron, he's all lovey-dovey. They resent it." Bernstein says that mutual children often operate as a distraction from unfinished stepfamily business with older children, which can spell problems down the road.

So Charlie and I thought about it a bit, then decided it was crazy. The critical issue for me was respecting my own human limits. We already had four children who needed love and attention and good parenting for a good many more years, and now I had a husband who also needed and had every right to expect love and attention and tending. If I had a baby, someone who was already here would end up neglected, probably the one who complained the least. I had this feeling when I got pregnant with Jesse—that I had to "divorce" David a little bit to be able to love a second child. It wasn't really like that, but by marrying Charlie, I'd had to pull back a bit from my own children to make room for Charlie and his. If I had a fifth child, I'd be pulling back even more. It wasn't worth it, even if she was a Penny.

But even after our decision not to attempt a pregnancy, our Charleen sightings continued to haunt us. Finally Charlie admitted that maybe there was something about the Charleen fantasy that was about our lost youth.

"Our lost youth?" I asked, confused.

"Our lost youth together," he said. "It's about what we don't get to have, which is a marriage that starts out when you are young and hopeful and full of dreams."

I know what he means. I've sometimes wondered what life would have been like if we had met when we were young. I've often wondered what our children would have been like, particularly since we are more like each other than either of us was like our first spouses, the pairings that produced our existing children. I think that is part of the pull of Charleen, the mystery child that would combine our best qualities.

"She might be one hell of a musician," I say.

"She would probably be one hell of a writer, too," Charlie says.

But there is also the dark side. "Maybe she would be a huge worrywart," I muse. "Worse than either of us."

"She'd want to organize both the library and the kitchen!" Charlie says.

"What if you combined your attention to detail and my compulsiveness?" I tell him. "She might be anal-retentive!"

So we sit down with our wonderful, interesting boys and appreciate what we have. Sometimes Charlie looks down at Rex, the dog that is our constant companion, the child that never has to go to another house.

"We already have a love child," he says, patting Rexie. "We don't need another."

So we bumped along during those early months, me reading stepfamily advice books and popping Zoloft, Charlie trying to build his consultant business, the boys flailing their way through the necessary adjustments and instant messaging their friends late into the night.

And then, on September 11, the world exploded. I was at work that morning, Charlie at his desk at home, the boys far-flung at their different schools. When a colleague broke into a meeting of my department to tell us what was happening in New York and at the Pentagon, I ran back to my office and called Charlie.

"Get home," he said. "Get off campus. Just drive home. Don't go anyplace public. I'll figure out what's going on with the kids."

At that point there were reports of possible other hits in the D.C. area, and we weren't sure what to do. It chilled me to the bone to wonder what target the hijackers had in mind for the plane that crashed in Pennsylvania. It had been headed for Washington. My ex-husband Ron worked just blocks from the Capitol, and many of my other friends toiled within spitting distance of the White House. We managed to collect the boys by midday, then sat huddled with them around the TV. I suddenly was overwhelmingly glad to be a family, intensely grateful that I had a strong, capable husband to turn to for help. That I could make dinner and gather my children around me that night, talking quietly, letting them relax a bit after the tension of the day. The next morning, when the papers arrived, I took Adam aside and we strategized about whether to keep any of the photos or stories from Jesse or Matt. Each boy had a different take on events, which gave us a window into their hearts. It was a day when kids needed parents and parents needed parents. For the first time I could feel the strength of being a family together, particularly as the calls started coming in from our worried relatives in other parts of the country.

"I'm so glad we are a family today," I told my father-in-law when he called from New Mexico.

"I'm so glad you are a family today, too," he said. "I'm glad you and Charlie have each other."

What I suddenly saw that day was that this wasn't just a marriage for me, but that this larger extended family could provide a strong support for all of us. What we had built by marrying was something risky, yes, new and mostly untested, but it was already throwing off a glow.

CHAPTER TWELVE

The First Holiday

IT'S A CRAZY FALL. I drive by the Pentagon, where my father worked for many years, feeling sick to my stomach when I see the gaping hole left by the terrorists. In the weeks after the attack, there are several bomb scares at my university, emptying campus and wreaking havoc with the class schedule. My students, young journalists running around town chasing down stories, are nervous and edgy, and their parents are frantic for their safety. When the anthrax scare hits, things only get worse. Charlie and I joke about who should get the mail—ours goes through the ill-fated postal service processing center where two postal workers died—standing on the porch and waving it around in the air before bringing it inside. This is before we find out how little anthrax it takes to make you sick. Capitol Hill closes for three days. There are rumors about truck bombs on the Beltway and mysterious packages on the Metro.

But by Christmas, the tension starts to ease. My sons have survived the first semester of their new school and give all indications of thriving in the more competitive atmosphere. Our house renovation is nearly finished. The kitchen cabinets are in, even if few have drawers. Still, it's a kitchen we can cook in, so we revel in the space and load it with goodies. As the holiday approaches, I start my usual planning: What thoughtful gifts can I get for everyone? Which cookies shall I bake this year? What should I put in the kids' stocking? What should I say on the Christmas card? As I start my usual ramping up for the holiday, however, it occurs to me that it will all be more difficult this year, and not just because we have more children.

The biggest problem may be my husband.

"I love Christmas music," he says, turning up the car radio so that the Messiah is blasting through the speakers. "It's the one thing about Christmas I love."

"There's only one thing you like about Christmas?" I squeak, not sure I've heard him right, not sure I want to hear him right.

"Well, it's so overcommercialized, and I don't like the whole gift-giving thing. The fact that gift-giving sends you out into the crowded malls with that appalling piped-in music."

"You don't like that you have to find people presents?"

"Well, it's not that exactly," he says. "I just never know what anyone wants, and most of my family has plenty of possessions, and it seems silly to just get something because the calendar says it is Christmas. I can't see the point of giving people things just to give them something, so I paralyze myself trying to find the perfect gift."

I know Charlie is hardly Scrooge—he's too warm and generous for that. But this gift-giving problem makes him seem a bit Scrooge-like.

"Aren't you going to get me anything?"

"Of course, sweetie. Just tell me what you want. Or maybe we can pick it out together."

My vision of opening surprise packages under the tree from someone who knows all my secret desires and who has listened carefully for months as I've dropped hints is fading quickly. I don't know what to say.

"I like the whole Christmas tree thing, too," he adds, trying to brighten me up. "Getting the tree and decorating it. I love how they smell."

"Aren't you going to get the boys presents?"

"Well, yes, but I'm not sure what they need or want." He turns to me with a big smile. "That's where you come in. What do you think my boys would like? Oh, and I love all the food around Christmas, pumpkin pie, that cranberry relish like my mom makes, the turkey dinner with all the trimmings, things like that."

I look out the car window so Charlie won't see the disappointment on my face. I hadn't realized until that moment how much I was counting on the Christmas season to leaven my spirit. Now it looks as if my main job is to cook and run a gift-buying service. I come from a family that lavished lots of energy and love on Christmas celebrations, often because they were bright spots between my father's trips at sea with his ship. He missed lots of birthdays, so my mother would try to make it up to us at Christmas, and the tradition stuck. We were the kind of family that always tried to find the tallest tree, led carolers around the neighborhood, organized the church pageant, threw intimate Christmas Eve parties, and treasured our traditions for Christmas foods, from my father's fish chowder to the oysters Rockefeller and plum pudding blazing with brandy.

"What did your family do at Christmas?" I ask Charlie, trying to figure out how we will connect these two traditions. Or, rather, my tradition and his nontradition.

"Well, my parents weren't into the commercialism either, so we had a tree and a party. I don't remember what else."

If there is anything that throws the cultural differences between families into high relief it is a big, honking holiday—one with high expectations and studded with childhood memories and lots of activities.

And holidays reveal the deep irony in remarriage. I thought that by remarrying and expanding my family I would be going back to familiar territory. But in actuality, remarrying is more like going to live in a foreign country. You may have a companion again, but you quickly discover that you and your partner speak different languages and are used to different cultures. Your new family members may seem no more familiar to you than people from Sri Lanka, and sometimes a good bit less friendly.

I didn't realize until that first Christmas what a big cultural gap there was between me and Charlie and the two families we had created years earlier. Every family has a culture—that thick web of habits and preferences and rituals and values and inside jokes that gives each family its unique ecology. Some families thrive in an environment of constant motion—kids rushing about with endless activities, cell phones buzzing, cars pulling in and out of the drive all day. Other families like to nest and have a strong preference for quiet time on the sofa or lingering over meals taken together. Some families prefer a life filled with spontaneity and last-minute decisions; others like routine and schedules. Some tend to openness, with lots of sharing of family gossip and concerns, while others are more private about individual and family matters. Some families are intensely into togetherness, while in others, family members may tend to go their own separate ways. It's not that some cultures are better than others, it's that they are different, and for adults and children who have developed an individual family culture, mixing with a different family culture can feel—in the beginning—like living with another species.

"Kids have their established way of being in a family, and they don't like giving that up when they blend with another family," says my therapist friend Dorree Lynn when I ask her if this is a common problem. "Besides, their other biological parent may be maintaining that old way of being, and that's hard. The way of being defines who they are, and when you create a stepfamily you are trying to define a new way of being. What you are talking about here is like trying to build a United Nations."

Beneath the daily differences, says Lynn, lie the values that make up a family's worldview, the conscious and subconscious choices we make about how we are going to live. They are an expression of who we are, as individuals. They are the fabric of a life, the habits we will carry forward into our futures, the culture that comforts us, the qualities that make up our sense of being home. Because they are values in everyday wrapping, they help us decide what to do and who we are going to be, which is why it is particularly troubling for children to lose their culture. They end up feeling like they have lost the map to their life.

The questions that reveal a family culture are fascinating. Do we value athletics over academics, or vice versa? Do we try to decommercialize Christmas; do we push our kids to do community service or attend church? What kind of discipline do we employ, and when is it called for? Do we allow our children a lot of freedom, or do we keep a tight hold? Do we believe in equalizing goodies and benefits, or do we fit them to the individuals? Do grown-ups have more privileges than children? What are our political convictions, and how do we feel responsible to them in our daily lives? How do we communicate, and how well do we resolve the inevitable conflicts we face?

The Christmas issue was complicated a bit by the fact that Adam and Matt's mom is Jewish. It wasn't clear to me, however, quite what they had celebrated in the past. As far as I could tell, there seemed to be a lite version of both Christmas and Hanukkah, depending a bit on who was visiting. I didn't really know if the boys would be expecting Hanukkah presents or not, or celebrating Christmas at her house.

On top of that, the gift-giving tradition for Charlie, or at least the under-the-tree part, seemed mostly childcentric. When he asked what I wanted, I invariably told him "Earrings!" and he invariably said, "Let's go pick them out together." It certainly saved on wrapping.

I guess I knew there were families that operated this way, but I'd never spent a holiday with one. In my family, gifts were the way people expressed their attention and love. For years we ran different present exchanges, with Secret Santas either filling a stocking for someone else or conducting covert investigations trying to figure out what single gift would really knock the recipient's slippers off. We sat around Christmas morning slowly opening these treasures, one at a time so everyone could watch, while we nibbled on muffins and sipped coffee and champagne. We were the kind of family that was still waist-deep in Christmas wrap at noon.

For my newly configured family, however, gift-giving seemed both loaded and a little unnatural. Not only did Charlie dislike the commercialization of the whole gift thing, the kids had no idea how, why, or what to give to their new stepbrothers and stepparent. It was bad enough finding something for their own mom or dad. If there was going to be anything under the tree, I was going to have to figure out a gift-giving scheme that would get everyone involved before they thought better of it.

The first problem, however, was assuring that the schedule was clear. We were supposed to have the boys, but we still needed to give each of our ex-spouses a chance to connect with the kids for some holiday time. Ron and I had a long-standing tradition around this—giving one parent Christmas Eve day and the other Christmas Day—but we weren't sure if that would work when folded in with Charlie's kids' schedule.

As we struggled to figure out where they would be and when, I began to understand why this complexity issue felt all out of proportion. Scheduling this holiday was not just about our four boys. It was also about their two other biological parents, Adam and Matt's new stepfather, and then the huge web of grandparents, aunts, uncles, and cousins extending out in all directions. Thanks to divorce and remarriage, our four boys technically have eight different family units of grandparental people out there totaling thirteen individuals, all wanting a piece of their schedule. Actually, that's simply my best guess—I don't even know for sure how many different "grandparents" are in their lives.

Emily and John Visher, early organizers of the stepfamily movement in this country, quantified this problem of how a stepfamily grows as different units split and recombine with other individuals. In a traditional nuclear family with two children and two sets of grandparents, there are eight people, who can be paired off 28 different ways. When you start grouping the eight people in larger subsets, there are 246 alternatives. I like to think of this as if members of the family get into cars in varying groups. Now, here is the interesting part: In a typical stepfamily, where there are several children on each side, the numbers take off in an exponential streak. In an example based on a real family, there is a central remarried couple who have brought five children to the marriage. One of the ex-spouses has remarried, and there are six sets of grandparents connected to these five grandchildren. In all, there are 22 individuals in this extended family, who can pair up in 252 ways, or split into any of over 8 million different group combinations. That's 8 million variations on who might show up when David graduates from high school.

This helps explain why Charlie and I keep track of who will be living with us—who is actually a residential member of the family—on the calendar. It explains why I have a long list of emergency phone numbers over the phone. Why those maddening school forms that have only one space for a parental address make my teeth ache. When I married Charlie, my kids' school secretary updated the school directory in such a way that it looked like Charlie married Ron, and I moved into my ex-husband's house. We're confusing, if nothing else. I call family therapist Peter Gerlach of Chicago, who has built an extensive website on stepfamily dynamics for the Stepfamily Association of America, and he tells me there are nearly 100 variations of different kinds of remarried families, when you consider variables such as remarrying after a death, after a divorce, with kids from one side, kids from another, varying custody schedules (legal, full physical, shared, visitation), half siblings, full siblings, stepsiblings, and "mutual" babies. "The net effect of all this variation is that each family feels alone in their experience," Gerlach says. "It feels to each that there is no one else like them, so no one understands."

This also helps explain why it is so frustrating when someone expects people in remarried families to be able to behave like they live in nuclear families. When my mother was trying to get me and Charlie to commit to our holiday schedule, I finally admitted in frustration that we were waiting to hear from Charlie's ex-wife, who had to get clearance for her plans from her brother before we could say what we would be doing. It sounded absurd, but it was true. People I have never even met hold sway over my life.

. . .

As Christmas nears, I get that itch to make cookies, which I often give to friends and neighbors. I'm not sure, however, how this would be read by the neighbors on Charlie's street, many of whom knew and liked his ex-wife. Will they like me? Will this look like I'm trying too hard? Do people even exchange gifts in this neighborhood? Many people stop us while we're walking the dog and ask how we are doing and how the renovation is going. Everyone seems curious about us. And then one day we get a call: Can we host the block holiday party?

"Can we?" Charlie asks, looking at me hopefully.

I just shake my head. Because the kitchen isn't quite finished, the dining room is still stacked with boxes. I'm still knee-deep in grading final projects and exams, and most of what I consider to be the Christmas tasks—cards, the tree, buying presents and wrapping them—hasn't even started. "Honey, look at this place."

"I guess you're right," he says. "But everyone wants to see what we've done to the house."

"Next year, sweetie. Tell them the renovation isn't done, but we'll do it next year."

In my gut, I know the neighbors want to see more than the new kitchen. There's a palpable—though polite and sensitive—interest in us on the street. How does our family look on the inside? Is the place a mess or has order been restored? Do the kids seem to get along? Who's bunking with whom? Who's in the basement? There's a lot you can tell about a family from the inside of their house. I'm not sure I'm ready for the world to see us yet. We're still making our life, and there's a lot that's unsettled.

As I weigh these deeper tensions, I am reminded of how loaded the holidays are for me. My first husband, Ron, grew up largely independent of his family, with little regular contact. By the time we married, he had a history of feeling lonely and depressed on holidays, and that sometimes lapped over into our experience. Early in the marriage I learned to retreat to my own family of origin if I wanted a warm, happy holiday, and in time Ron became more comfortable in their company. After I divorced, holidays often felt like the nadir of my single life. Even though I was used to sharing the boys with Ron, it always felt wrenching around holidays. On the holidays I had the boys, I tried to coordinate with my parents or siblings, to give my kids that warm experience that was so dear to me. The holidays I didn't have them, I sometimes spent with other family members or sometimes sat alone, feeling empty and bleak. In time, I learned how to plan my way through the rough days—connecting with other single friends or latching on to childhood buddies who would take me in as family. But it was never easy.

Holidays are difficult in part because they are a time when everyday actions take on added meaning, a time when people expect the bonds of family and love to find expression in everything from gifts and favors to sumptuous meals. But every family conveys love differently, and to varying extent. And for many remarried families, who may not even all love each other, the whole notion of a time of heightened emotion can be threatening.

One night I sit down to write a chatty holiday newsletter, as I have for years, and I find I can't do it. I have no idea how to sum up our first year together. There are many highlights, but I know that's not the whole picture. Instead, I finally write a far-cical version of the twelve days of Christmas—hardly original, but I manage to capture the mayhem of our household without the dark underside I sometimes feel. "Eight maids IM-ing, seven phones aringing, six people showering, five guys who shave!" I paste this over a picture of the six of us at the wedding and send it out, first to my friends and relatives, then to a list of Charlie's old acquaintances.

"This is the first Christmas card I've sent out in years," he tells me. "Thanks."

Many of the self-help books for remarried and stepfamilies say that rituals and traditions are an important tool for family-building, but that it is important to pick rituals carefully. One book suggests that instead of bringing traditions from either family's previous life, the newly blended family should create entirely new traditions for the holidays. "Avoid the temptation to recycle old traditions that may not feel inclusive to everyone in the new family."

Recycling? Is that what we were doing when we bought a Christmas tree? Decorated it? Sang a Christmas carol or ate a Christmas cookie? I loved Christmas because of all the recycled traditions—I wasn't about to dump them and start over. After my divorce, I leaned heavily on these traditions to give my children a rich holiday experience, despite my exhaustion and unhappiness as a single mom. If I told my kids we were going to give them up, perhaps because they were not a tradition for Charlie and his kids, I would have had a rebellion on my hands. I'm not sure what family this advice works for, though it does raise a point. Traditions may need to adapt to bridge the culture gap between families. That I could understand, and the idea of possibly building new ones to add to the mix. The more the merrier, was my mantra. The more the busier.

For our first newly transformed tradition, I suggest we hang Christmas stockings for everyone, then all help fill them. I want the boys to buy everyone else in the family a gift, something they would like, because it will get them thinking about each other and not just themselves. But I also don't want this to become a big deal. Something thoughtful but small. So Charlie and I take the boys one night to a nearby drugstore and fancy food emporium, and give them each a basket and the instruction to get two things for each other person in the family.

They skulk around the store for nearly an hour, whispering to each other, trying to keep their baskets hidden, laughing over the joke presents and rummaging through the jars of specialty jellies to find something unusual. Since we have spent most of our communal time at the dinner table, they all knew each other's preferences. It works like a charm. The gifts are funny, thoughtful, and sweet. And I didn't get stuck doing all the Santa duty.

By the time Christmas finally rolls around, I am exhausted but feeling that we have some good planning in place. Charlie and I go to considerable trouble to get a foosball table for the recreation room, believing that something communal would foster better stepbrotherly relations. On Christmas Eve, our kitchen cabinet maker still hammering away, we decorate our tree, blending the two collections of ornaments, and I give the boys each something new of their own to hang among the others. It is a heavily laden but happy tree. For dinner that night I start a new tradition: We unwrap several baskets of goodies from cousins and grandparents, and lay out a feast of little treats. I serve mulled cider and cut a loaf of specialty bread, and we have a meal with almost no effort. After dinner, I tell all the boys it is time to wrap their stocking gifts. There is much banging around upstairs, and finally a plea for help from Adam, but soon we are filling the stockings, laughing and elbowing each other over the Christmas cookies.

Christmas morning is a little tense and a bit of a crash: it's over in half an hour—a far cry from the ordered coziness of my own family—and there are a couple of disappointments among the kids. In the middle, our cleaning lady shows up, confused about the holiday and determined to vacuum. The boys bounce around the house the rest of the day, jockeying over the foosball table and playing Internet-based games with each other from their separate rooms—togetherness of a sort, but mediated by the digital environment. They are fine. Still, it doesn't feel much like what I knew of Christmas, and by the time I have cooked, served, and helped clean up the turkey dinner, I am in tears in the darkened kitchen, wrung out. The angel in the house has been running around all day trying to make everyone happy, and now she is having a nervous breakdown. It doesn't help that I miss my own family, which is gathered together at my parents' home, just a two-hour drive away. We aren't with them because I was concerned that my new family—the six of us—would have added too much confusion to an already full house. My father had just had prostate surgery and was still recovering. I knew, however, that if it had just been me and my two boys, we would have been there. And it would have felt more like Christmas.

Some families, the psychologists point out, are more highly ritualized than other families, and I can sense that Charlie's instinct is distinctly nonritual. For me, a holiday (like vacation time) is sacrosanct—a time to stay home, nest with the family, talk, and make a big meal. For Charlie, a day when most others are home can be a great day to shop or get out. Done with the Easter egg thing? Let's go to a movie. "It's not worse," I say to myself through gritted teeth. "It's just different."

But there was no denying this culture thing was tricky. Even though our kids lived equal time in both houses, I had to be careful not to impose my family culture on top of the culture Charlie and his boys shared. At first they seemed to have the stronger hand. As the resident family of the house we moved into, they had all kinds of squatter's rights. I sometimes felt that Charlie's way was the default way; if I didn't change something, it went back to the way he did it. I had worried that our more organized style of living would get sucked into their, shall we say, more fluid approach, because chaos always devours order. In truth, though, I had to realize that as the wife I had enormous power to control the culture of the house, even if Charlie was right beside me discussing laundry protocol and picking out curtains. Sometimes my stepsons complained that in my effort to re-create the intimate life I had always shared with my sons, I had imposed much of my motherly culture on all of them. But I wasn't their mother, and sometimes that chafed.

Psychologists who work with remarried families say these families often tend to split into factions of insiders and outsiders, and cultural differences can exacerbate those divisions. Many stepfathers say they often feel like outsiders, because their own children tend to spend less time with them, and instead, step-dads spend most of their time with their new wife's children.

In stepfamilies, there are all kinds of imbalances. The outsider experience, the therapists will tell you, is one of isolation and exclusion, and nearly everyone in a stepfamily experiences moments of feeling excluded, pushed away as unnecessary, perhaps even as unwanted at certain times.

I was having coffee one day with my friend Daniel, who had recently divorced his wife, when he started talking about feeling like a perpetual outsider during his marriage. His wife had a six-year-old son from her first marriage, and she often shut Daniel out of decisions regarding his stepson because, her theory went, he didn't know how to parent because he had never been a parent.

"It was a major problem in our marriage, and one of the things that led to our divorce," he confides. "Even after we had Michael, she still kept me out, just changing the excuse. After that, she said I didn't know how to parent because my family had been so dysfunctional. The truth was, she was used to doing things her way, and there was little room for compromise. It wasn't that one way of parenting was good and the other bad; they were just different. And she could never deal with that. It had to be her way or the highway."

A few weeks later I was talking with my graduate school friend Nancy, whose second marriage broke up in part because of this problem. "Sometimes I didn't even feel as if I belonged in this house with them," she says, describing life with her former husband and his children. "Particularly when we just had my stepkids, it often felt like I was the fifth wheel. The irony was, we were living in my house. I would sit there wondering how this happened."

Stepparents say they are routinely cut out of activities where they might actually be able to lend some expertise, simply because they are not the primary parent to a child. Many stepparents report feeling shut out of helping with homework or college applications, or coaching on a sport or musical instrument, often by the children's own parents, who may feel threatened or are unwilling to cede control.

One of things Charlie and I loved about each other was the wisdom and insight each could lend in raising the other's set of boys, but when we got down to discussing specifics, we often found the biological parent barring the way to genuine participation by the stepparent. We often found it hard to let someone else into decisions about the boys, because we both had to consider the kids' other biological parents, and sometimes that just meant there were too many factions to deal with happily. Sometimes, as my friend Suzanne used to say, it took too much explaining to explain.

Some stepparents report feeling like a piece of furniture when they are barred from having a say in what happens with the family schedule or children's activities just because they are not one of the biological parents. When Charlie was trying to decide on rules about driving for his eldest, the first in the family to get his license, Charlie's first inclination was to talk with

his ex-wife. That made some sense, but I told him he als
needed to talk with me. Our boys were going to be sharing
these rules. Just because one of my kids wasn't first up on the
roster didn't mean I shouldn't have a say in determining the
driving tradition in our family.

Then there is spending: the great sucking sound on the
family bank account. Spending is largely a family culture issue:
How much do we spend on presents, how much on vacations?
How often do we eat out or buy expensive food? Spending habits
and their corollary, saving habits, get handed down through
generations, and may be an intrinsic part of how a family
defines itself. Are you thrifty? Do you fold up the Christmas
wrap each year like your mother did to save for next year, or do
you stuff it in plastic garbage bags and toss it into the alley? Do
children get things when they want or need them, or do they
have to wait for birthdays or holidays? Chores and allowances
are all part of the family culture around spending, and traditions can run deep, which is another reason many merging families are loath to talk about these issues. Just setting up an
allowance system and chore schedule that would work for our
two sets of boys took an MBA (Charlie) and the patience of Job
(me). Fairness and equity loom large in such discussions, and
quickly reveal the different approaches biological family units
may have followed in the past.

Our original approach toward the four boys was a principle of fairness and equality for all. But we had to rethink that
the first time one of our guys had a legitimate need the others

couldn't match. When he said, "No one can be special anymore?" that made us think. Maybe fairness across the board made the family a little too much like a communist country. How do you reward a child who makes a special effort or who, like this one, has a special need? Of course they are all special and they are all different, and we've had to reassess our approach to sharing the resources of the house so that we don't end up hamstrung.

Spending and trust issues can also raise their ugly heads when children reach the age where they need to start learning to manage their own money. Many remarried partners find they have varying approaches to teaching money management, and may have differing levels of trust for the kids in their household. How child support gets spent, who manages it, how much it is, and whether both partners feel the child support issue is fair (whether it is flowing in or out of a house) can also raise issues of trust and stewardship. Particularly if resources are pooled, spending and household management can become a minefield if the expectations and concerns are not aired regularly.

But the biggest culture clash in our family, it turned out, was the unbridgeable animosity between my cat and Charlie's dog. I used to think they would look so cute in the Christmas photo—two solid white pets, with big red ribbons, perched at our side. But we were never able to get them anywhere near each other, much less in the same photo frame. We finally took Snowy out to live at the farm, where we needed a good mouser.

Our tenant, who lives in the barn, makes sure he has enough food, and we built him a pet door to get into the basement at night to stay warm. He lives there today, strong and muscular, stalking the horses and enjoying the easy pickings. And when we come to visit with the dog, he takes off for the hills.

CHAPTER THIRTEEN

The Wicked Stepmother

I'M SITTING IN THE FRONT row of the darkened theater at my stepsons' school, between Charlie and David, with a passel of little girls at my feet. It's squeeze-in room only for opening night of the school's spring musical, *Cinderella*. Adam is singing the role of Prince Charming, looking handsome and deeply conflicted as the prince who doesn't want a wife. When he comes onstage, the little girls gasp. He's tall, dark, brooding, with a royal blue sash across his chest. If I were little, I'd gasp, too. Oh, fun, I think with a smile. Something to tease him about. He's the newest heartthrob of the under-ten set in suburban Maryland.

But as the play unfolds, I start to squirm in my seat. For this story is not really about the prince. It's about Cindy, there in her own little corner, and that overdressed creature who is the wicked stepmother. She's played by the school's reigning comic actress—all screechy and patronizing and saccharine and insincere. Her daughters are equally cartoonish—fat, ugly, ill-mannered, and stupid. Cinderella, of course, is winningly human and real, despite her rags. Plucky, sensitive, humble, and hard-working. Her stepmother taunts her, occasionally dangling a bit of sympathetic motherliness before her but then jerking it away. This play is all about the cruel cat-and-mouse of bad family relations, and it makes me so uncomfortable I can barely keep my seat. When the fake mist that accompanies the good fairy godmother momentarily obscures the audience, I'm glad to be hidden. I don't like sitting in the front row for this play. I can't *stand* this play.

It doesn't help that Adam's mom is in the audience as well, and probably drawing connections between me and the stepmother on stage. Our relationship, which never got the space or attention to develop, is awkward at best, sometimes tenser than that. I know she has disagreed with some of the rules Charlie and I tried to establish for our household. I think my stepsons would tell you I don't have many mean moments, but like every human, I have my weaknesses and faults. I'm sure that to her, the protective mother hen of her boys, I'm an enigma, someone she isn't sure she can trust. It turns out that there is a lot of natural antipathy between biological moms and stepmoms, much more than for biological dads and stepdads, theoretically because biomoms and stepmoms compete more for their children's loyalty and love. I think that is less true in a situation like ours, where our children are older and my stepsons' dad, Charlie, does most of the heavy parental lifting for them in our household. Still, it isn't a natural liaison, moms and stepmoms. Almost as if our biology can't quite accommodate it.

There isn't a little girl alive who grows up wanting to be a stepmother, yet many of these young beauties lined up at my feet ogling my handsome stepson will find themselves in the role one day. As portrayed in myth and fairy tale—not to mention Hollywood movies and some recent sociological research—the stepmother is invariably greedy, unkind, and self-promoting. In contrast to a real mother, a stepmother seems almost unnatural, as if the order of the world only allows one mom per child. And the message is clear: If you're a stepchild, watch out.

Of all the new roles I've taken on since remarrying, being a stepmother is the most uncomfortable. It is the role I was least prepared for, the role nobody really talked about, the role most wrapped in social stereotypes. Thanks to folklore, there seem to be just two models: wicked and angelic. (Surely an angel in the house would figure out how to navigate the difficult shoals of stepmothering without running aground as often as I have.) And that's the problem. If you are not inhumanly wonderful and perfect in the job, if you occasionally have a real moment and crack under the stress, then by default you are evil.

"Anyone who would be willing to take on a role whose most common adjective is *wicked* has got to have their head examined," says my friend Nancy, who took on the job of stepmom when she married a man with custody of three children from his previous marriage. "No matter what you do, how you try to be patient or bite your tongue, there will be a moment when the kid pushes your buttons and you react. Your wickedness—your human frailty—flickers through, and you and your stepchild never forget it."

Many remarried people say they are surprised when they find themselves in the position of a resented or besieged step-mom or stepdad, particularly if they have been successful parents to their own children. One of the most unnerving aspects of my remarriage is that, at age forty-seven, I've had to learn how to do something new and different, something that challenges all my assumptions about myself. I thought I had the mom thing down. I thought I was pretty patient, flexible, tolerant. I have been those things with my own children and with a generation of students. But it turns out that I'm not always patient, and I'm sometimes irritable. And I don't think that is just depression. I have a new, humbling understanding of my limits.

But stepparenting is harder than parenting. Why? For many reasons. Because it is largely thankless, no matter how hard you try. Because kids don't want to be parented by a stand-in; they want their own folks. Because kids sometimes go back to their biomom and complain about their stepmom, especially if she did something heinous, like make them eat their peas. Because stepparents have no legal rights to support their role in the lives of their stepchildren, and are sometimes cut off from kids they have helped raise through a second (or third or fourth) divorce. Because there are 20 million stepfamilies in America, but schools and hospitals don't seem to have noticed. Because kids don't want to accept rules from a stepparent. Because some biological parents fail to support the stepparent spouse, and may even undermine his or her authority, particularly if the two parties cannot agree on rules or parenting policies. Because many of the people who second-guess a stepparent have never been in the role and have no idea what it is like.

There have been many attempts to locate the source of the myth of the wicked stepmother. Psychologist Bruno Bettelheim suggests that children need to split their feelings about good mothers and bad mothers into discrete objects so as to better understand them, which is how we end up with the stepmother serving as the evil mother. Earlier versions of the Cinderella story had evilness lodged in actual mother figures, and some scholars have argued that it was shifted to stepmoms only during the Victorian era, when there was a move afoot to sanctify moms. No wonder I'm having trouble being both a stepmom and the angel in the house.

Others have argued that the Cinderella story served as a vehicle for natural mothers to send a coded message to their children that stepmothers were not to be trusted. Women were usually the tellers of these tales to children, and many of them feared dying in childbirth and knew that their children could easily end up as stepchildren to someone else. Warning their children against evil stepmothers might inoculate them from transferring their loyalty from their original (dead) mother to the new stepmother. In cases where mothers suspected their husbands were already pursuing younger women outside the marriage, women who might end up as stepmothers to their children, the story could serve as a sort of revenge. Ironically, the story has instead worked against women who go beyond what might seem natural and provide love and support to children born of another womb.

. . .

What's interesting about the stepmom problem is that I don't really have big problems either stepparenting or being with my stepkids. In fact, we are doing relatively well. What I dislike is being identified as a stepmom.

Marilyn Coleman, a sociologist at the University of Missouri who has studied stepparents, reports that this isn't unusual. "The stepmothers we have interviewed were usually so freaked out by the idea of being perceived as a wicked stepmom that they wouldn't even claim they were mothers to their stepchildren," says Coleman. "They will admit they do mothering things—feeding kids, doing laundry, helping with homework— but they will not claim the term *stepmom*. They say they are afraid of challenging the biological mother if they claim that role. The problem, of course, is that their reluctance probably gets in the way of their establishing a close relationship with their stepkids."

I can't imagine why we would feel this way.

In a recent study at Princeton University on how much money families spent on food, researchers concluded that stepmothers spent about 6 to 7 percent less money on food eaten at home than biological mothers. The media then offered up this tidbit as proof that stepmothers were stingy, even to the point of starving their charges.

But to me, reading between the lines on this study, there are a host of unanswered questions. The data in fact seems so limited I'm surprised any self-respecting scientist bothered to reach conclusions from it. No one tested the stepchildren to see if indeed they were malnourished or reported being hungry or suffering from any ailments. No one asked if these kids were being spoiled with expensive treats by their biological mothers, who must have lost some degree of custody (or there wouldn't be stepmoms in the family equation) and might feel guilty about that. No one asked if they were being spoiled by their stepmothers, who might be taking them out for McDonald's every time the stepkids whined. The study, after all, looked only at how much money was spent on food eaten at home, not spent on food generally. But frankly, the biggest unanswered question is, Where the hell are these kids' fathers? If their children are being underfed in their households by their second wives, possibly to the point of neglect, where are these dads? Haven't they noticed? Why don't the researchers admonish the dads, if someone needs to be admonished for neglecting children, which is a big leap, given the limited data. Why are the women the only ones in the kitchen doling out the food?

Kay Pasley, a psychologist and leading researcher in the field of stepfamily dynamics at the University of North Carolina, Greensboro, also has big problems with this study and its conclusions. She says the researchers had not allowed for the fact that most children living with stepmothers also spend substantial time visiting with their biological mothers—more time, on average, than kids do who live with a stepdad and visit with a biological father. That would mean, argued Pasley, that the children were not in the stepmother's home for as many meals, a fact that could easily explain the statistical difference. There could be other reasons, too.

"It may well be that these stepmother families have fewer resources to allocate because of their spouse's responsibilities of payment of child support and/or alimony, and the authors acknowledge this," says Pasley. "To conclude that stepchildren in stepmother families are not fed as well as children in biological families simply does not reflect their findings."

In fact, it is unclear if much of the purported science about stepparents is more helpful or hurtful. The topic seems hopelessly caught in the political funhouse that is the debate around family issues in America. For stepparents, it certainly feels as if there are more unhelpful myths and factoids than there are useful models, and that is part of what makes it so challenging.

Studies such as the Princeton food allocation study raise troubling issues, and have launched a national debate over the naturalness or unnaturalness of stepparenting, with the most conservative voices suggesting that stepfamilies are actually dangerous places for children. These conclusions are then used as evidence that divorce and remarriage should be discouraged through social and governmental policy.

Biologists will tell you that some species, including many mammals, have a tradition of males routinely killing infants when the male has taken over a new female who brings along babies sired by a previous mate. In most of these cases, the goal of the male is to bring the female into estrus more quickly by shutting down her milk production. If the nursing baby is eliminated, she soon becomes ready to mate with her new partner. Biological equivalents of stepparenting among other species—that is, the raising of children by adults who are not related to them—are scarce indeed.

In one unsettling volume called *The Truth About Cinderella: A Darwinian View of Parental Love,* sociobiologists Martin

Daly and Margo Wilson of Hamilton, Canada, claim to have reviewed the research about stepparent abuse of children and conclude that "having a stepparent has turned out to be the most powerful epidemiological risk factor for severe child maltreatment yet discovered."

They examined records of fatal child beatings and found that, while some people kill their own genetic children, a child has a far greater chance of being killed if he lives with a stepparent. They also found that stepparents who killed children were more likely to do so by assault than were biological parents, who generally used less brutal methods—often killing the children while they slept. Biological parents who killed children were also more likely to have diagnosed psychiatric conditions. Stepparents rarely had diagnosed psychiatric conditions.

Daly and Wilson also looked at reports of sexual assault by stepparents. A 1996 study from Finland found that, of 9,000 fifteen-year-olds questioned, 3.7 percent of the girls living with a stepfather said they had been abused sexually by their stepfathers, compared to 0.2 percent of teen girls living with biological fathers. They say that recent studies from Hong Kong, Korea, Nigeria, Japan, and Trinidad also find that kids living with stepparents are more likely to report being beaten than children living with two biological parents.

Daly and Wilson conclude that from a Darwinian perspective, stepparenting is hardly an adaptation that promotes passing on one's genes. An evolved human psyche, they write, "that treated stepchildren and genetic children exactly alike would be a psyche vulnerable to exploitation, and would be evolutionarily unstable in competition with more discriminating alternatives.

There is, then, a strong theoretical rationale for expecting that the evolved human psyche contains safeguards against allowing a mere stepchild, however appealing, easy access to that special mental category occupied by genetic children, the appropriate objects for the most nearly selfless love we know."

When I read this treatise, my first reaction is that it's a long way from resentment over a stepchild's messy bedroom to a fatal child battering or sexual abuse—and most stepfamilies will never even *start* to go from one to the other. And we are humans, thinking animals, capable of a high level of social conditioning and adaptation, with complex psyches. Also, fields such as sociobiology and evolutionary behavior are new and undisciplined, with few standard scientific protocols for comparing behavior between humans and other species.

In fact, the very suggestion that humans may be hard-wired to be bad stepparents seems to be little more than irresponsible political grandstanding, considering how little real science has been done to establish such a connection. It is certainly depressing to feel, as many stepparents do, that we must fight this negative image before we are accepted by society. And it has also been particularly troubling to those who work to promote strong stepfamilies.

Margorie Engle, president of the Stepfamily Association of America, is more blunt: "If you look at the studies of child abuse, in actual numbers, it is the biological fathers and biological uncles that win that race," says Engle. "These findings are terribly distorted in lots of ways. It is just part of the political movement to promote first families to the exclusion of all other types of families."

However shoddy the science behind them, these studies get headlines in most media, accompanied by little scholarly context. The result is that, for many people, being a stepparent feels like a particularly potent sociological test of essential goodness. Several sociologists who study stepparents report that many stepmothers actually exhaust themselves overtending their stepchildren, haunted by the idea that they are being watched and judged by the wider public world.

For children of all types, the deliciousness of the Cinderella myth is not the raw undercurrent about motherhood, but the contrast of good, sweet, long-suffering Cinderella with her two evil stepsisters, who are usually portrayed as ugly, whiny, weak, and dishonest. It's sibling rivalry, squared. Cinderella's stepmother favors them wildly despite their flaws (giving them dresses, allowing them out in society, forcing Cinderella to serve as their maid), which is why Cinderella needs outside help, in the form of a fairy godmother, to reveal her worth and elevate her to her rightful position as the loveliest, the one with the delicate foot that fits the slipper, the one who will be chosen by the prince. In part, this is a story about rewarding the virtuous Cinderella. Yet it resonates with the conflict around resources and the charges of favoritism that plague many modern-day stepfamilies. It picks at the question of who gets to hold the remote.

Without doubt, an underlying tension runs between stepparents and kids. I met a woman at a party several years ago when I was just beginning to think I might marry Charlie. I knew a bit about her already, from a mutual friend, and knew that she was a special education teacher, someone patient, kind,

a rock for her school and her community. That night we chat-
ted at length about her recent remarriage to a man who had
two sons who lived with them for several months of the year.
Despite the fact that this woman was obviously loving, openhearted, and patient, her brow crinkled with tension when she
got to talking about their life with her stepsons. "I don't know
how they could be worse," she suddenly said. "They are messy
and inconsiderate, and I just don't understand why they can't
pick their towels up off the bathroom floor."

At the time, I had two sons who rarely picked their towels
up off the bathroom floor, and it registered as a mere annoy-
ance. What could possibly be wrong with this woman that she
couldn't handle something like that more gracefully? She even
had a son of her own, and he probably wasn't a paragon of
good behavior. Did she have a hidden evil side, was she really
incredibly impatient at home despite her outside reputation?

So I think of her now as I contemplate another teenage
infraction—messy counters, wet towels, backpacks sprawled in
the front hall—and realize that if the mess belongs to my sons,
it registers as a blip, kids not paying attention to the rules. If it
belongs to my stepsons, it often registers differently, more like
kids not respecting the rules.

And I think of myself as rational.

It may be hard to be a stepparent, but what does it feel like
to be a stepchild? I did not grow up as a stepchild, nor did I
know any growing up. But I can try to imagine what it must be
like to suddenly have to go live with a strange adult—a momlike
figure—when you are little. It must feel like being kidnapped. It

must feel like a complete and utter dislocation, especially if you are too young to really understand what is happening. When I was a child, my mother was everything—the rocks, the trees, the entire landscape of my life. My father, the Navy officer, moved in and out of my life more easily. His travels created relatively little stress because my mother was always there. I can't really imagine what it would have been like if she had vanished, or if my connection to her had been broken by a joint custody schedule and a stepmom. I went to stay with cousins once for a week, and by the time it was over, I had decided my kind and loving aunt was a complete witch. And we were related.

Most people who remarry do so fairly quickly after their divorce, so it is little wonder that kids feel whiplashed by the changes in their lives. They often end up feeling treated like possessions—schlepped around, passed back and forth, argued over, but rarely consulted. So it isn't surprising that they rebel or get depressed or get angry in their new stepfamily. Many kids in stepfamilies say they believed when they were little that their parents' marriage broke up because of their new stepparent, even when it is clearly not the truth. Children of divorce often say they don't quite trust their parents' version of events, and may suspect their parents are glossing over tough facts. Besides, it's easier to blame the stepparent than some vague story about lost love.

"When my dad remarried, my stepmother was trying to deal with me and my two brothers, and we were a handful," says my student Tim Brennan, who was thirteen at the time. "I remember thinking that she had taken my dad away from my mom, so that made her the enemy. We did lots of things to make her miserable and, I guess, to punish her. Years later I found out that wasn't how it happened, and I felt terrible. But she forgave me. We have a great relationship now."

Many stepchildren undoubtedly bring enormous resentment to their parents' remarriages, and this can be difficult to overcome, no matter how kind or patient the stepparent. Psychologist James Bray, who has studied stepfamilies for years, says that stepkids usually feel more resentment and project more rejection and lack of appreciation than positive feelings for their stepparents in the first few years, regardless of whether the stepparent is loving or cold. In fact, he found this to be so common he dubbed it the good father syndrome.

"A number of stepfathers were sensitive, understanding, empathic, and enthusiastic. In short, they possessed all the qualities parenting experts describe as essential to winning the heart of a child," says Bray. "Yet we found that very few of these men won any hearts in their stepfamilies. More often than not, they ended up being ignored or rejected by a stepchild."

Children in stepfamilies also struggle with loyalty issues, especially if their parents are still fighting. Remarrying can cause old problems between divorced spouses to flare into open conflict, which can make children feel caught in the cross fire. If the relationship between the biological parents deteriorates when one remarries, kids will often blame the stepparent.

Stepparents, in fact, say that stepparenting is hard in large part because of things that have little to do with the stepchildren: the jealousy of biological parents, unclear roles and expectations, and limited time with the stepkids.

As many stepparents discover, the world often reminds them

they are *just* stepparents—even if they are supplying the lion's share of the parenting. My college friend Laura, whose step-daughter lives with her full-time, says that even though her stepdaughter's mother is an alcoholic and completely absent from Sophie's life, Laura is still struggling to get Sophie to accept her with few conditions. "When she needs me, then I'm everything to her," says Laura. "But when she's angry at me, then she turns to her dad and acts like I'm not even in the house. I keep reminding myself that it is not about me. I just repeat that: It's not about me."

The reasons kids resent stepparents seem to have more to do with the job title than with the stepparents themselves. "You could be a complete saint and your stepkids will still resent you sometimes," my therapist tells me. "You have to realize it's the role you are in. You are naturally the target."

One night, trying to sort out my feelings about my wicked stepmotherliness, I stumble across a stepmom's website with a robust discussion going about the perils of stepparenting in this day and age. Maybe men don't talk about this stuff publicly, or maybe the issues aren't quite as loaded for stepdads. While there may be more stepdads than stepmoms in America, the number of stepmoms is growing, and they are increasingly less isolated from each other. As more men lobby for joint custody or succeed in winning generous visitation schedules, more and more remarried women are finding themselves in the role of stepmother. And thanks to the Internet, stepmothers today can find their peers online.

And when they do, watch out. *Robust* is putting it mildly.

As I scan the different discussion strings, I feel as if I've stumbled out of the mist and into a circle of women gathered around a bubbling cauldron, the cackles rising with the steam. The talk occasionally gets wild and woolly, but it is clear from the intensity of the conversation that this community provides something that keeps these women from running screaming down the streets. I certainly feel better the more I read: Compared with some of these families, my stepsons and I are paragons of every possible virtue.

There are stories of stepchildren stealing from stepparents, kids taking cars when they know they've been grounded, kids openly defying their stepparent's authority, often with the support of their biological parent. There are daughters who insist on holding their dad's hand whenever he sits with his new wife, kids who throw tantrums when they are barred from the parental bedroom, kids who throw objects when they can't have what they want.

Not surprisingly, some stepparents admit they are less than happy in their stepchildren's company, and a common theme on the stepmoms' website is the problem of contentious visitation, including the disruption of the household and the additional work stepmoms take on when their stepkids are in the house. The complaints are legion: stepchildren who disrespect rules or who leave the house looking like a disaster zone; biomoms who undermine stepfamily harmony by complicating visitation schedules or fostering resentment in their children; husbands who dump kids on stepmoms and go golfing, instead of spending their visitation weekends with the kids at the latest Disney flick. But woven between the howls and outrage are the responses from the other stepmoms: messages of compassion and understanding, with a heavy dose of tough love on the side.

"Just calm down and deal," writes one woman in response to a post suggesting that the author is considering getting an apartment to live in until her stepson goes off to college in a few months. "Don't move out on them. Communicate your problems and insist they go for help!"

Another woman tearfully describes finding that her fiancé gave his ex-spouse expensive jewelry for Christmas. "Boy, I wouldn't marry the guy until he can prove he is OVER his first wife," writes another member.

"Excuse me, but your stepchildren have a right to live in your house, if that is where their dad lives," counsels another, after reading a post complaining that the author doesn't mind opening her home to her new husband, but can't understand why he needs to bring his daughters along for the ride. "You married the family, not just the dad. You are not locking those stepchildren out of the house."

When I read these comments, I'm chastened. I think of my friend who moved out the day her stepson smashed the glass coffee table and her husband just sighed. I have been very lucky in my stepsons. While we struggle occasionally to coexist—primarily over the state of the kitchen—our problems are small potatoes compared to many of the conflicts stepfamilies develop.

Even my friend Barbara is having a harder time than I am. "At the beginning I thought of this as one big adventure, and I would go out of my way to plan fun stuff for the weekends my husband's two kids were with us," she confides. "Now it's more like a chore. My stepdaughter often hides in the closet and makes long phone calls to her mom on her cell phone, even though she knows that's not allowed. We have a hard time going out to do something fun because she is usually having a meltdown. With seven people in the family now, we don't always have time to check everyone's emotional temperature before we go. Her problems have made it hard for everyone to enjoy the weekends."

I'm even more worried about my friend Lisa, who is engaged to marry a widower with an angry teenage daughter. "What happens to me is a complete dichotomization of my feelings," she tells me. "On the one hand, I think, oh, this poor, motherless child. No wonder she is a mess. Then in the next moment, I want to wring her neck. She has complete power to make us miserable, and often uses it. I've never felt like I was living with such a split in my life."

It is without a doubt a challenge to live with children you have not raised and may have little authority over. I think I respond with more frustration when my stepkids leave a mess than when my children leave a mess because I have a lot less power to make it right. If my kids are the offenders, I can yell at them to get their little selves down here right away to clean it up, and pronto! But I never yell at my stepkids and rarely even ask them to do a chore. Picking on them is their dad's job, and I wouldn't dare wade into those waters. But sometimes that powerlessness leaves me grinding my teeth.

One might think this would be the wrong approach, but apparently the relatively hands-off system I've blundered into turns out to work best for most kids, as long as the stepparent can stand to live on the margins. According to Bray, successful stepparents are those who chose more of a monitoring role than a strict parenting role. "The monitoring stepfather was usually not involved in the child's emotional life, but he knew a lot about the child's daily life: where she was, whom she was with, and what she was doing," says Bray in his book *Stepfamilies*. Bray said he expected that such a detached form of parenting would be unhealthy for kids, but it turned out that stepparents who functioned as monitors in the first few years, while they were building a bond with their stepchildren, developed better relationships with these kids than stepparents who assumed a more authoritarian role from the beginning. Kids understood that monitoring and companionship indicated affection and concern, which made them feel valued. Monitors helped biological parents by providing a second set of eyes and ears, but usually got out of the way when the more serious parenting decisions needed to be made.

Despite the fact that stepparenting is a central issue for most blended families, few couples ever talk about it before marriage or discuss ways they can encourage or develop the stepparent-stepchild bond, Bray says. But by the time they are several months into the remarriage, most couples recognize that the issue will need to be resolved.

I met a stepfamily once with a wicked stepmother, and they gave me the willies. The father was handsome and easygoing, with a gosh-darn quality about him and the way he talked about his family. His wife, the allegedly wicked stepmother, was thin and plain, with a tautness around her mouth and eyes.

She was British and he was an American army officer. They met and married in Europe, then came back to the United States to take custody of his two teenaged daughters. But things are not going well.

"When he travels, the girls follow my rules, but when he comes home, they ignore me," says the wife, sitting stick-straight in her chair. Her handsome husband lounges next to her, shaking his head as if to discount her problems. "I came from a family with strict rules," she continues. "I don't know why a stepfamily cannot have the same rules a normal family would have. Am I not supposed to have rules for them, just because we are a stepfamily? But I can tell they resent it. So when he comes home, I step back. The girls and I don't have much of a relationship."

I watch them talk in this group meeting, and I can see their breakup just over the horizon. He's forced her to play the bad cop while he gets to be the hero. She's doing all the hard work with these kids, and he gets to parachute in for the fun and the affection, undermining her system and standards. I can see the anger building inside her. One day soon, she's just going to walk out the door because the only thing she's getting back is low self-esteem. No wonder she looks tense.

One of the things that has always bothered me about the Cinderella story is the absent father. Like the dads in the food allocation study, Cindy's dad is missing from most versions. In some, he's dead, but not all. In some versions, he's just not paying attention. There are no wicked stepdad stories (or damn few), mostly because women rarely abandon their kids to the care of stepdads. But dads often ask stepmothers to carry the burden of their children. What is surprising to me is that society doesn't find the missing-father syndrome more troubling. I'm not sure why, but it seems easier to blame the stepmom.

What the sociologists will tell you is that if stepparents are going to have a chance in a stepfamily, they need to be supported by the biological parent. In fact, poor relationships between children and stepparents can sink a remarriage faster than almost any other pressure, says Emily Visher, who founded the Stepfamily Association of America with her husband John and studied stepfamily life for many years as a therapist in California. Visher says she tried for years to write about the remarried couple relationship as separate from the parenting, but became convinced that it was impossible to disentangle the couple relationship from the complex web of child relationships that make blended family life so challenging.

If a stepfamily is going to make it for the long term, stepparents must have a real role. Visher says that stepparents often become the scapegoat for problems in blended families, but in reality, it is the biological parent in the household who holds the power to make the relationships work.

"The parent has the love of those children, and can set rules and limits," says Visher. "He or she also has to protect the stepparent from abuse, gossip, and rudeness from children. The parent needs to be considerate of the stepparent, and include him or her in family activities and planning." In short, it is critical that the parent and stepparent work together to run the household, and that the children witness that cooperation. When that doesn't happen, stepparents often get hung out to dry.

"I'm not a real disciplinarian, but I was more strict with my stepson, and later my son, than my wife would have been," says my friend Daniel, whose marriage broke up in part because of disagreements over parenting. "With my stepson, whenever I did something she didn't like, he got snatched away. In time I just disengaged. I couldn't be engaged and feel like I was being graded all the time. She even did the same thing with the son we had together. I saw it as a father/mother difference, but she saw it as a real parent versus stepparent thing. In time, I just checked out of that relationship."

.

One of the great advantages stepparents can offer kids is that—like teachers and coaches and other adults not caught up in the angst of the parental tie—they can sometimes see solutions to problems with kids because they bring that alternative vision, that fresh perspective.

When Charlie and I first faced the idea of having four teenage boys learning to drive, he just wanted to go hide. He was terrified by the thought of any of them behind the wheel. His solution was to delay their learning until they were eighteen, so they could drive only when they were more mature.

This approach worked with my first stepson, who didn't really care that much, but my second stepson wanted more independence sooner. Fortunately, he is a mature, careful, attentive kid. I knew he would make a fine driver, and I supported his campaign to get his dad to put his anxiety aside and let him learn to drive at a younger age.

My friend Jim Caine, who married Maggie when her children were teenagers, may have perfected the role of monitor. Maggie had a "challenging" ex-husband, a man who had bullied her into giving up substantial custody time with her kids when they were little and who still needed to be considered first at every family function. Jim and Maggie, mild-mannered and generous of soul, always told her children that it didn't matter. Now, after ten years of keeping to the background but also keeping up with the family, Jim is the favorite of both his stepchildren.

"By taking the backseat, he ended up in the driver's seat, in terms of those relationships," says Maggie today. "He's always there if they need him. My son often calls him up just to chat. He's a big influence on them."

Despite the care and concern that most stepparents extend to their stepkids, stepparents are sometimes accused of not loving their stepchildren, or at least not loving them the way they love their own children. Many stepparents berate themselves for feeling different about their stepchildren than about their own kids, thinking that those bonds should look and feel the same.

In fact, most studies of stepparents find that they willingly admit they do not love their stepchildren in the same way they love their own children, although the vast majority also say they care deeply for their stepkids, some even saying that they love them as well. Even if stepparents are not reporting strong love for their stepkids, most provide substantial emotional, financial, and logistical support to stepchildren, say the researchers, no matter what the feeling is at the end of the day.

This question reminds me of the lament of the wife in *Fiddler on the Roof*. When her husband asks her if she loves him, instead of saying yes she answers instead that she cooks for him and takes care of the house, and if that isn't love she doesn't know what is. Love is a slippery thing. Who is to say when care and support equal love? Who can measure it, and how can types of love be compared?

When I first remarried, I decided I would offer my stepsons what I offered my students: wholehearted support, affection, concern, and help. At that moment, I had no other models. I didn't know what precisely I was to give them, so I looked for a model that was familiar and would not overwhelm them. Over time, though, my relationship with my stepsons has evolved into something closer to what I feel for my nieces and nephews: a much deeper affection and love. I expect it will grow someday to be something even more special than that. It may never be like the love I feel for my own children, but I clearly feel related to them and morally responsible for their care and happiness. And maybe that's the key.

The truth is, love can't be measured or quantified. People can just know what they feel in their hearts, and should not be judged by the larger world, particularly those who have never been asked to love or live with a stepchild. Most stepparents behave as if they love their stepkids, even if they have moments of gnashing their teeth later in the privacy of their bedrooms. And that's okay.

CHAPTER FOURTEEN

The Neglected Self

SHORTLY AFTER WE HAD MARKED the first year of living together, I went off for a few days to a yoga retreat center in New England. It was my birthday present to myself, and also a dash for sanity. I was knotted by the stress of managing the boys, my stepsons, our ex-spouses, everyone's conflicting schedules, our complicated lives. Nothing seemed easy, and everything seemed critical, from each kid's homework to every interaction over the breakfast table. The first morning at the center I sat in a welcoming circle of other retreaters, who were all saying something about why they had come. Most people gave lengthy explanations, but when it was my turn all I said was: "I'm here because I live with four teenage boys in a stepfamily." There was no need to say much else. That simple statement won me three days of tender care and concern, as if I were a war veteran hospitalized for shell shock.

But as I padded around the retreat center in my socks, I wasn't quite sure why I was there. Ironically, I missed the hubbub of our warm kitchen at home. When I went through the vegetarian cafeteria line I wished the boys were there to laugh with me at the unusual food. Why did I need this modern equivalent of forty days in the desert with the locust eaters to find my center? Wasn't my center back home, making turkey tetrazzini?

Yes, but . . . something about me was different, unsettled, agitated, and it confused me. I knew who I was before I remarried, but now I wasn't so sure. Remarriage had destabilized my sense of self, my idea of myself, in ways I was just beginning to understand. Here I was, forty-eight years old and in the middle of another identity crisis. Divorce and an earlier career change apparently hadn't been enough. Now I was in another period of redefinition, and this time I wasn't sure what I was encountering.

The truth was, remarriage had forced me to confront my dark side—the impatient, strung-out, angry, grieving Wendy. For years I had thought of myself as patient, kind, levelheaded, and strong. But now I suspected I was those things only when I could control my environment, which I couldn't anymore. Not only did I fear I was turning into someone far more flawed than felt comfortable, but remarriage had forced me to do this with an attentive audience: my husband, the boys, our ex-spouses, the curious world. There was no crawling into the shadows and licking my wounds, as I did after my divorce. This time I was front and center, and it felt like everyone was ready to judge.

If there was ever a path to Zen Buddhism or some sort of spiritual detachment, it is stepfamily living—which perhaps explains why I was at a yoga retreat center. If you believe the universe sends us messages, living in a stepfamily is like having billboards on the front lawn reading: DE-STRESS NOW BEFORE IT'S TOO LATE or DETACH BEFORE YOU GET EATEN ALIVE. Particularly for women, who usually run the household, the life of a blended family is full of snags. I had come off my antidepressants after the first year but still struggled with our bumpy path. We had hit more than a few holes—we were way off the beaten track, compared to most nuclear families. We weren't even sure we had a map for the territory we were in. We didn't know if we were a family, or if so, what kind of family, because the rules and expectations for a regular family never seemed to apply. A simple milestone such as the eldest child getting his driver's license triggered complications of nearly every stripe: fairness, parental panic, parental authority, money, philosophical differences between households, and territoriality issues. The boys were doing their best, but it was hard to live in two homes, particularly when those households differed in lifestyle and outlook. I didn't know if I had any authority to ask my stepkids for help or if I should back off completely to ease the tension. My own kids, my husband, and the dog and the kitchen and the closets all needed attention. And my stepsons may have, too, but they sure didn't seem to want it from me.

I knew from all my reading that most merged families stumble through a predictable series of stages, and that we were doing better than most. Stepfamilies tend to start off idealistic. Then they wake up to the hair-raising reality of what they've done and go through a stage of confusion as some members persist in the romantic haze of denial while others howl at the moon. They break through into real hell when they acknowledge life sucks, take off the gloves, and wade into the power struggles. At that point, many families split into factions, often based on biology, and others splinter. If a family is going to make it through this firestorm, they need to learn how to handle conflict and to negotiate differences without fighting or polarizing— or doing too much damage. If they make it through, there is the coming-together stage, followed by the resolution stage, when optimism returns and the future brightens. Family members accept each other, for better or worse. Ties strengthen as shared history and experiences accumulate over time.

According to the experts, this whole process can take anywhere from four to nine years.

As I plod through a labyrinth of stones at the retreat center, trying to attach to the idea of serenity, I do a few mental calculations. I'm not sure what stage we're at, because everything seems so muted, especially with our boys. Nobody's acting out badly—just some peripheral grumpiness. I find it hard to figure out what is normal teenage behavior—Adam is a bit tense these days, but he's also in the middle of applying to college—and what is a more serious problem. The truth is, Charlie and I, like David and Goliath, seem to be the elected champions of our teams. We're expected to do the real fighting, then get back to the others with the results. If that's true, I calculate that we are at the gloves-off stage, because my wrangling with Charlie is getting a bit more pointed. I am torn constantly between think-ing I should speak up about something that bothers me and feeling that I should shut up so this marriage has a chance. My therapist's comment about tolerating neuroses and irritating habits echoes through my head. I sit in meditation and wait for answers.

Charlie and I didn't even have a fight until after we mar-ried, which was three years into our relationship. At the time, no one believed me that we didn't fight, and I worried that per-haps it wasn't such a good thing. If we weren't fighting, maybe it meant we were too afraid to fight, that the relationship was too fragile. But the truth was, we didn't fight because we were both working so hard at understanding the other that we never retreated into opposite corners. We certainly had heated discus-sions, but the goodwill was thick and generous in those days, and it carried us through many disagreements. We were both eager to compromise, eager to work out our differences. And we were eager to prove that our relationship was different from our first marriages.

We had our first fight about a week after I moved in. It wasn't a great moment for either of us. We had been out at the farm for a long weekend with my parents, and were back at the D.C. house for one night, doing everyone's laundry and repack-ing so we could stuff everyone back in the car and head for Cape Cod the next morning. I was exhausted, and beginning to worry that marriage to Charlie meant I would never again have enough time to do everything. We had five loads of laundry stacked in the hallway when the washer and dryer shut down. This was mystifying, as they had both been working earlier that week. Then we noticed the lights were dim—we were in a sum-mer brownout, due to a power outage elsewhere in the city. Within a few hours the lights were back, but we were still doing laundry at about two A.M., when Charlie and I got into some-thing heated, probably having to do with fairness and the boys. This was one of our hottest topics that first year, all the balanc-ing between everyone, and it brought out the female lion in me, protective of my cubs when I suspected Charlie's boys might get preferential treatment. The discussion escalated until Charlie suddenly referred to me by his ex-wife's name. It stopped both of us cold.

"Boy, I must have really hit a nerve if you got us confused," I said, deeply offended. "Let's stop."

I don't remember now just what the issue was. Mostly the problem was that we were tired, and I was dreading this next trip—back into the territory that had been loaded for us in the past. I often felt, that first year, that things were just happening too quickly for me to keep up emotionally. I had barely pro-cessed my remarriage and my move, and now we were going off for a family vacation, all together, back into terrain that had proven difficult for us in the past. My mother turned to me once during those early months and said, "Don't let Charlie drive you into the ground. You guys are doing a lot. Give your-self a break sometimes." I married Charlie in part because of his hard-charging energy, and was often impressed by how much he accomplished in a day. But sometimes I felt like I was being dragged along by wild horses, and I often worried that I wasn't doing my share. I couldn't have done more, but I wor-ried that he could have done more in my shoes, and that must mean I wasn't trying hard enough or carrying my load. He often rose early in the morning because he couldn't sleep and would announce at breakfast that he had already paid all the bills and e-mailed a bunch of people and worked on some project for a couple of hours.

All I had done was read the comics.

Charlie, to his credit, never expected me to keep up with him, though I did feel a gentle push sometimes to do more of the things that improved me—exercise, eat the right foods, practice my piano, write another article. If I had a problem with perfectionism, he was obsessed, as he recognized. He often hesitated to make decisions because he wasn't sure what was quite the right way. Me, I would just leap, figuring that making any move was sometimes more important than making the best of all possible moves. He often had lots of ideas about how something could be done, often solutions I would never have had the mental energy to come up with. Sometimes this brought tangible benefits—a better hotel room, cheaper airfare, the perfect view. Other times, it meant we could never relax because the effort to improve was never finished. We teasingly called him the great maximizer.

Sometimes I would catch him trying to maximize me. Early in our relationship he would often check the route I was planning to take through rush-hour traffic. He was the kind of guy who loved to monitor the traffic websites and guide family members around the problems by cell phone. But sometimes I found this maddening.

"Sweetie, I've lived in Washington most of my life," I would tell him. "You don't need to approve my route."

"Well, it might take you a long time if you're trying to go left at that light onto Colesville. Trust me, it's a bitch at this time of day."

Usually he was right, which only made it worse. "That's okay," I learned to say. "I love getting stuck in traffic. It's a Zen thing. You know, a chance to practice detachment."

I'm not sure why, but I didn't like these adjustments. "Don't act like my supervisor," I would tell him. "Don't parent me."

Some of this was oversensitivity on my part, I realized. My first marriage was studded with criticism of my alleged ineptness. Charlie said, again and again, that he didn't consider me inept. I knew that his meddling was a function of an overactive brain rather than criticism, but sometimes it was hard to tell the difference.

Back home in the fray, I decide I need to talk with my real estate agent and friend, Mary Lee. Not because I'm planning to move, but because she has been married three times and divorced three times, and raised a son in a stepfamily, and has watched her own child divorce and remarry, and still has a great relationship with his first wife as well as the second. She knows a thing or two about remarriage, Mary Lee does, and so I quiz her relentlessly.

"Why is this so hard? Is it all the cooking? The guy thing? Or is it because I'm not a good wife?"

"The cooking thing is just superficial, though sometimes you'll want to throw the frying pan right through the window. No, remarrying is hard because it forces you to face things about yourself you'd just as soon not know. I found myself doing and saying things and thinking, Is that me? But it was me, and it was better to know myself."

"That's right," I tell her. "I thought I was a good person. I thought I was patient. I thought I was a good mom. I thought I would make a good wife. Now I'm not so sure." I tell her about the stages. "How am I supposed to make it through all these stages and hang on for nine years without going insane?"

"Oh, you do everything quickly. I'm sure you'll get through in six or seven."

"By then all the boys will be in college," I say.

"Exactly." She smiles. "And you and Charlie will be fine."

But I'm not sure I'm going to last that long. Except for the first few harrowing months after separating from my first husband, I don't think I've ever felt as lost or dislocated as I have since marrying Charlie. And the way I deal with it is to attach to everything. I try to fix everything, smooth everything, be there to make sure nothing gets lost or forgotten or ignored or stepped on. I don't always appear like the angel in the house, but I carry her around like a monkey on my back. By the end of the day I'm huddled under the comforter, inevitably exhausted or frustrated or defeated by the fact that these efforts rarely bring the peace and ease I try so hard to achieve. Every harsh word, every teenagey harrumph, every mess and territorial infraction sticks to me. I think of myself as Velcro girl, attracting all the shit in the household. I am able to function, but often feel irritable and sad, missing my old life. Secretly, I wonder if my deepest fear—that I am too emotional or weak or sensitive to be a good wife—is coming true. That I'm not holding up under the pressure. What I keep telling Charlie is that "I just don't feel like myself."

"Maybe it's time-of-life issues," Charlie delicately suggests.

"You mean perimenopause?" He knows I've missed a few periods. Things could be winding down in there.

I'll admit, I told him once that a guy willing to marry a woman headed straight into menopause should be given a medal. Maybe that is part of it. Perhaps this is hard because my body and mind are not primed for this much change at this point in my life. Maybe remarriage is unnatural, at least biologically.

The tensions in every remarriage can make life feel unstable, even as it looks settled from the outside. For many remarried people, life continues to be unpredictable, more chaotic, less solid than first marriages, often for many years into a remarriage, and this instability can keep remarried partners in a state of stress and dislocation for many years. It was this stress that worried my own doctor and prompted him to give me antidepressants.

Psychologist Bray found that adults in second marriages recorded stress levels much higher than those of adults in nuclear families. Women in new stepfamilies, in fact, reported stress levels three times higher than women in nuclear families, and men in new stepfamilies reported stress levels about two times higher.

"Stress often interfered with a woman's ability to attune to her children—to track their thoughts, feelings, and needs carefully," says Bray, who says this stress often functioned like fog in the family, confusing everything. "Preoccupied, the mother would miss the youngsters' distress signals."

Bray also found that highly stressed newly remarried partners often resort to what he calls a blunt shorthand of poor communication skills and regressive behavior when they feel overwhelmed and disheartened by the stress and difficulty of remarriage. Instead of becoming better in their new marriage, people revert to the bad old habits that undermined their first marriages, making "the incidence of marital conflict soar in new stepfamilies," he says.

As remarried people struggle to get their feet under them in their new lives, their attention is focused on nearly everything but themselves. They have a new spouse, a person whose needs and desires have to be considered, and they often have a new household that must be tended, and then there are the children— one's own, who may be feeling ignored and need reassurance, and stepchildren, who want some kind of attention but can be hard to please and easy to irritate.

The one person we have no time for is ourself.

"If I didn't have my job to go to each morning, I would go mad," says Barbara as we huddle again in one of our midday talkfests. "Sometimes I look around the house and here I am doing this little wifey thing, feeding the kids, taking care of the baby, and I don't recognize myself," she says. "If I didn't go to work, I'm not sure if I would know who I am."

Barbara understands my quest for sanity, and also how it feels even harder as the second year of a remarriage dawns. "It's like college," she says. "The first year you know things are tough, but you think you're doing okay. But you have no idea really, because you're an idiot, you don't know anything. The second year, you realize how lost you are. The bad grades start piling up and you start to panic. Maybe in the third year, we'll get our feet under us. At least that's my hope."

When I sit down with my therapist, I find myself talking about self-esteem.

He listens, slightly baffled. "Self-esteem? You're having self-esteem problems?"

"Yes," I tell him. "It feels like I can't do anything right. I feel like an idiot half the time."

"Describe being an idiot."

"Someone who fails to remember to write down phone messages. Someone who gets irritated when the kids ring the doorbell instead of using their keys. Someone who lets the dog out, then forgets about him and he runs away. Someone who leaves the laundry in the washer overnight, and it gets hopelessly wrinkled."

"You sound overwhelmed, not like an idiot."

"I know these seem minor, but when you add them up, I'm really beginning to think I'm slipping."

"This, from a woman who runs an academic department with, what, several hundred students and twenty faculty?"

"Oh, yeah," I say, waving away the discrepancy. "That's my work persona. I'm fine there, no self-esteem issues there. It's at home. I burn something in the kitchen and feel like a bad wife."

"I burn things all the time, and we just go out for pizza."

"I cooked a turkey but roasted it upside down, then nearly

burst into tears," I tell him. "Isn't that stupid? But I wanted it to be perfect. I couldn't believe how stupid it was to cook the thing upside down. I feel like a teenager myself."

"I think the key here is the perfection problem. Who is asking you to be perfect? Is Charlie or are you?"

When I considered my patient, tolerant husband, I couldn't figure out why the perfect-wife problem had moved into my heart and set up camp. When he asked me what I was worried about, I would say I didn't want to disappoint him. Maybe that was the fear—that I would disappoint him and he would begin to reject me, as I had felt rejected by my first husband.

But Charlie always said, "I can be disappointed that something happened, but it doesn't mean I'm disappointed in you. I'm never disappointed in you."

I just couldn't understand why I didn't believe that.

Psychologists say that the many new roles and stresses of remarriage can weaken self-esteem, particularly if one fears the remarriage is fragile. Just the thought of another failed marriage is so humiliating, unhappy remarried spouses feel isolated and are unwilling to go for help. Remarried people may feel so overwhelmed by demands from the family that they ignore old friends, give up hobbies they loved, or leave jobs if they have to move or stay home with children. Breaking these old ties can lead to further isolation, as well as the abandonment of good self-care and health routines. This further exacerbates low self-esteem.

I didn't think the marriage was fragile, but I wondered about myself.

"Remarrying can be extremely tough on a stepmom's self-esteem, and on the rest of her, too," says Karon Phillips Goodman, author of *The Stepmom's Guide to Simplifying Your Life.* I've picked up her book because the idea that I might be able to simplify my life a bit looks like it might be the key. Goodman's a stepmom herself and a psychologist, so I've contacted her online to get a direct infusion of intelligence. "Frequently a new stepmom has left behind a life in which she was in complete control, where she felt great confidence in her abilities, often after surviving a shattering divorce and becoming far more capable than she ever thought she could be. Then she remarries and feels inept to do anything, because steplife is like nothing she's experienced before."

Goodman says that having no history with stepchildren makes it tough to build a relationship with them, and this is often made worse by an ex-spouse who may be trying to prevent a relationship from forming between a stepmom and her stepchildren. "The stepmom can feel like her life isn't her own anymore," says Goodman. "Everyone else seems to have more say and power than she does. And the person who should be her greatest ally, her husband, may not understand at all."

I've joined the discussion on the stepmoms' website, and when I raise the issue of self-esteem, mail comes flooding in my direction. "I can't begin to explain how fractured my emotions have become," one woman told me. "I bounce from happiness to anger, guilt, jealousy, resentment, insecurity, relief. Is there anything I left out?"

"Sometimes I hardly recognize myself," says another, echoing a common theme. "I'll be irritated by something that seems so small, but it's connected to something bigger, and that to something even bigger, and it all makes sense to me, but everyone else thinks I'm crazy. I guess that's it. A lot of people think I'm a little bit crazy these days."

Several women tell me they are doubly surprised by the emotional roller coaster of remarriage because they felt that if they could survive their divorce, they could survive anything. "But apparently not," one tells me. "What I learned from surviving my divorce is no help now. In fact, sometimes I think that's part of the problem. That old independence gets me into trouble now that I'm remarried."

I remember my post-divorce period as a time of slowly discovering and then redefining who I wanted to be as an adult, outside the stressful life of my first marriage and the restrictions set by my first husband. I got to decide what kind of parent I would be, how important family would be in my life, whether I would attend church or take up bird-watching or build my career. I had plenty of time to indulge in me-oriented activities— my book club, exercise, visiting with friends, learning yoga, working late into the night on evenings my kids were with their dad. When I wasn't taking care of my children, I was free to do whatever I wanted, and I protected that autonomy even when I dated people and got pulled into their lives. I had learned to love my solitude and I needed my space.

Remarriage is different. If divorce leaves you alone in a quiet place to think, remarriage feels more like losing your mind in a crowd. Since I've remarried, my "space" has dwindled to a corner of the house and a few bits of time between work and the demands of my much larger family. I no longer have an hour of quiet alone time before bed. Now Charlie and I struggle just to find twenty minutes at the end of the day to talk with each other before collapsing. On the nights I really need to bury myself in a book for a few moments I feel selfish and cruel that I'm not willing to share that time with my hurt husband. So I constantly give it away—compromise on my need for quiet, share my space with someone else.

On the face of it, this loss seems a silly one. In fact I'm often ashamed to even admit I need more quiet. I remarried, after all, largely because my quiet life often left me lonely and bored, as much as I loved my solitude. I hated the years Charlie and I were dating, when we would often end up cuddling with the phone, trying to have that shared experience with each other while we curled on our own beds in our own houses, several towns apart. I couldn't see my sweetie or lean against him or feel his hands on me, and when one of our psychologists suggested we wait seven years until all the boys were in college to marry, every fiber in my soul yelled "Not fair!" I remarried because I wanted this closeness, the proximity, the shared life.

But sometimes it feels like a cage, and even worse, sometimes I'm not even sure who I am.

Remarriage usually brings a welter of confusing new roles, often at a time in life when we thought we knew what we were doing. On the stepmoms' website the women debate their role, with no clear definition: mom, maid, babysitter, dad's companion, friend or mentor to stepkids. I thought it would be easy: I would be the wife and mother, queen of the house. But how do you feel like the queen of the house when you don't even know where everything is? When your stepkids feel that it is their house more than yours, because they've lived in it since they were babies? And who's to say they aren't right?

It is disconcerting to be having another midlife crisis, and I'm sure that my family and friends are probably muttering under their breath that it is time for me to grow up and sort this out and just get on with it, for crying out loud. Sometimes I say that to myself as well.

And then I go to sign a check or a credit card receipt and I can't remember what name to sign because I've changed it again, this time back to my maiden name.

The last time this happened, I had to cross some of my signature out. The clerk studied me, suddenly distrustful. He then made a big show of comparing it, complete with the crossed-out words, with the signature on the back of the credit card.

"I just got married," I say, wagging my ring finger. "I'm just confused. Honest."

But he watches me carefully until I leave the store. Can't be too careful.

"I'm not sure who I am anymore," I tell my therapist. "I used to feel like I had a strong moral compass, but now I feel like I question that compass all the time." The problems in my life don't have simple, straightforward answers. It's not clear to anyone what the right solution is sometimes. Charlie and I will be trying to negotiate a policy about, say, curfews and having friends over on weeknights, and we look at each other, both buffaloed by the variability of our children, our former rules, our parents' rules, our new rules, the rules in the kids' other houses, their opportunities for meeting girls, the odds that any of them have encountered drugs, and the possibility that their friends have their driver's licenses. Some of this is having teens, but it's compounded by the complexity of our lives. We're making it up as we go along, and that's exhausting.

One day my counselor asks me—after listening to another tiresome story about some problem we are having—"You used the term *run interference*. Do you feel you have to run interference between everyone all the time?"

I used to do twenty minutes of yoga each morning while the boys readied themselves for school, but once I married Charlie, I gave up the yoga so that I could, well, run interference in the kitchen during that mad half hour when all four of our boys were down there, colliding over the toaster oven and rooting through cupboards looking for snacks. I was so concerned that they would resent each other or be upset if they couldn't find what they needed that it was impossible for me not to go help. I had set up the kitchen the way I wanted it, and because of that, I felt responsible when no one could find anything.

"Aren't you supposed to be upstairs doing downward-facing dog?" Charlie would ask, eyeing me suspiciously.

"Well, I want things to go smoothly down here," I would say, handing someone a knife, finding the new jar of peanut butter for someone else. "I'm the greaser of the skids."

But when my counselor and I pull this apart, what becomes clear is that I was really trying to be the emotional referee for the entire family. I was afraid that if I wasn't in the middle of things, they would get out of hand. That the boys, when left to their own devices, would get divisive—maybe physical. And that seemed like the worst possible outcome. So I stood in the middle, monitoring conversations, springing to action if anyone needed something, always smoothing the way. No wonder I was exhausted.

"You've heard of triangulating?" he asks me at my next visit.

"Yeah," I reply. Triangulating is my life, so this conversation makes me a bit nervous.

"Well, maybe that's part of the problem," he says. "The family dynamics people would tell you it is very dangerous in families."

"Dangerous? How can being the referee be dangerous?"

"Because," says my counselor, "everybody in your family needs to be free to make their own relationships. You're protecting everybody from everybody else. Get out of the way, go somewhere and shut the door so you can ignore them, and let them fight it out. Until you do that, they won't have a chance to get to know each other in any substantive way."

That night I decide to let the mayhem roll instead of going down to help through the dessert hour, a special activity in our house. Usually I make milk shakes for my kids and offer something to Matt, though he likes to get his own. Instead, I settle back in with Goodman's book.

"Because a stepmom's life is full yet unfamiliar, it's easy to feel overpowered by obligations, whether real or imagined," says Goodman. "In your efforts to do all and be all, you may use a shotgun approach. Since you're unclear about where to direct your efforts, you aim at everything in sight."

That was certainly me. I wanted my stepfamily to be some sort of miracle—to blend in significant, heartfelt ways without any of the pain of readjustment, without anybody really taking anyone on, without any blood on the floor. I would manage this miracle by managing everybody else.

And that's the trap, says Goodman. Many of us, Goodman suggests, think that we will be able to beat the odds for stepfamilies, and then set ourselves up for disappointment when our unrealistic expectations fail to come true. Instead of trying to manage everything and everybody, like some sort of puppeteer, Goodman—like my own counselor—suggests stepping back and getting perspective. If you are ever to simplify the demands of remarriage, she says you must first test your expectations to make sure they are realistic, then try to focus on your true obligations. An expectation, she says, might be trying to always feel warm and fuzzy toward your stepchildren. That's admirable, but probably impossible to get right every day. Instead, she says, your obligation is to be patient and supportive of your stepchildren, even if you don't feel warm and fuzzy. The obligations, she suggests, are often simpler and easier.

When I divorced ten years ago I struggled for several years to find out who I was without the needs and expectations of my husband defining me. The life I built around that person who slowly emerged from the rubble is a key to helping me understand what I really need in this new, remarried life. When I was divorced I had lots of solitude and quiet. I've lost both those. Regaining a portion of that solitude should help me feel less emotionally exhausted all the time. I used to spend lots of time with women friends and had extra time for work. I still need those escapes, particularly given the number of men in my house. I'm finding that I can't just trade in the old me for this remarried person. Most of us have a few things that we compromise on only at our peril, and it is better to have those non-negotiables stated upfront so that everyone in the household can understand them. I feel guilty even admitting I have non-negotiables, I'm so quick to give myself away. But the key to finding my peace in this life is to claim what I really need, then hold on for dear life.

I still exchange e-mail with Louisa Smithfield, whom I met at a yoga conference the year before. She has one son of her own still at home and serves as a full-time stepmom to her husband's daughter, and when I ask her how she deals with the stress of her remarried life, she e-mails back: "The airport. I just hop on a plane and go somewhere.

"When I can't take it anymore, I just leave for a few days," she says. "I go to a conference, or book myself into a yoga retreat center and go. It's easier to do that now that the kids are a bit older." Louisa says that her relationship with her step-daughter continues to be difficult, particularly as the child reaches her teen years. "The emotional bank account gets over-drawn a lot, with regard to her," says Louisa. "I've adopted this Buddhist attitude of nonattachment. What I've gotten from Buddhism, among other things, is the idea that desire can create suffering. I had this misguided dream that I would provide my stepdaughter with what she didn't get from her mom, and that would heal her and we would have a close relationship. Unfortunately I've had to let that go. That wasn't going to happen."

Louisa says her work as a yoga teacher has gone a long way toward helping her detach. "What I'm learning is the sweet grace of forgiveness for myself. Most of the time, I'm really in there and engaged with the kids, because it is my nature to be dynamic. But sometimes I need to go heal myself."

So I got more serious about my yoga practice (though it often gets interrupted by one of the countless distractions in this house), and I got more serious about the idea of detachment.

At the stepmoms' website, detachment is one of the pillars of advice. Detachment, according to these women, means being able to distinguish between your business and everyone else's business, and then letting go of the things that are really someone else's responsibility. There's quite a bit of debate about what detachment looks like in operation. Does it mean we don't talk to our stepkids when they are rude? Does it mean we don't offer to drive them to school when they fail to get up with the alarm clock and their dad has already left for work? Does it mean we rent a hotel room if the evening at home is just too fractious to bear? The concept isn't set in stone, but when applied with flexibility (flexibility is another pillar of the stepmoms' advice portal), detachment can come in handy. It can be a cure for that Velcro feeling, and many second wives report it is the best way to get fathers to step in and parent their own children.

Goodman says the key to sanity is letting go of those things you can't control and focusing on those you can. She also says it is important to "get in touch with the strong person who still lives inside" and stand up for your rights in the household, establish your limits, and set goals for the family. Sit down with your partner and let him know what you need to be happier. If it is dinner with everyone at six P.M. every night, then try to get a commitment to that, serve dinner then, and let those who miss it eat leftovers. Set standards, but implement them flexibly, so you don't drive yourself and everyone else crazy.

In time, I learn that the real key to my sanity is to relax my standards a bit, focus on the moment in front of me, and let other things go. I need to give up the effort to control everything, because it will just pull me under. My former identity as scrappy independent single mom is getting in the way. I don't have to be a lioness for my kids' sake anymore. What I need to become is more tolerant and less reactive. Someone who can listen quietly when mayhem is breaking out and figure out what to do.

I'm learning. I no longer expect the family to set off for a long car trip without multiple stops before we break free of the Washington Beltway—the drugstore for CD batteries, the library to return books and let someone else have ten minutes (only ten!) filling his book bag, the video store (more returns), and usually a fast food joint, because we've now killed two hours and logged only five miles. This drove me insane the first time I experienced it. Now we laugh.

I've also been helped by the sudden realization that if I am not careful, my children will grow up while I'm busy having a nervous breakdown. That we really only have a few more years together, and I better start paying attention. That while the adults are going through their divorces, their single get-your-feet-under-you lives, their romances and remarriages, the kids are living their childhoods. The truth is, I'm not going to be a mom to four teenage boys for much longer. Now, instead of feeling burdened by making dinner again, I'm more likely to get someone to help me bake something special midweek as a surprise. My mother suggested the other day I simplify my life by complicating my sons' lives—making them all do more chores. I like this so much I e-mail it to Smithfield, which triggers a flight of fancy about all the ways we could complicate our children's lives. Under the ruse of "you will need to know how to do this in college," we are getting them to do laundry, cook more, keep their own stuff better organized. I'm learning to divide and conquer—reveling in the private time I get alone with one kid when I'm driving him somewhere, hiding in the kitchen so I can listen while someone else practices his voice lessons or guitar in the other room.

Remarried people almost invariably report that their lives are so busy they have trouble finding time to do the things important to keeping their own sanity, but everybody seems to have a few escape routes. During a period when her stepdaughter was testing the adolescent waters, my friend Mimi Schumer took up oil painting, taking a full-day class once a month that served as a mini-retreat. "If I hadn't done something like that, gotten away a little bit inside myself, I'm not sure I could have survived the turmoil," Schumer tells me. "I needed some sort of mental vacation, and painting gave me that. Maybe you need something like that."

In this spirit, I sign up to take piano lessons again for the first time in twenty years, sinking into the long-familiar music and losing myself in the mental gymnastics. It helps, because it is something all my own. But my favorite way to detach now is to go draw myself a bath, pour in some bubbles, and get in. I like this because while I'm in the bath, I can't easily leap up and run out to settle an argument. I can't be the referee without my uniform on. So I strip down, ease myself into the water, and try to ignore the clamor outside the door.

What I'm learning is what I suspect the universe has been trying to get me to understand for years: that the beauty of life is not found in perfection but instead in the rich tapestry of a life fully and not always gracefully lived. That being in this chaotic family, with no clear rules or guidelines, gives me tremendous freedom to just enjoy it for what it will be. I've been given the gift of extra children—boys I can take pride in and support, and whose history with me grows every day. My own kids have been given the chance to be part of a larger family, and a wonderful stepdad for life. Every time we take off for a vacation together, I brace for mayhem. And mayhem we get, from the day we sent forty peaches rolling across the baggage claim area of the Providence airport, to the night we touched down in Bozeman, Montana, at two A.M. only to find we could barely get ourselves and our ski gear in the rental van and had to drive, exhausted, for hours in a blizzard.

But there is a crazy pleasure to the larger crowd, and sometimes there are precious moments of stillness. One night while we were waiting for a table at a crowded restaurant on Cape Cod, the four boys sat on a bench, reading. Two of them were engrossed in the latest Michael Crichton, and were actually sharing the book—one reading the beginning, the other the ending, with the middle pages standing up between them. The oldest was skipping through Nietzsche, his choice for beach reading. An elderly couple tapped my shoulder. "What attractive young men you have," said the woman. "And so well behaved." I looked at her, a bit dumbfounded. But then I looked at the boys. There they sat—handsome, engaged in their books, good kids adjusting surprisingly well to the curveballs life had thrown them. Boys to be proud of.

"Yeah, they are, aren't they?" I said, with a laugh. I thought for a minute that I should explain—they weren't really all mine, that we had blended the set, I couldn't really claim credit for all of them, but then I decided, the hell with it. I'd earned this. "Thank you," I said like any mother. "We've decided to keep them."

CHAPTER FIFTEEN

Finding Our Balance

I KNEW WE WERE GOING to beat the odds the day I missed Jesse's first play.

Jesse should have been a natural for the stage, because he's always been a clown, but somehow he chickened out whenever play tryouts were announced. After a few years of living with Adam, however, Jesse was starting to reconsider. Adam had been in nearly a dozen productions through high school and Jesse could see how much fun he was having, so he screwed up his courage and went out for a middle school production of *Much Ado About Nothing*. He got cast as the drunken hooligan who, for a fee, besmirches Beatrice's reputation—just his kind of role. He was excited but nervous, afraid his mustache might fall off or that he would garble his lines. I was all set to go with David when the school shifted the schedule and I was caught in one of those working mom's nightmares: I had to give a talk the same afternoon as Jesse's play. I wasn't sure I would make it to the school in time for curtain.

When I told Jesse of my dilemma, he looked crestfallen. I sneaked in the back of the theater for the dress rehearsal, determined to see it in some form, but it wasn't the same. Because I knew I would probably miss the real show, I asked Charlie if he would take David and clap loudly for Jesse.

"Sure," he said. "I might even see if Adam and Matt will go."

"Well, it's middle school Shakespeare," I warned him. "Sort of stiff and hard to hear, if you know what I mean. I'm not sure they would enjoy it much. It might be too much for Jesse if the older boys bring their, shall we say, critical faculties to bear."

"We'll see," he replied, smiling at me. "Go to your talk. Don't worry about us."

I wished Jesse the proverbial broken leg, then went off to give my speech. I finished as quickly as possible and rushed back to Jesse's school, hoping to catch at least the last few scenes, but I could see from the clock that I was probably too late. As I wheeled into the parking lot, I spied Charlie, with Adam and Matt and David, crossing to the car, the three boys jostling one another like a pack of wolf cubs.

"Hey, guys," I yelled, pulling up. I couldn't believe all of them had come. "Did I miss it?"

"Oh, yeah," Adam laughed. "And you were right—stiff and hard to hear, but Jesse was really good."

"Yeah, he was one of the best," said Matt.

"Well, you guys were really sweet to come," I said. I was

surprised they would give up precious Saturday-afternoon time for this. "Above and beyond the call of duty."

"Yeah, well." They shrugged. "No big deal."

"Thank you, sweetie," I whispered to Charlie as I reached up to give him a kiss. "I'm sure that meant a lot to Jesse, to look out and see you guys all there."

"No big deal, honey. We had fun. We cheered."

Later when I asked Jesse how he thought he did, he looked at me with a proud smile. "Adam said I was really good, Mom."

"Well, there you go. If Adam said you were good, you were probably terrific."

When I told Charlie I would marry him nearly three years ago, I had no idea that remarriage would rock my world as deeply as my divorce had ten years earlier. My brother-in-law, a guy who has weathered some real crises in his life, told me before I got engaged that remarrying and blending families was the toughest thing he had ever done. I listened and nodded, but I didn't really believe it at the time. I had watched him and my sister parent their two kids, and thought they had done a marvelous job. They had done a much better job together than they ever would have apart. I knew it wasn't effortless, but they were so right for each other I somehow figured it hadn't been that hard.

Now I know that being right for each other doesn't make the process any easier, just perhaps less likely to fail. Every couple who remarries will have to go through all the adjustments before they reach sanity. There's no skipping steps or taking the easy route. There's only one way through, and that is through the crucible, that furnace that changes you forever into something different than before. David and Jesse and I are no longer the shy, nested, small-horizon family we were when I met Charlie. We've been blasted out of our comfort zone simply by the effort of keeping up with Charlie and his boys. In the beginning, I sometimes worried that I didn't want to be as voracious and large-living as Charlie's gang. They, on the other hand, resented some of my civilizing influences—the insistence on writing thank-you notes, the clean-counter protocol, the color-coded bathroom baskets. It felt as if the harder we tried, the stronger the centrifugal force was that threatened to spin everything apart. I remember the hot summer day just a few weeks after our wedding when Charlie and I, trying to get our fractious children to agree on a fast food restaurant, finally parked at a busy intersection, handed them each five dollars, and told them in disgust to go get their own meals. So much for family time. We sat there watching the heat rise from the pavement and just shook our heads as the boys scattered to four different restaurants.

If they had all been my own kids, my own biological children, I would have just picked a place and told those who didn't like it to lump it. But two of these kids weren't my own biological children. In fact, they had been related to me for only a month. I couldn't boss them around the same way because I was in that stepmom probationary period. I didn't want to appear too evil (too much like a real parent) just as we were getting to know each other, so I kept my mouth shut.

But then I would notice my kids watching me as I agreed to

things I never would have agreed to or allowed when I was just their mom, and it made me uneasy. They didn't know what to make of it, and neither did I. But at the same time, this disruption in my parenting method let in some fresh air for my kids. When David, my easy child, hit that delightful teenage phase when all they do is argue and complain, Charlie was there supporting David's right to disagree, even as I glared at him to back off. When I said I didn't think Jesse would want to see *Porgy and Bess,* Charlie insisted we take them all—the grown-up culture would be good for them. At every turn, Charlie pushed me to let go, lighten up, and open the windows to the world for my boys. And then sat with me while I fretted about the consequences.

One of the most challenging tasks for remarried couples is establishing what kind of family you will be, and we struggled with that mightily. What do you do when one person doesn't like skiing or someone else can't stand cats? Do you enjoy political debates at the dinner table or stay up late watching basketball? What do you allow and what do you restrict? Each bold stroke calls for compromise, for individual sacrifices, for everyone to learn to share and take turns and bend. Stepfamily experts call this investing in the we that is the core of a successful remarriage. Charlie and I work harder to create this we than the kids do, but they have been coming along. I put pictures of our vacations into collages and hang them on the walls, to remind us of the family unit that will be the bedrock of our future together. Charlie organizes trips that everybody will enjoy—even the guy who isn't wild about skiing. If we're trying to pull off a special surprise for one of them, we get everybody in on the ruse.

Over time, our biological boundaries have started to soften, though I would hardly say we are a blended family or that we look anything like a traditional nuclear family. Charlie and his sons sometimes go on trips without the rest of us; sometimes we go visit my parents without them. Other times, we all go together. Sometimes I think we should push for more togetherness, but then reality hits me in the face. Their sports and activity schedules are so demanding, there is no way one parent could tend to all of them with anything like the level of attention our kids get from the two of us operating our own subfamily units. It's taken several years for me to absorb the history on my stepsons—their emotional challenges, academic ups and downs—and I still don't know the half of it. It's a challenge to feel like a family when you don't even know each other that well.

Truth be told, our kids were less than enthusiastic about living with each other. They didn't necessarily like each other and they were worried about losing their privileges and parental attention. In the beginning, this worried me more than anything. In those early months I watched their interactions like a playground monitor: ready to leap in and break it up if things got dicey. But after a while I relaxed. They have too much respect for their parents and too little personal agony to really go after each other. They circled for several years, not sure they liked their new relatives, but now are closing in slowly, as teenage boys will do, connecting as much as they can without embarrassing themselves. Every Christmas they buy each other more presents, because they know each other better. They tease, they compete, they challenge each other with math problems over the dinner table. They are boys, after all. Sometimes they advise each other, talk about colleges, encourage each other, and offer help. I know they will never feel like blood brothers, but I hope that as they grow older they will seek one another out more, enjoy one another's company at family events, rely on one another as Charlie and I age. I hope their children will feel like cousins.

When Charlie and I married, we made a deal: no matter how hard it got, we wouldn't divorce for five years. By then most of the kids would be off to college, and we figured we would have a chance to renew our relationship if it had weakened under the stress of raising the four boys. I had read the harrowing statistics on remarriage failure and was determined to outlast them, if nothing else.

When a remarried couple can't hold it together, the familiar disintegration often happens shockingly fast. Unlike first marriages, which usually enjoy several years of romantic bliss before problems start to emerge, study after study confirms that the majority of remarriages, particularly those with kids, will struggle through the first two to five years, as everyone fights to adapt to the new family, new territory, new rules, and new family culture. Unfortunately, about half of those will not make it through that testing period. Once people decide it isn't working, they tend to move out quickly—sometimes, the therapists say, before they've even tried to make things better.

What goes wrong when remarriages fail? Is it always about

the kids, the enduring reality that blood is thicker than water and that loyalty questions will always result in a balkanized household—mother with her kids on one side, dad with his kids on the other? In the course of trying to negotiate the new marriage, a day inevitably comes when one partner turns to the other, in a moment of pain and disbelief, and says, "Are you asking me to choose between you and my kids?"

This is the most harrowing of questions, because it reveals the very core of what drives second marriages apart. But I believe that the question itself—and the tendency to see things as a struggle between the marriage and one's children—is the problem, not the answer. When this moment came in the second winter of my remarriage, over some question about discipline, I instinctively backed down. I was mad as hell at that moment, but I could still see the big warning sign flashing in my head.

"No," I replied, "I will never ask you to make that choice." I knew in my heart that I would only lose. So I backed up, asked myself some hard questions about my own contribution to the problem, and let go of my resentment. When I had calmed down, I went back to Charlie with some ideas and solutions, rather than ultimatums.

What I'm learning is that the path to a resolution is never straight for us. We meander, try new things, go back, get help, look at maps, dig tunnels. Sometimes we get there faster than other times. I'm learning to trust the process and count forward motion of any sort as a blessing. For someone who has always been results oriented, this Zenlike approach to life is not easy. In fact it is often frustrating, but in time I think we will find our way through the maze and discover that we have built support for each other in the process.

Ironically, the experts say it isn't necessarily the loyalty problems and fights that doom a remarriage as much as how people fight and whether they can ultimately resolve their problems. Psychologist E. Mavis Hetherington says she was surprised to find that frequent fighting was not a good predictor of remarital breakup—it was more how people fought. In her study she found that high levels of contempt, hostile criticism, and withdrawal were the most clear predictors of marital breakup whether in a first marriage or remarriage.

Psychologist John M. Gottman of the University of Washington has done fascinating studies of interpersonal behavior between married people, and found that he can predict which couples are headed for divorce by the degree to which they display what he calls marriage's Four Horsemen of the Apocalypse: hostile criticism, contempt, denial, and withdrawal. Couples who indulge in this kind of disdain and rigidity need help, and need it fast.

These qualities feel familiar, because I saw them emerge in my first marriage. I know how corrosive contempt can be in an intimate relationship. I know that there are points past which a marriage cannot recover. What Gottman has discovered is that our marital interactions—in fact, all our social interactions—are composed of hundreds of emotional bids for connection between people. "These bids can be a question, a look, an affectionate touch on the arm, or any single expression that says 'I want to feel connected to you,'" Gottman says. Those bids, and whether they get a negative or a positive response, create the fabric of a relationship. We know when we are ignoring or dissing someone, as my children would put it—and we do it at our peril.

According to Gottman, the success of a marriage is dependent in large part on how we live and behave every day, not just on whether we occasionally take time for a midweek date. He suggests couples work consciously to manage their reactions and words, and try to avoid escalating discussions into confrontations, particularly when talking about touchy subjects. He also says that couples should set limits on hurtful behavior from each other. Those that do better are partners who establish high standards for the marriage from the very beginning.

Gottman also says a couple must learn how to repair a bad situation and exit an argument before it gets completely out of control. Repair attempts include things like using humor or reaching out to touch each other to defuse the tension, trying to establish common ground, backing down from a position, or registering appreciation for the other's feelings. He also says happy couples generally focus more on the bright side, and know to go for help early when things get difficult.

Charlie is the master of the repair attempt, often throwing in one of his classic wordplays when conversations get tense. My wise mother told me once that no matter how mad she was at my father, they always felt as if they could still touch each other, sneak a foot over to the other person's side of the bed or lean up against each other—and it was often that little touch that allowed them to make up.

Remarried couples will inevitably struggle—for example,

about money issues or harassment from ex-spouses, or resentment and disrespect from children—but most can survive if the couple that holds the entire house of cards together is willing to adapt, stay close, learn tolerance, and develop the skills to resolve their problems. Rigidity, intolerance, withdrawal, and resentment are not helpful. Those who do better are the people who can continue to talk with each other, work out little issues before they become big and overwhelming. I caution myself to watch my impulsive emotionality—those sarcastic comments, eye rolls, exasperated grumbles. In this marriage, I try to be a grown-up in the best sense of the word.

One of the more interesting lessons of remarriage is that the family will usually do better if the individual parents can loosen their grip on their children, something that is often a challenge for people who have survived the tumult of divorce by holding on to their kids for dear life. But in a remarriage, balancing the emotional needs of children and the emotional needs of the adult relationship is key. If one spouse stays deeply enmeshed with his or her children, to the exclusion of his or her mate, the couple is going to have problems. If a husband ignores his children's needs because he is overly attached to his new spouse, he is going to have a different set of problems.

Charlie and I were lucky in that we brought almost equal burdens to the marriage. We each have two sons, and the teams of brothers present similar challenges. In families where one parent has brought a very difficult child or a particularly bitter ex-spouse, the other partner can feel unfairly taxed. For us, the family feels balanced, even when we are wrestling with problems.

Somewhere around the middle of our second year, the tension in the house eased. For one thing, the unexpected blessings started coming faster and faster. The boys were helping out in the yard and kitchen with considerably less grumbling. We took a trip to California and the boys worked out a fair and equitable seat-trading system for the rental van entirely on their own, without parental intervention. We had the smoothest trip of our marriage mostly because we were learning to function as a team—all six of us, not just me and Charlie. At the airport two of the boys would help me with the bags in the ticket line, and the other two would head off to get breakfast for the rest of us while Charlie parked the van. Everyone met at the gate in twenty minutes. We don't look like newbies anymore. We are adopting the swagger of veterans.

Today I can sense the growing comfort in the house, the subtle adjustments everyone is making. I am happier as the months go by, feeling more and more like the mom of the hearth in this different but lively and entertaining family. My boys are thriving, my stepsons are thriving, my husband is happy, and the dog doesn't run away anymore. Whether we make it five years, ten years, or—Charlie's goal—fifty years may matter less than how we live each day.

I believe that the biggest challenge is to build that marriage partnership—not just for the health of the marriage, but also for the health of the family. And I don't mean just building the love relationship: I mean building a true and equitable partnership in which you work together to make decisions and support each other in managing the family. In which you don't rearrange everyone's schedule at a request from an ex-spouse without consulting your new partner. In which you fight the temptation to isolate yourself when the going gets tough. In which you refuse to allow the household to split into competing camps. In which you stay interested and involved in your stepkids' lives and work to build a bond, even if they do not accept you as an authority. In which you throw bids of affection and connection in everyone's direction every day.

In the process of my remarriage, I've learned some eye-opening things about myself: that I will get depressed if I don't fight for the things I need in my life, but that I don't like fights; that my patience is more limited than I ever imagined, now that it has really been put to the test; that I can be judgmental and rigid if I don't watch myself; that I am less resilient than my own children; that living with other people's teenagers is a constant seesaw between love and frustration; that the woman in the house, no matter how much lip service is paid to alternative lifestyles, will end up making dinner unless someone orders out. That I don't like sharing control but I don't like being responsible for everything, either. That I'm petulant and sometimes seem to nurse my own irritation, as if I need distance but don't know how to ask for it nicely. Sometimes I look in the mirror and wonder if I'm getting less mature every day.

Fortunately, most everybody still seems to like me anyway, which may be the biggest lesson and blessing of this whole enterprise. When I lived alone with my two small boys, I could be the perfect parent—at least in my own estimation. There was no one around to question my judgment on a daily basis. I could indulge my boys, write the rules, nip problems in the bud.

Now I'm often challenged on a decision, and sometimes find I don't have a good reason for what I'm planning to do. Sometimes I want to spoil a kid just because I'm too tired to fight. Sometimes I set down a rule and realize, when the kids push back, that it is unnecessary or ridiculous. I've discovered that like most people, I tend toward bossiness and rigidity when I get anxious. I'm getting in touch with the human weaknesses that keep me humble. As a result, I doubt myself more than ever before, but also find I am more thoughtful, more open to other ideas and positions. I'm growing and changing. For someone approaching fifty, whose body and mind wants to calcify rather than stretch, this is challenging indeed.

But most important, I've learned to ride the storm. I've learned to admit my mistakes and then forgive myself and others. I've learned to apologize and to accept apologies and be done with it. I've learned that there will be friction and problems but that they are not, in and of themselves, catastrophes. The catastrophe happens when the family's response is to shut down, get resentful, and stop trying. In time I hope to learn how to detach when I need to take a break, get away, breathe, and regroup.

When Charlie and I first talked about merging these sets of brothers, among all the plans for housing and schooling and discipline and responsibilities, he kept saying: "Let's make it fun." Sometimes I thought he was crazy. Was doing all that laundry going to be fun? How about the inevitable fights over the remote? The bickering between brothers that would escalate when they didn't feel they could pick on anyone else? But as we started trying to plan for fun, we got better at having a good time together. Big families can be a gas, something our generation seems to have forgotten. Just cramming all of us, our luggage, and the dog into the family van will make somebody start giggling, even if someone else is complaining. So we try to listen to the giggler. Dinner table conversations are often hilarious; there's always something outrageous just bursting to be said, and the bigger the audience, the better the response.

And we don't just plan for fun at holidays and vacations. When we see a tough stretch ahead—exam week, Mom on a deadline, Dad on travel—we schedule in treats or special activities. We consciously build the memories, because that is what we want them to take into adulthood: the lobster night tradition on Cape Cod, the goofy word games we play in the car when we're all bored to tears, the chess tournaments and algebra challenges, the endless rounds of Murder in the Dark.

As Gottman would say and many other researchers have confirmed, you can make your remarriage a self-fulfilling prophecy. If you spend too much time worrying about the weaknesses and failures, you can end up with a failure. Or you can focus on the bright side, the things that are working, and it may turn out to be a success. What I'm learning with this marriage is that it can bump along in all its glorious imperfection, and gradually—if we all keep trying and giving and holding on—it will grow into something strong and resilient. Something that will provide a foundation for my boys as they grow into men who may try someday to marry and build a family.

The other day Charlie, who has a wicked sense of humor, cracked a particularly twisted pun at the breakfast table. Everyone winced except me, who laughed out loud.

"That's your job, I guess," Adam said to me with a wry smile. "To support the illusion that Dad is funny."

Later David, who is thinking a lot about girls and relationships these days, said, "Mom, I think that's so great that you always laugh at Charlie's jokes. You guys are perfect together."

If there was one thing I hoped my remarriage would give my children, it was the model of a good marriage. It was the only thing I couldn't do for them on my own as a divorced single mom, and along with filling my own deep need for companionship and love, it was the dream of a good marriage that propelled me forward through all the difficult, trying, and nail-biting moments.

When I was on the brink of divorce thirteen years ago, a very wise therapist said to me, "You will never know for sure if you are doing the right thing, because you will never know what you saved your children from." I look at where we are today, with my ex-husband living a full life just two blocks away, still close to his boys, supportive of my marriage to Charlie; with all four boys doing well in school and busy with their friends and many activities; with a sweet, forgiving, funny, tolerant man in my life, who is doing his damnedest to make me happy; with a big, comfortable house, even if it always seems a bit messy; with work that satisfies and a loving extended family and friends, and I know I've landed in a fertile place. It may sometimes seem like a teeming, overgrown garden, but it is a garden in the best sense of the word. It's a place where I can put down roots and find the sustenance I need. The world of divorce always felt to me like an open, barren plain—windswept and empty. Like trees that grow on stormy coasts, the life I built on that plain was small and closed in on itself, and it needed to be carefully tended so it wouldn't get blown away. Today I'm in a sheltered place, and we have the luxury of growing large and weedy. We can relax back into the reassuring support of home and family, we can finally let go.

There is one hell of a debate raging out there about the health of the American family, and to listen to it can be discouraging, especially for stepfamilies. Margorie Engle, president of the Stepfamily Association of America, says, "Given the extraordinary vulnerability of all the participants in stepfamilies, the current national adoration of first marriage can be brutal for us." Some religions actually banish divorced and remarried families from their congregations, saying that to remarry is an abomination before God because it violates the sanctity of the original marriage. Some sociobiologists say that stepfamilies are dangerous places for kids, and most media stories focus on the small percentage of stepfamily kids having problems, ignoring the 80 percent of kids in stepfamilies who do as well as kids in nuclear families.

Perhaps the most retrograde attitude is that concerning stepparents: that they are inferior and suspect parents because there is no biological tie with the child. The mythology of the wicked stepparent is alive and well.

There is an interesting irony to this. If I adopted an older child, I would be a local hero, no matter how good a parent I was to that child. But if I take on two stepchildren, I'm hardly nominated for a medal. Instead, my behavior is watched, judged, criticized. Yet there is little difference: both parents lack a biological tie with the child, both situations involve parenting a kid raised by someone else, and both acts are choices, consciously made out of love and kindness. So why do we retain this age-old prejudice? Yes, it is true that some stepparents—as is true about some biological parents—are bad parents, people who abuse or hurt kids. And it is probably true that the lack of a biological tie can make that line a bit easier to cross, although why that does not seem to be true about people who have adopted infants (who are no more likely to abuse kids than birth parents) is not addressed by the sociobiologists. I personally believe that poverty and despair are greater predictors of child abuse than biology or stepparenting, but the statisticians are still debating these issues.

I do know that living with children who have been raised differently than you would have raised them is a challenge for any adult. But most stepparents should get medals for what they accomplish: building a loving, supportive environment for their stepchildren, despite the lack of a biological bond. Those who have not challenged themselves to help raise a stepkid probably will not ever really understand what it means. To do it, you need to believe in your heart of hearts that all kids deserve as many loving, helpful adults in their lives as possible, and that if you are one of those adults, you have a moral responsibility to be there for that kid. That doesn't mean you serve as slave or ignore your own needs and other responsibilities. It means that you weave that child into your life to the best of your ability, whether the child rejects you— out of loyalty to the biological parents—or puts up barriers that make it difficult to fully engage. You do what you can and trust that you will grow to love that which you tend. It's worked for me.

The fact of the matter is that remarriages and stepfamilies are here to stay. If society is concerned about the health of our families, and strengthening families as a way to provide healthy homes for kids and better support for adults, then we need to be there for every family, no matter what it looks like. There is no single model but only the multitude of variations that is the modern family. Researchers in the remarriage field say they are constantly stymied by what they call the individuation of each family. They set out to find trends and end up with a hundred case studies. Each family is a world unto itself. Each family will find a different solution to the problem of how to live, and some of those will look unusual. When I try to explain our varying custody schedule with the four boys—week on/week off with one set, a split week with a Tuesday-night individual kid switcheroo for the other set—many people give me a look of alarm. "Boy, how do you keep it straight?" Well, these are our children, not visitors. We know the schedule because they matter to us. Beyond that, we just keep plenty of food in the refrigerator and give everyone a key. It works for us.

Do we feel broken? Like half a family? Hardly. When you add up all the loving adults in my children's lives, it's more the plus model than something reduced. There are five parents among our four boys. They get presents and kudos and special attention from many sets of grandparents. They have scads of aunts and uncles and nieces and nephews. They have relatives all over the country. There will always be somebody there for them.

· · ·

I've always known that the classrooms at my university were peppered with kids who had grown up through divorce and remarriage. But I never appreciated how big a groundswell was sitting right under my nose until several years ago when I hosted a panel of policy pundits and reporters discussing how the news media and entertainment industry portray the American family. There were many other interesting events on campus that night, including a basketball game, but the hall was packed with students. To present a balanced perspective, we had invited both liberal and conservative voices for the panel, and true to form, several conservative speakers decried the demise of the nuclear family, blaming divorce and remarriage for the decline of American society. When we asked for comments from the audience, scores of students rose and paraded to the microphone. "Excuse me, but I don't feel broken," they said one after another, in a long line that wound out the door. "I come from a divorced family, and I'm fine," or "I was raised in a loving stepfamily and we are just fine." They were polite but insistent, proud and clear. By the end of the evening, the conservative pundits had little to say.

One of the things that has sustained me through my first few years of remarriage is the collection of stories I've heard from these students about their experiences as stepkids in blended families. "Oh, yeah, it was awful at first, but now I really like having all these siblings," one boy told me. "It took a while, but now we're really close," said another. "I love my baby brother," said another girl. "My stepmom is really a big part of my life," said a young woman from Pennsylvania. "I mean, I'm still close to my mom, but my stepmom sometimes understands where I really am because she doesn't get as anxious as my mom does."

What my students provide is the voice of experience, the perspective from a child who has grown up and matured and can now see, from a greater distance, the difference his parent's remarriage has made in his life. And most of those kids say they are just fine.

And truth be told, I usually can't even tell which of my students come from nuclear families and which come from stepfamilies. Sometimes the strongest, most squared-away kids show up at graduation with two sets of smiling, teary-eyed parents, eager for me to meet them all. And it is always an honor. If we no longer live in the proverbial villages it takes to raise a child, then maybe an extended stepfamily will do.

Maybe the most important thing I've discovered is that the home I was so desperately seeking when I remarried was actually right there next to me the whole time—in Charlie's heart. Something in me knew this as soon as I met him, but it's taken years for me to believe it, to trust it. At the very core of this big, cumbersome enterprise known as a blended family is the sacred space in our hearts where our promises to each other, given in a garden two years ago, live and flourish. I know he will always listen to me. I know he will be patient and try to fix what is wrong. I know he will try, every morning, to have me laughing within moments of our waking up. If the home I live in is to be filled with forgiveness and tolerance, than I have to hold that uppermost in my heart. To be happy, I didn't need to marry the perfect person or be the perfect wife. I just needed to find someone who would leave a light on in the window and always take me back in.